Shakespeare's Vast Romance

Shakespeare's Vast Romance

A Study of
The Winter's Tale

Charles Frey

University of Missouri Press
Columbia & London, 1980

Copyright © 1980 by The Curators of the University of Missouri
University of Missouri Press, Columbia, Missouri 65211
Library of Congress Catalog Card Number 79-3063
Printed and bound in the United States of America

Library of Congress Cataloging in Publication Data

Frey, Charles, 1935—
Shakespeare's Vast Romance.

Includes index.
1. Shakespeare, William, 1564-1616. The winter's tale.
I. Title.
PR2839.F7   822.3'3   79-3063
ISBN 0-8262-0286-1

For A. H. F.

Preface

I first saw *The Winter's Tale* as a young boy and first wrote on it in Maynard Mack's Shakespeare course twenty-five years ago. This book issues from successive expansions and revisions of my first study, and my indebtedness to Shakespearean researchers and interpreters of widely differing interests and persuasions is apparent throughout.

I thank all my friends for their steadfast encouragement and wise counsel. Maynard Mack, Dustin Griffin, Kathleen Blake, and Susan T. Frey read and improved the drafts. My students have taught me more, of course, than I have taught them. Still, despite all the help I have received from readers, students, editors, and others, I remain keenly aware of how far beyond my ken *The Winter's Tale* serenely glides.

The reader will find the relatively few references to primary sources clustered, for the most part, in notes to the second chapter. In accordance with the general practice of interpretive works such as this, no citation list separate from the notes is provided. My sources are mainly other interpretations, and I gratefully acknowledge the substantial aid of prior interpreters. I apologize to all those, moreover, who have written on *The Winter's Tale* and remain unmentioned here. We labor together in silent communion.

A portion of the fourth chapter was published in somewhat altered form in *Shakespeare's Romances Reconsidered*, edited by Carol McGinnis Kay and Henry E. Jacobs (Lincoln: University of Nebraska Press, 1978), pp. 113–24, and is reprinted with permission.

C. F.

Seattle, Washington

May 1978

Contents

Introduction

In the past few decades, no group of Shakespeare's plays has increased more in public and scholarly esteem than the four late comedies —*Pericles, Cymbeline, The Winter's Tale,* and *The Tempest* —generally collected in modern editions under the heading "Romances." Major summaries tracing the rise in critical fortunes of the romances reveal that the shift in appreciative estimate has been accomplished by the collective efforts of many persons pursuing varied interests and approaches.[1] Much of the effort has gone to create a new space in critical and theatrical consciousness for a kind of drama that reaches beyond conventional categories of comedy or tragedy. We now accept the challenge and significance of this new kind, variously denominated "tragicomedy," "repentance play," "comedy of forgiveness," "pastoral romance," or, perhaps most simply and clearly, "dramatic romance."

Most of the longer studies have treated the plays as a group, inviting observation of similarities more than singularities.[2] We

1. See Philip Edwards, "Shakespeare's Romances, 1900−1957," *ShS* 11 (1958):1−18; Philip Edwards, "The Late Comedies," in *Shakespeare*: *Select Bibliographical Guides*, ed. Stanley Wells (London: Oxford University Press, 1973), pp. 113−33; Norman Sanders, "An Overview of Critical Approaches to the Romances," in *Shakespeare's Romances Reconsidered*, ed. Carol McGinnis Kay and Henry E. Jacobs (Lincoln: University of Nebraska Press, 1978), pp. 1−10, and see the extensive bibliography of over 650 items in that volume, pp. 182−215.

2. E. M. W. Tillyard, *Shakespeare's Last Plays* (London: Chatto and Windus, 1938); G. Wilson Knight, *The Crown of Life: Essays in Interpretation of Shakespeare's Final Plays* (London: Oxford University Press, 1947); E. C. Pettet, *Shakespeare and the Romance Tradition* (London and New York: Staples Press, 1949); Derek Traversi, *Shakespeare: The Last Phase* (London: Hollis and Carter, 1954); Northrop Frye, *A Natural Perspective: The Development of Shakespearean Comedy and Romance* (New York: Columbia University Press, 1955); Frank Kermode, *William Shakespeare: The Final Plays* (London: Longmans, Green, 1963); Carol Gesner, *Shakespeare and the Greek Romance* (Lexington: University Press of Kentucky, 1970); Howard Felperin, *Shakespearean Romance* (Princeton: Princeton University Press, 1972); Joan Hartwig, *Shakespeare's Tragicomic Vision* (Baton Rouge: Louisiana State University Press, 1972); Hallett Smith, *Shakespeare's Romances: A Study of Some Ways of the Imagination* (San Marino, Calif.: The Huntington Library, 1972); Douglas L. Peterson, *Time, Tide, and Tempest: A Study of Shakespeare's*

have begun, however, to separate out Shakespeare's four romances into their distinctive personalities, worlds, orchestrations, and metabolisms. The evidence of books and articles about individual romances suggests that the focus of interpretation is shifting to cover the romances in an order that reverses their chronology. The concentration of the 1920s and 1930s upon *The Tempest* has given way to a broader interest in all the romances but particularly, in our era, *The Winter's Tale*. Future decades may see *Cymbeline* and then *Pericles* enter more fully into the new collective prominence of Shakespearean romance. Right now it appears specially fitting to attempt one or more synthesizing, synoptic, holistic accounts of the play that, to judge from the large numbers of contemporary performances and interpretations, has evidenced a peculiar attraction for us.

This book is designed to provide one such relatively comprehensive account of *The Winter's Tale*. My method involves a kind of triangulation whereby I provide, first, a selective history of recorded responses to the play. Second, I consider certain problems concerning the play's background, including sources, Shakespeare's own development, and a few analogues of the time. Third, having repositioned *The Winter's Tale* or, more accurately, the reader's mind within important contexts of the play I provide a brief account of what a fresh seeing or reading of the play may yield to a reasonably well-informed spectator or reader. My overall purpose is to weave together some of the major strands in history and criticism that should become part of the play's interpretive fabric.

The Winter's Tale is, even for a Shakespearean play, surprisingly difficult to approach with confidence. In *The Tempest*, the presence of Ariel and Caliban, the declaratory speeches of Gonzalo and Prospero on the commonwealth, the meaning of art, and the power of forgiveness, and the laboratory focus of the play on three groups, three masques, one isle, one afternoon, all invite the sort of schematic, philosophical criticism that *The Tempest* has generated so abundantly. *The Winter's Tale* is not like that. It is the opposite of a philosophical play. It is not a drama of ideas so much as a drama of actions that

Romances (San Marino, Calif.: The Huntington Library, 1973); Barbara A. Mowat, *The Dramaturgy of Shakespeare's Romances* (Athens: University of Georgia Press, 1977).

are sudden, spontaneous, manifold, and only mysteriously gathered, if at all, toward some final significance.

A substantial chorus of interpreters agrees that *The Winter's Tale* has its imposing life and makes its mark in the theater, during performance, but leaves little in the way of "deeper meanings" for conceptual analysis. Elsewhere I have outlined some of the problems that have been posed for these and indeed all interpreters by the play's protean resistance to such analysis.[3] I have argued that, given the play's resistance to conceptual analysis, a sound interpretive strategy, for the moment, would be to provide not post-play rumination but a collection of materials most useful to pre-play preparation, that is, to inform, strengthen, and encourage intellects that would re-encounter the play for themselves, the play in its irreducible mystery. My triangulation of chapters that follow attempts to provide one such collection of preparatory materials. In ordering and presenting these materials, I seek, particularly, a recurrent focus upon the developing, cumulative drama of the play in performance or reading and upon the uses of a temporal-affective criticism responsive to that drama. In addition to my search for a helpful mode of interpretive response to the play's progressions and climaxes, however, I search as well for a response that answers to the play's vastness and opacity. The full winter's tale—whether play or season—includes both fall and spring in its disturbing and hopeful embrace. If we would appreciate a bit better how the play makes its own embrace as great and as creative, we need an interpretive vision that can focus upon connection and evolution yet open itself peripherally to unresolvable diversities and incommensurables.

To emphasize the paradoxical amalgam of coherence and vastness in *The Winter's Tale* is to encourage modern interpreters toward more innovative methods than have been generally employed so far. We need constantly to reposition the play amid changing notions of its prehistory (sources, backgrounds, Shakespeare's development) and post-history (staging and criticism) that evolve with our evolving points of vantage. We need also to experiment with a variety of fresh interpretive "performances" of *The Winter's Tale*. Such performances should not be seriatim readings that detail the critics' succes-

3. Charles Frey, "Interpreting *The Winter's Tale*," *SEL* 18 (1978):307–29.

sive and, often, highly subjective responses to each scene in sequence; they should be comprehensive efforts at marking out major dramatic patterns that give the play its distinctive presence and progress. One such pattern, for example, is the tightly structured alternation—through the first three acts, of (on the one hand) long, loud, crowded scenes in which Leontes appears, berates women, rejects his associates, threatens death and (on the other hand) brief interstitial scenes in which pairs of lesser characters meet in amity and hope.[4] In the final chapter herein, I detail a few of the remarkable effects of this alternating rhythm and then trace the way the rhythm shifts in the latter part of the play. There, a similar opposition between mistrustful and faithful characters—this time Polixenes against Perdita and Florizel—is regularly interrupted and partly dissipated by the parodic intrusions of Autolycus. Tracing out the progress and the implications of such patterns helps sensitize us to shifts of pace, of tonal quality, and of attitudes generated by the play. It also does much to explain the dramatic functions of Autolycus that have long puzzled interpreters.

If we view the statue scene, similarly, as climax to a sequence in which Hermione, Paulina, and Perdita are made still centers of attention coming from uncomprehending bystanders who stimulate and witness radical transformations in the central woman, then we can respond more readily to the impact of the final scene: the chapel-gallery setting, the bystanders shown to be more stone, less real, than the statue, the aura of religious veneration, the conjunction of "faith" and "wooing," the mixtures of satire and seriousness, miracle and mockery, comedy and high reverence. We need, in other words, to work with whole-play features, devices, and patterns in sustained attempts to make more palpable and effective the full drama of the play.

Amid the general consensus that *The Winter's Tale* now makes new and impressive claims upon us, but facing the general vagueness of and disagreement about the exact nature of those claims, contemporary critics have been ever more insistently asking just what kind and degree of "faith" or belief in its action and world the play demands. Again, however, their

---

4. This matter is taken up in the final chapter herein, a portion of which has appeared in somewhat different form in my essay, "Tragic Structure in *The Winter's Tale*: The Affective Dimension," in *Shakespeare's Romances Reconsidered*, pp. 113–24.

brief inquisitive essays fail to include enough of the play's full working to provide convincing answers. Too often, the interpreters divide into (1) formalists who defend the play's artistry against detractors who think it broken backed, lacking in unity, shallow in character portrayal, strange in style, and so on, and (2) non-formalists or contentualists who face more directly the "message" of the play. The first sort of defense is exemplified by articles such as one titled "Style in *The Winter's Tale*" which argues that the abstract patterns of the play render it "not sparse but dense":

> Shakespeare has left nothing out. Rather he has crowded into the frame of one play the patterns of many. The King is jealous, the Queen is falsely accused, the Queen dies. The Prince in disguise courts the Pauper, the Prince is discovered, the Prince flees. The play has no shortage of plots, but such summaries of its action are almost all that are given to us. Neither event nor character is fully amplified. Much is alluded to. Almost nothing is explained.[5]

The Winter's Tale, it is concluded, creates a world of absolute, artificial, abstract "intelligible forms," a world that "demands of us the kind of intellectual assent that is ultimately more binding than the plausible surfaces of *Othello*." Without ever really saying what the play is about, the author urges us to admire this sort, or "style," of art and give it not just aesthetic but intellectual assent.[6]

The second mode of defending *The Winter's Tale* tries to explain its mysterious power to move an audience, a power seemingly incommensurate with the play's apparent quaintness and artificiality. Whereas the formalist critic argues an aptness of style in this romance but tends to abide the mystery of its power to affect us, the critic oriented toward content may try to look directly at that mystery. Attention centers, of course, upon the statue scene, a scene that contains, according to G. Wilson Knight, "the most strikingly conceived, and profoundly penetrating, moment in English literature."[7] One interpreter in this mode rejects all lesser versions of the "miracle" of Hermione's restoration and argues that she was dead and is

5. Marion Trousdale, "Style in The Winter's Tale," *CritQ* 18:4 (1976):30.

6. Such formalist praise takes another shape in an article that describes effective repetitions of words and actions in the two halves of the play: Richard Proudfoot, "Verbal Reminiscence and the Two-Part Structure of 'The Winter's Tale,'" *ShS* 29 (1976):67–78.

7. *The Sovereign Flower* (London: Methuen, 1958), p. 240.

brought to life; the play asks us and, apparently, persuades us to believe in the "one wholly satisfying solution to the problem of death." "It is a very difficult truth for many, but it is the truth of the play."[8] Another writer in this vein, who also concedes the power of the play's ending, "its capacity to convince us," asks again: "To what are we required to lend our faith?" His answer is that the statue scene appeals to our deepest wishes and desires for a miraculous renewal of lost life. We give our assent to the restoration of Hermione as an accurate reflection of our greatest hopes. But, at the same time, "*The Winter's Tale* pushes comedy to the limits of the form." The radiance of the statue scene only accentuates our dark knowledge of permanent loss, the reality of death, the evanescence of attempts "to evade the enormous price of a thing done."

> Life is not like art, and does not afford us this miraculous im-
> agined redemption. Life renews itself through new gener-
> ations—Perdita, not Hermione. The dead stay dead. Not all our
> tears change that. . . . Beautiful and heart-thrilling as *The Winter's
> Tale* unquestionably is, in the end we must say of it something like
> this—it truly reflects our human wish, but if we think of another
> final scene where a woman as loving and true as Hermione lies
> dead as earth, we shall not confuse that wish with truth.[9]

To the question, What kind of assent does *The Winter's Tale* demand from us?, we thus get two dramatically opposed answers: (1) religious affirmation of personal immortality, and (2) near-tragic reflection upon the finality of death. These dissidents agree with the analysts of style that the play attempts to body forth a golden world and to awaken faith; they disagree, however, as to the depth and lastingness of that awakened faith. A middle mediatory position emerges, inevitably, in the arguments of another critic:

> Shakespeare has made Paulina's art as suggestive and ambigu-
> ous as possible: is it true or false, good or evil, magic or theater?
> The dual nature of Paulina's magic is also that of Venus, of female-
> ness itself in the play: the corrupt and destructive "seeming"
> Leontes imagines or the grace and fertility which transform
> Leontes' sterile order. It is the duality of the fallen world, as
> reflected in the play, and particularly in the Renaissance pastoral
> romance, in which . . . "we find two worlds juxtaposed: the actual

8. Robert R. Hellenga, "The Scandal of *The Winter's Tale*," *ES* 57 (1976):18.
9. F. H. Langman, "The Winter's Tale," *SoRA* 9 (1976):203–4.

world of human experience, and a kind of inner circle, a purified abstraction of that world, or 'Arcady.' " . . . It is also the duality of Shakespeare's art in particular, and even more in particular, of *The Winter's Tale*: a celebration of the power of art in the context of all-embracing illusion.

Without ever answering the question of how fully and completely we are made to believe in Hermione's restoration, this interpreter ends with paradoxical hints that the "old tale" hides within it a "divine reality." "As the play's title reminds us, its truths are fiction. Yet it moves and convinces; it brings itself to life."[10]

For these interpreters of *The Winter's Tale*, plainly, a crucial issue, if not the crucial issue, is the exact quality of conviction or life contained in or evoked by the play. These attempts to pay homage to the play's peculiar power all falter, in my view, to the extent that they overstress, on the one hand, constructive artistry or stylistic integrity and overstress, on the other hand, the play's presentation of miraole and its demands for religious faith. In the first place, the generations of readers and spectators who have testified to the confusing shifts in the play from one style to another, one mood to another, one place and time to another, cannot be so easily dismissed. *The Winter's Tale* is, above all, vast: vast in its scenic, characterological, and tonal range. It is a romance of "rough magic" and should not be simplified through a formulaic conception of its style. Relatively brief pieces, such as the articles cited, tend, perhaps inevitably, to miss the sense of teasing complexity and strangeness engendered by the living play, and that is one reason for believing that a longer study, one that examines the full length of the play and its contexts of origin and reception, may help us become more responsive to its vastness. In the second place, the issue of the play's demand for "faith" can hardly be settled definitively, if at all, in essays that concentrate only on the final scene or in essays that overplay as do the last three discussed, the issue of "miracle" by suggesting that Hermione really died and then came back to life in the statue scene. Hermione herself delcares to Perdita:

I,
Knowing by Paulina that the Oracle

10. Patricia Southard Gourlay, " 'O my most sared lady': Female Metaphor in *The Winter's Tale*," *ELR* 5 (1975):394−95.

> Gave hope thou wast in being, have preserv'd
> Myself to see the issue.[11]

Hermione's statuesque pose is at best analogous to the sleeps of Thaisa in *Pericles*, of Imogen in *Cymbeline*, and of many another Sleeping Beauty. It is a standard feature of romance — non-Christian and Christian — enshrined in a thousand stories from ancient times to the present. Again, to work with the full play in its many informative contexts helps to remind us that the statue scene represents much more than faith in personal immortality. To judge, in particular, from the various scenes of waking sleepers and of art ceremonies interrupted by intrusive "life" in the late plays, Shakespeare was less intent upon proofs of immortality than upon showing ways in which waking and dreaming, truth and illusion, life and art interpenetrate and create each other's meanings. In the romances, disenchantment soon proves itself a dream. In the romances, smaller revels dissolve but only into grander ones. To apprehend the vastness of the process may help to save us from naive, polar commitments. It may also help us to awaken our own dreams of faith.

Though past critics have sometimes responded to *The Winter's Tale* with admiration and delight, modern interpreters are the first to intimate that the play presents a radical, shocking, soaring vision of regeneration and redemption that may take lasting hold upon readers and watchers. What has been for a long time the play's tragicomic veil of strangeness may now be parting, like Paulina's curtain before the statue, to reveal life within re-creating art, an art that might impel us some way past illusion, maya, and bafflements of hope. My main purpose here is to make more accessible for readers and spectators of *The Winter's Tale* its artful life, its vital grandeur, its plain humanity, its lasting countenance of affection.

---

11. J. H. P. Pafford, ed., *The Winter's Tale*, Arden ed. (London: Methuen, 1963), 5. 3. 125. All references from this edition are cited by act, scene, and initial line numbers, unless noted otherwise. Quotations from Shakespeare's other works follow the *Complete Works*, Alfred Harbage, gen. ed., Rev. Pelican ed. (Baltimore: Penguin Books, 1969).

Chapter II.

Views and Reviews

Viewers and readers of *The Winter's Tale*, both past and potential ones, may profit from considering certain selected responses to the play, responses recorded through time since the play's inception. Though the history of such responses is, in part, a history of truncated performances and distorted readings that tell us more about tastes of the times than tests of the play's worth, still, our perceptions of past inadequacies imply an image of potential wholeness. We see, for example, that Garrick's pastoral pastiche fails to satisfy fully because the audience was not made to suffer a near-tragic confinement and waste before the pastoral; the audience was not asked to experience three acts that make the pastoral deeply refreshing. We see that the Victorian *Winter's Tale* isolated Hermione and Leontes in tableaux scenes and bravura set speeches, to promote character and spectacle at the expense of scenic continuities and progress of the action, to make the play solid and heavy in terms of personalities but void of that great ascent through related climaxes—accusation, trial, betrothal, and statue scene—to which the text so plainly bears witness. We see that recent interpretations of the play as "pastoral" and "romance" have emphasized its skeletal affinities with literary, often nondramatic, traditions but have also neglected the play's peculiar dramatic structure and its particular rhetorical strategies.

Stage history, by itself, presents a limited guide to what has been made of the play. For centuries, readers of Shakespeare's works have been at least as numerous as viewers, so that responses to the printed play and to writings of others about it have influenced both productions of and responses to the presented play. If we seek to inform our own responses as both spectators and readers, we need to know not only how the play has been conceived and received in production but also how the play has affected readers. To this end, the shaping or educating of response to *The Winter's Tale*, I trace a selective history here of its life among significant producers, actors, spectators, and readers.

The Jacobean Winter's Tale

I

The first recorded performance of *The Winter's Tale* took place on 15 May 1611, at which time Simon Forman, an astrologer and doctor, wrote this account of it:

In the Winters Talle at the glob 1611 the 15 of maye ♀ [i.e., Wed.] Obserue ther howe Lyontes the kinge of Cicillia was overcom w ^{t} Jelosy of his wife with the kinge of Bohemia his frind that came to see him. and howe he Contriued his death and wold haue had his cup berer to haue poisoned. who gaue the king of bohemia warning therof & fled with him to bohemia / Remēber also howe he sent to the Orakell of appollo & the Aunswer of apollo. that she was giltles. and that the king was Jelouse &c and howe Except the Child was found Again that was loste the kinge should die without yssue. for the Child was caried into bohemia & ther laid in a forrest & brought vp by a sheppard And the kinge of bohemiā his sonn maried that wentch & howe they fled into Cicillia to Leontes. and the sheppard hauing showed the letter of the nobleman by whom Leontes sent a was that child and the Jewells found about her. she was knowen to be Leontes daughter and was then 16 yers old

Remember also the Rog that cam in all tottered like coll pixci/. and howe he feyned him sicke & to haue bin Robbed of all that he had and howe he cosoned the por man of all his money. and after cam to the shep sher with a pedlers packe & ther cosoned them Again of all their money And howe he changed apparrell w ^{t} the kinge of bomia his sonn. and then howe he turned Courtiar &c / beware of trustinge feined beggars or fawninge fellouss [1]

Did Forman see substantially the same play as that printed in the First Folio? He mentions no statue scene. He has Perdita carried "into" Bohemia and laid in a "forrest" instead of being left on shore; perhaps he infers a forest from the presence of the Bear, but he fails to mention him.[2] He says that Perdita and

1. As transcribed from Bodleian manuscript, Ashmole 208, F. 201v−202r, by J. H. P. Pafford, ed., *The Winter's Tale*, Arden ed. (London: Methuen, 1963), pp. xxi−xxii.

2. The so-called Padua First Folio Promptbook, perhaps used by amateurs performing in England circa 1625, indicates no appearance of the Bear. Gwynne Blakemore Evans, ed., *Shakespearean Promptbooks of the Seventeenth Century* (Charlottesville: University Press of Virginia, 1963), Vol. 2, pt. 2.

Florizel marry in Bohemia, whereas, in the Folio version, their attempt to marry is thwarted by Polixenes. He also misquotes the Oracle which, in the text, refers only to "that which is lost" (3. 2. 135). Still, the play Forman reports is recognizably ours.

How may Forman's account affect our conception of the play? Whatever he saw, it is clear that Autolycus was, from the first, mightily impressive and quite capable of stealing the show, at least to the didactically minded. And Forman's specification of the lost "Child" instead of the more vague "that which is lost" suggests how easily and quickly spectator and critic may lessen the full complexity of dramatic ambiguity. But the report of the play does not necessarily distort the experience. Though Forman does not mention Time's speech, for example, saying merely that Perdita was "laid in a forrest & brought vp by a sheppard," nonetheless, so calm a reduction of sixteen years to an ampersand may only indicate that he, like others, was totally unconcerned about the unity of time. It may also point to a rapid pace and to a seamless continuity in performance.

Though Forman, who summarized in similar style two other Shakespearean productions, seems to have been insensitive to broader emotional and intellectual meanings beyond plot outline and moral lessons, his words supply a useful point of view. He covers the essential action with little hint of the remorse or the laughter, the music or the beauty. If one knew no more about the play than Forman's account, one would assume that it consisted mainly of jealousy, attempted poisoning, flight, and cozening. Neither the penitence arising out of the trial, nor the "mirth o' th' feast," nor the waking of Hermione is mentioned though each contributes vitally to the final reunion and spirit of reconciliation. Forman's example is the first of many to show how easily, in the case of *The Winter's Tale*, one may learn the plot only to lose much of the play. On the other hand, it is useful to be reminded that the play does work, at least partly, in realistic and solid terms: emotions of fight and flight and the functional objects upon which Forman centers his attention—money, peddler's pack, oracle, letter, jewels, ragged costumes, and other apparel. Beneath whatever romantic or mythic gloss one may put on the play, there remains its familiar physical action, which was much in evidence at the Globe, at least to one Jacobean spectator.

Not only does Forman remind us that the play proceeds through the factuality of common emotions and objects, he points, indirectly, to the basic search in the play for health within the body politic and within the domestic scene. He identifies the characters not by name but by terms denoting familial or societal positions—wife, friend, issue, son, daughter, king, cupbearer, shepherd, nobleman, rogue, poor man, courtier—and he abbreviates the action to its essential movement of flight and discovery. The plot, justifying attention to role and status, turns upon relations of kingship, marriage, parenthood, and friendship. "To mingle friendship far, is mingling bloods," says Leontes at the onset of his jealousy (1.2.109), and the play proceeds to examine meanings of friendship and mingled bloods, painfully disproving the assertion of Leontes only to prove it again in the union of Perdita and Florizel.

The major scenes—Leontes' outburst of jealousy, Hermione's trial, Florizel's and Perdita's attempted betrothal, the final reconciliation—treat expectations and duties of friendship and kinship. Minor scenes explore them as well. Ordered to poison Polixenes, Camillo, according to Forman, "gaue the king of bohemia warning therof & fled with him to bohemia." This subsidiary scene, necessary as part of the plot only to maneuver Polixenes and Camillo to Bohemia, goes well beyond such bare maneuver and furthers inquiry into ties between servant and master, subject and king, son and parent. Camillo, having agreed to poison Polixenes, is left alone onstage (1. 2. 350). Polixenes enters. He knows that something is amiss, because Leontes has failed to respond to "customary compliment." When Camillo hesitates to inform him, Polixenes adverts to the bond of gentleness that should unite them (1. 2. 390), and, invoking norms of a father-son relation, Camillo and Polixenes gradually draw together in spiritual and physical companionship (even joining hands [1. 2. 447]) as they recede toward their exit.

Forman speaks of the two men fleeing; their gradual affirmation of trust is the only "flight" portrayed onstage, a flight from the oppressive atmosphere of Sicilia. Forman also mentions the flight of Perdita and Florizel, and again it is a decision to flee, based on the slow dawning of Florizel's faith in Camillo, that constitutes the scene. In successive stages, Florizel reveals his increasing acceptance of Camillo's advice:

> How, Camillo,
> May this, almost a miracle, be done?

That I may call thee something more than man
And after that trust to thee. (4. 4. 534)

                              I am bound to you:
There is some sap in this. (4. 4. 565)

                                        Camillo,
Preserver of my father, now of me,
The medicine of our house, ... (4. 4. 586)

Examples could easily be multiplied of such subsidiary scenes in which characters work their way toward a common bond of hope and trust (see, for example, 1. 1. 8—36; 5. 1. 177—232; 5. 2. 124—75). The point here is that Forman, through his simplistic concentration upon the mechanics of plot and role, draws attention to the play's striving toward community. From the jealousy of Leontes to the warning of Camillo, from the abandoning of Perdita to their eventual welcome, the play pushes toward proof that men may and must share common bonds of humanity. Forman helps us engage the play by forcing our attention upon its rudiments—objects and costumes, the status of each character, their plainly antisocial or socially supportive actions. An insistence on the palpable reality of the play as an experience of plot and properties grows out of Forman's flat account, and an awareness that the play deals in pervasive patterns of jealousy, fear, friendship, and love rises from his prosaic summary.

II

This view of an early performance of *The Winter's Tale* by a Jacobean who was not among the literati provides a usefully plain and logical approach that accords the play a substantial reality and shows it to be less ethereal than some would have it. For, from its inception, the play has been steadily categorized as unrealistic.

Ben Jonson, in his induction to *Bartholomew Fair*, purported to complain of plays that "make nature afraid," "that beget Tales, Tempests, and such like drolleries" with attendant "concupiscence of jigs and dances."[3] Jonson remarked to William Drummond that Shakespeare wrongly attributed a seacoast to Bohemia,[4] and in his prologue to *Every Man in his Humour*, he

3. Eugene M. Waith, ed. (New Haven: Yale University Press, 1963), Induction, ll. 115—17.
4. E. K. Chambers, *William Shakespeare* (Oxford: Clarendon Press, 1930), 2:207.

complained of plays (such as *Henry V*) in which a "*Chorus* wafts you ore the seas."[5]

Discounting first the suggestion that the play is only a drollery, one may reiterate that the characters' continuing search for relationships of trust (analyzed in the flight scenes) is anything but whimsical. If the antics of Autolycus seem droll (we will not second Forman's perverse moralism in treating them as Shakespeare's warning against coney catchers), the general effect of the shearing festival is not. The clowning of Autolycus plays a decidedly subordinate role to the love play of Florizel and Perdita. Jonson complains also of the dances, yet, during both of these, characters onstage converse, and the plot moves forward. The dancing serves to heighten and express the nuptial tension at the center of the scene. If it is the satyrs' dance that Jonson glances at in "concupiscence," he may be right about the tendency it was given but is certainly wrong in isolating it from the play—and especially from the play of attitudes, both refined and earthy, that form the defining ambience of Florizel's and Perdita's union—for the dance marks the moment the lovers join vows and hands, turning from a game of courtship to the more serious troth of marriage.

The shearing festival, clearly, is no airy-fairy memory of a golden age. From Forman's description of Autolycus as a tattered cozener and the Clown as a poor man, one would gather that the "shepherds" and "shepherdesses" were presented as contemporaries of the Jacobean audience, figures more up-country than out-of-country. Such staging makes sense of its text. The rarefied Greek air breathed at the beginning of the long pastoral scene by Flora and her Apollo-citing swain inserts itself only fleetingly into the harsher northern climates whose natives think upon Puritans and lawyers, codpieces and cutpurses, money and pins.

Complaints of the Bohemian seacoast and of a chorus conducting one from country to country become, in the direct experience of the play, equally frivolous. Shakespeare found the Bohemian seacoast in his source, Greene's *Pandosto*. To have changed it in the name of mimetic accuracy would have been as misguided as to fashion Autolycus's ballads to suit the truth-loving rustics (4.4.262–85). Even if taken as an unintended error, it only bothers one who applies to the play Procrustean tests

5. Chambers, 2:205.

developed in the study. In the theater, as a recent editor has observed, "these things do not worry . . . : they cannot indeed be noticed in the quick movement of the play."[6] But suppose that the error was intended. Suppose that Shakespeare knew as well as the next man that he was telling a "fabulous" tale and that the association in space of a seacoast with Bohemia was no odder than, say, his association, in time, of Julio Romano with the Delphic oracle, and that both associations could help support an atmosphere of dreamed reality—what then? It is not past belief that Shakespeare deliberately incorporated what he knew to be a violation of actual space in order to signal to the knowing that in this world space is every whit as mythical as time. Time the Chorus, similarly, performs no calendar functions but simply introduces the willing spectator to a new time and season, a time for things newborn, coaxing him openly toward fresh attitudes and expectation. We know from the prologues in *Henry V* how effectively a Chorus (and characters in the nature thereof) can appeal to the "quick forge and working-house of thought" (5. Pr. 23) to enlarge perception. Time's address fulfills that same function here.

In explanation of Jonson's criticism in the induction to *Bartholomew Fair*, it has been asserted that "spectacular production" contributed to making the Jacobean *Winter's Tale* "decidedly unrealistic."[7] If so, the principal points where spectacle might be stressed other than in the shearing festival, where it has already been discounted, are the trial and statue scenes. Yet there is no indication in the Folio, Forman's account, or elsewhere that spectacle (in the sense of large crowds, lavish backgrounds, props, machinery) was actually employed. The trial scene, apparently out of doors (3. 2. 105), would seem to require only imagined scenery like most Shakespearean outdoor scenes. It requires no large number of actors.[8] In the statue scene, Leontes has to look around for the statue, which could suggest that, even if veiled, it was not obtrusively or elaborately presented. The remainder of the scene is marked by reverential restraint in reactions to Hermione's waking, in Per-

6. Pafford, *The Winter's Tale*, p. lii.
7. Waith, *Bartholomew Fair*, p. 32 n. to ll. 113−15.
8. Compare William A. Ringler, Jr., "The Number of Actors in Shakespeare's Early Plays," in *The Seventeenth-Century Stage*, ed. Gerald Eades Bentley (Chicago: University of Chicago Press, 1968), pp. 110−34, and Chambers, 2:86.

dita's silence, and in Hermione's brief speech; it seems likely that the staging would follow suit. Indeed, as one scholar has observed, the entire *Winter's Tale* suggests the use of "a staging simplicity that would not tax the barest innyard stage."[9] If, moreover, *The Winter's Tale* was played at the Blackfriars theater during the winter season, there is little reason to suppose that its staging there differed greatly from that at the Globe.[10]

That the play may be spectacularly staged to suit the taste of some audiences was proven later in the productions of Charles Kean (1856) and Beerbohm Tree (1906). To argue that its Jacobean staging was less than spectacular is not to argue, of course, that it should always be played on a bare stage with a minimal cast, avoiding all pictorialism for the sake of an idealized verbal purity. On the contrary, the play at every point has a pronounced visual appeal that should be artfully emphasized in whatever fashion may help a contemporary audience to comprehend the whole.[11] The point here is that Jonson's lighthearted jibes are not proofs of unreality in the play.[12]

9. J. W. Saunders, "Staging at the Globe, 1599-1613," in *Seventeenth-Century Stage*, p. 239.

10. See A. M. Nagler, *Shakespeare's Stage* (New Haven: Yale University Press, 1958), p. 102, and Daniel Seltzer, "The Staging of the Last Plays," in *Later Shakespeare*, Stratford-upon-Avon Studies 8, ed. J. R. Brown and Bernard Harris (London: Eduard Arnold, 1966), pp. 128–29. Production of the play was never recorded at the Blackfriars theater though it has been argued that the play was written for that theater. See Gerald Eades Bentley, "Shakespeare and the Blackfriars Theatre," *ShS* 1 (1948): 46–49; C. B. Purdom, *Producing Shakespeare* (London: Pittman, 1950), p. 56; Irwin Smith, *Shakespeare's Blackfriars Playhouse* (New York: New York University Press, 1964), pp. 212–13. The play was presented at Court in 1611, 1613, 1618, 1619, 1624, 1634, and perhaps other years. Chambers, *Shakespeare*, 2:342–52. Since the masques presented there often employed elaborate stage machinery, it is possible that *The Winter's Tale* received more ornate production there than elsewhere. Compare Nagler, p. 104. A repertory company like the King's Men, however, probably would be unwilling to sacrifice a basic continuity in performing style. Insertion of spectacular effects would inevitably disrupt accustomed stage business, cues, and general timing. Compare Bernard Beckerman, *Shakespeare at the Globe: 1599–1609* (New York: Macmillan, 1962), p. 213. If, therefore, masque-like elements appear in *The Winter's Tale*, it is still permissible to doubt that they were staged with masque-like spectacle.

11. Compare G. Wilson Knight, *Shakespearian Production* (London: Faber and Faber, 1964), pp. 234–41, warning against neglect of Shakespeare's visual artistry.

12. Jonson may have been trying to pay Shakespeare back for references in *The Winter's Tale* to a dance of satyrs as a "gallimaufry of gambols" (4. 4. 329) and "homely foolery" (4. 4. 334), because there are indications (particularly in the mention of dancing before the King (4. 4. 338) that Shakespeare was

Within the aggregate of his complaints, however, there lies a weightier questioning. What sort of play is it? Beside the massive naturalism, which is one element in much of Jonson's comedy, parts of *The Winter's Tale* do appear capricious and fanciful. How is it that the dances, the country hopping, the wide gap of time, and the stagy last scene can possibly be integrated with the rest? If Forman leads one to see the non-literary, nonromantic underworkings of the play, its repetitions of domestic and social strife, its didactic thrust, then Jonson leads one to acknowledge the tension of romance in the play, its a-geographical and anachronistic unconcern, its dances and emblematic tableaux. Embedded in the text is a rendering of sordid jealousy that is realistically clinical in some respects ("No barricado for a belly" [1. 2. 204]; "My wife's a hobby-horse" [1. 2. 276]). Equally embedded are seemingly irreconcilable scenes of aphoristic detachment ("A sad tale's best for winter: ... There was a man— ... Dwelt by a churchyard" [2. 1. 25]). Dream vision (Antigonus's) yields to low comedy (Shepherd and Clown). Exalted lyrics ("When you do dance, I wish you / A wave o' th' sea" [4.4.140]) share the scene with a bawdry that sharply questions their attitude ("Will they wear their plackets where they should bear their faces?" [4. 4. 244]). Jonson, quite appropriately by his own dramatic principles (as argued in *Timber*), if not practice, took exception to this apparently Janus-faced play.

III

Jonson's complaints promote inquiry into reasons for both the appeal of *The Winter's Tale* to Jacobean audiences and its subsequent decline in popularity. As far as is known, the play was among the most popular presented at court prior to the

---

alluding to Jonson's masques, such as *Oberon* (performed 1 January 1611). Polixenes, however, speaks of the dance as refreshing, and, as in *Oberon*, it comes at and marks a moment in which passionate energy encounters a benign order. Compare Stephen Orgel, ed., *Ben Jonson: The Complete Masques* (New Haven: Yale University Press, 1969), pp. 14–20. Shakespeare may have been offering a depiction and evaluation of the "anti-masque" dance whose full subtlety escaped even the wit of Jonson. It is important, however, that Shakespeareans not make Jonson their casual whipping boy. Obviously the author of *The Alchemist* and *Bartholomew Fair*, in many respects masterworks of free form and a highly qualified realism, can hardly be simplified to a neoclassicist stickler for all conventions or to a mere advocate of realism or antiromantic naturalism.

closing of the theaters. Put on for the less selective audience at the Globe as well, it must have been acted in such a way as to make it unified and complete. Surprisingly little, however, is known about styles of Elizabethan-Jacobean acting. Some scholars argue that the prevailing mode was formalistic, others that it was naturalistic.[13] Hence no one say can say just how *The Winter's Tale* was in fact performed. The most one can suppose is that the acting somehow responded to the play's demand for a similar counterpoint between the stagy and the realistic, homiletic declamation and intimate spontaneity, the formal constrictions of trial, betrothal, and statue scenes, and the exuberance that follows upon them. Convincing portrayal of the individual characters, moreover, must have covered a like range. As Hermione jests with Polixenes, discounting his formal protestations, risking double entendre, she must gather into her part a dignity and bearing that question the lightness of her speech and suggest that the banter may be only the spirited life of royal integrity. Similarly, as Leontes seethes in the first throes of jealousy, ranting through pseudological soliloquies, he calms himself intermittently and touchingly sympathizes with Mamillius, looking upon the boy's "welkin eye" and finding "comfort" in his words. The actor of Leontes' part must vary, as well, a harsh tone of accusation and command with a querulous or sometimes childlike questioning. Through the clouded tyrannical will peer gleams of a naive and hence redeemable quester: "Art thou my boy? Art thou my calf?" "How can this be?" "Is this nothing?" "Would I do this?" "Shall I be heard?" "How could that be?" "Have I done well?" "Hast thou read truth?" "How! gone?" The questioning side, indeed, must be shown as winning through. In the play's final scene, the King's questions point toward the life that art can and cannot instill: "Does not the stone rebuke me / For being more stone than it?" (5.3.37); "What fine chisel / Could ever yet cut breath?" (5.3.78).

13. Compare M. C. Bradbrook, *Elizabethan Stage Conditions* (Cambridge: Cambridge University Press, 1932), pp. 105−21; Alfred Harbage, "Elizabethan Acting," *PMLA* 54 (1939):685−708; S. L. Bethell, "Shakespeare's Actors," *RES* 1 (1950):193-205; and B. L. Joseph, *Elizabethan Acting* (London: Oxford University Press, 1951), pp. 60−82, 141−53, who argue that Shakespearean acting was formal, conventional, and rhetorical, to R. A. Foakes, "The Player's Passion: Some Notes on Elizabethan Psychology and Acting," in *Essays and Studies* 7 (1954):70; Marvin Rosenberg, "Elizabethan Actors: Men or Marionettes?" in *The Seventeenth-Century Stage*, pp. 94−109; and John Russell Brown, *Shakespeare's Plays in Performance* (London: Eduard Arnold, 1966), pp. 22−39, who argue that the acting can fairly be called realistic and natural.

Leontes the tyrant insists on rules of allegiance, stages trials at law, and accuses the world of general unfaith. Leontes the questioner puzzles his way toward a deeper sense of a more natural faith in human honesty, goodwill, and love.

Part of the answer, finally, to the problem raised by Jonson as to how a play of such shifting diversity could receive a coherent production lies in the characters' own sense of theatricality in their actions. Leontes (1. 2. 187), Hermione (3. 2. 37), Perdita (4. 4. 133), Camillo (4. 4. 594), and others conceive of their actions in terms of the stage and so invite the audience to keep in focus the theatricality of the whole. Such references are common in Shakespeare but rarely so intense as here. Open admissions of theatricality, such as asides and direct address to spectators — for example, Leontes: "I / Play too . . . And many a man there is (even at this present / Now, while I speak this) holds his wife by th' arm, . . ." [1. 2. 187]; Time: "Imagine me / Gentle spectators" [4. 1. 19] — have considerable impact upon a live audience, coaxing it to keep in mind the immediately dramatic but not necessarily realistic ceremony shared by all. One who considered the play from a more detached, critical view of probability and reality, on the other hand, would receive no such impression and would hence be more likely to find fault with the play's unreality.

Certainly the play, though difficult, was popular during its first decades. The above analysis should, at the very least, lay a groundwork for understanding why its popularity would decline in the eyes of later critics who were committed to purity of form and classical unities and were never privileged to witness the living play.

Neoclassic to Romantic

IV

"The Winters Tale was acted on Thursday night at Court, the 16 Janua. 163 [4], by the K. players, and likt."[14] This was the last recorded performance before the suppression of theaters in 1642. With the demise of the King's Men, the play was left to its place among the thirty-six texts of the First Folio, all vying for equal recognition. Prime interest shifted to works that could

14. From the *Office Book* of Sir Henry Herbert, then Master of the Revels, as printed by Chambers, *Shakespeare*, 2:352 (from the transcript made by Edmund Malone).

better hold their own against the ascendancy of Jonson and of Beaumont and Fletcher and against the influential rise of French neoclassicism.

Dryden, in 1672, as if seconding Jonson's complaint of "drolleries," included *The Winter's Tale* among plays "grounded on impossibilities" or "meanly writen." [15] It is likely that Dryden was more concerned about violations of the supposedly classical unities,[16] lately activated by Corneille and others — one day, one place, one action—than about the problem of Leontes' motivation or the reality of the statue scene. Though praising Shakespeare in his *Essay of Dramatic Poesy* (1668), he had even there complained of the long time periods encompassed by the history plays. His critique of *The Winter's Tale* occurs as part of a more general attack upon alleged defects and failures of Elizabethan drama: loose plots, coarseness, bombast, incorrect grammar and diction, excessive punning, carelessness, inconsistency, and frequent dullness.

Implicit in Dryden's disdain were an increasing depopularization of drama and increasing reliance upon norms of "criticism"[17]—correct generic form, faultless structure, and conventional, or scientific, truth. An almost grudging but real admiration for the liveliness of Shakespearean drama was held in tension with naive scorn for its irregularity and lowness. Not surprisingly, between a distaste for drama that lacked the formal intensity associated with adherence to unities and an affection for Shakespeare's original genius there evolved a compromise that worked to the detriment of *The Winter's Tale*. Regard for Shakespeare centered upon the depth and accuracy of his character studies, especially those in the major tragedies; where such studies appeared, incorrect plotting was momentarily excused. Pope was not atypical in purporting to absolve Shakespeare from noncompliance with Aristotelian formulas. But this does not mean that his allegedly loose construction was really overlooked or forgiven. A play like *Pericles*, which fails Pope's tests for both character and plot, was termed *wretched*. And, says Pope, "I should conjecture of some of the

15. *Defence of the Epilogue to the Second Part of the Conquest of Granada* (1672), in *Essays of John Dryden*, ed. W. P. Ker (Oxford: Clarendon Press, 1900), 1:165.

16. "Supposedly classical" because really traceable less to Aristotle than to Castelvetro, Scaliger, Sidney, and Jonson.

17. As in the work of decorum-conscious critics like Thomas Rymer.

others (particularly Love's Labor's Lost, The Winter's Tale, Comedy of Errors and Titus Andronicus), that only some characters, single scenes, or perhaps a few particular passages were of his hand."[18]

Augustan editors found the play archaic, indecorous, enigmatic. Theobald stumbled over words like *gest*, refused to let Paulina call Leontes a *fool*, and could not conceive of Time *making* error.[19] Samuel Johnson confessed ignorance concerning many of Shakespeare's terms, could not visualize red blood "reigning" in the winter's pale, and charged that the recognition of Perdita by Leontes should have been acted rather than reported.[20] These criticisms presented the play as foreign and obscure or occasionally as rough and foolish. Some editors openly attacked it. Charlotte Lennox argued that the jealousy of Leontes was too sudden and that other incidents were low and contrived.[21] Bell's edition jabbed the reader after the first three acts with the following comments:

> The first act resting almost on the childish irregular feelings of Leontes, can give little pleasure, less instruction.
> The second act . . . is better than the first, yet cannot we afford it much praise.
> The best of the third act is, its being short.

Shakespeare "was unconscionable enough to load" the fourth act with twenty-seven pages, and the fifth act is "languid" until the end.[22] Polixenes is called a "water-gruel character" and Hermione is "very near in the same stile" (154). Hermione's hankering after praise with its reference to being ridden with

18. Alexander Pope, " 'The Preface of the Editor' to the Works of Shakespeare (1725)," in *Eighteenth-Century Critical Essays*, ed. Scott Elledge (Ithaca, N. Y.: Cornell University Press, 1961), 1:228. Pope's inadequacies as an editor of Shakespeare were exposed by Theobald and others, but, though most of Pope's contemporaries may have believed the play to be Shakespeare's, defenders of it (such as Warburton) were not heard until the play was revived onstage.

19. In Theobald's 1733 edition, these items appear in 3:68, 106, and 112−13, respectively.

20. Samuel Johnson, ed., *The Plays of William Shakespeare* (London: J. & R. Tonson, 1765), 2:293 n.6; 323 n.; 324 n.6; and 341 n. Both Theobald and Johnson accepted Rowe's substantial emendation of Leontes' famous speech upon "Affection" (1. 2. 138).

21. Charlotte Lennox, *Shakespear Illustrated* (London: A. Millar, 1753), 2:75-87.

22. [*John*] *Bell's Edition of Shakespeare's Plays* (London: John Bell, 1774), 5:164, 176, 187, 211, 225. Alterations in this text were those of Thomas Hull (see note 28).

soft kisses and to heating acres, is cut out for being, as the editors explain, "quibbling and flat, conceived in terms, on the queen's side, rather childishly low, than maturely royal" (156). That Shakespeare may have wanted such innuendo available to the incipiently jealous Leontes and to his audience is a possibility that was never considered.

For all their loss of the play's spirit, these critics often hit unerringly at weak points in its overall structure. Bell's edition, for example, charges that the scene in which Florizel and Autolycus exchange clothes contains "unessential intricacy" (208). And the "precipitate retreat" of Polixenes is fairly said to abate his dignity (164). Shakespeare frequently shows in this play a kind of confident disregard for the probable expectations of his audience. Deference to normal desires for a briskly satisfying pace and for familiar characters is absent here. Preceding and succeeding centuries tried to find the subtler reward in Shakespeare's game, but the eighteenth century tended to resent it and said so.

The reservations of Restoration and Augustan commentators were influenced by the circumstance that the complete text was seldom, if ever, performed for them. It is most unlikely that Dryden, Pope, or any other commentator between 1642 and 1741 saw *The Winter's Tale* acted. And later critics fared little better. After the official reopening of the London theaters in 1660, Thomas Killigrew's company had obtained the exclusive license to present the play, but there is no record of any performance by Killigrew's or succeeding companies until the revivals of 1741. In January of that year, Henry Giffard, actor and manager of the unlicensed theater in Goodman's Fields, Whitechapel, put on the play and advertised that it had not been played for a hundred years.[23]

Despite the habit, indulged in by Davenant, Shadwell, and Tate, of redacting Shakespeare's plays (especially the lighter ones), Giffard may have staged a fairly complete version.[24] But

23. *The London Stage: 1729–47*, ed. Arthur H. Scouten (Carbondale, Ill.: Southern Illinois University Press, 1961), 2:881.
24. At least the cast list was fairly complete, omitting only Time, Archidamus, the Jailer, the Mariner, and other minor parts. Giffard, playing Leontes, staged his version eight times in January 1741, and it was popular enough that the Covent Garden management also presented it—four times in November and once the next January. The Covent Garden Bill (see *The London Stage*, 2:942) omits Archidamus, Mopsa, Dorcas, Jailer, Mariner, and other lesser parts—though they may have been played. The Bill lists Time

his production evoked no commentary that survives,[25] and after this the play was not seen for over a decade. The rest of the century saw only sporadic productions of altered versions.[26]

V

What the eighteenth century did with *The Winter's Tale* parallels what it thought about it. It is possible to trace graphically how the play was subjected to a "softening process" and "disintegrated into an idyll overlaid with quasi-heroic spectacle."[27] To stress those aspects of the play found most acceptable, the age tended to concentrate more and more upon isolated scenes and characters. The illustration to Rowe's edition of 1709, for example, shows a crowded statue scene with Hermione at stage left facing across toward Leontes. The light shines from stage right and spotlights equally Hermione, Leontes, and Perdita. In the edition of 1714, the same scene is copied but from much closer, as if the engraver sought a blowup. There are fewer characters, the principals are nearer together, the light now shines from behind Hermione and illuminates her chiefly while leaving Perdita in shadow. Not only does there seem to be some simplification (it is, of course, difficult to be sure how far the engraving imitates an actual production), but Hermione is certainly conceived as a sole, ecstatic source of feeling and en-

---

and interjects a "Diocles," probably not a misprint for "Doricles," Florizel's pseudonym at the shearing festival, because Florizel and the actor of his part are separately listed. Perhaps Diocles spoke a prologue or took part in an interpolated scene.

25. Giffard, an experienced and enterprising man of the theater (he first starred Garrick), sought to rival Quin and Macklin, who were bringing out at Drury Lane Shakespearean comedies long unplayed. See George C. D. Odell, *Shakespeare from Betterton to Irving* (New York: Scribner's, 1920), 1:220–21, 228. Concerning Giffard, see W. R. Chetwood, *A General History of the Stage* (London: W. Owen, 1749), pp. 166–67 (Chetwood is not always reliable.). See also [John] Doran, *"Their Majesties Servants": Annals of the English Stage from Thomas Betterton to Edmund Kean*, ed. and rev. Robert W. Lowe (London: J. C. Nimmo, 1888), 2:82. To account for the widening interest in Shakespearean comedy, Odell refers to "the rising tide of romanticism which was sweeping through literature and life" (1:222). And see Harold Child, "The Stage History of *The Winter's Tale*," in *The Winter's Tale*, ed. Sir Arthur Quiller-Couch and John Dover Wilson, New Cambridge ed. (1931; Reprinted, Cambridge: Cambridge University Press, 1968), p. 186. But the tide was not so sweeping as to keep *The Winter's Tale* long afloat.

26. See Charles Beecher Hogan, *Shakespeare in the Theatre: 1701–1800* (Oxford: Oxford University Press, 1957), 2:717.

27. W. Moelwyn Merchant, *Shakespeare and the Artist* (London: Oxford University Press, 1959), p. 209.

lightenment, whereas the text makes plain that the experience is collective. Whether it represents an actual moment of stage history or not, the illustration at least predicts what was to ensue. Efforts to unify the play by simplifying, reducing, and drawing conventional sentiment out of it multiplied from Rowe's time on. MacNamara Morgan, David Garrick, and Charles Marsh adapted it so as to serve the classical unities while shifting major attention to the later acts.[28] Garrick's, much the most popular of the adaptations, placed all the action in Bohemia. He cleverly eliminated minor characters and gave their lines to major ones, expanding the scenes with Autolycus as well as the statue scene. The general effect is one of greatly increased sentimentality. Upon seeing Hermione stir, Perdita says in Garrick's version:

> O Florizel! [Perdita leans on Florizel's bosom.]
> *Florizel.* My princely shepherdess!
>   This is too much for hearts of thy soft mold.
> *Leontes.* Her beating heart meets mine, and fluttering owns
>   Its long-lost half: these tears that choak her voice
>   Are hot and moist—it is Hermione! [*Embrace.*][29]

This sort of change suited audiences. Garrick as Leontes and Hannah Pritchard as Hermione, accompanied by new songs, dances, and stage business, were consistently liked. In the last quarter of the century, the vast conflux of forces associated with romanticism produced a climate more favorable to presenting the whole play. The influence of G. W. Lessing, A. W. Schlegel, and others who attacked the hegemony of French neoclas-

28. Morgan's adaptation (it is generally attributed to him) was produced at Covent Garden in 1754 and printed in 1755, 1762, 1767, 1784, and 1786. See Hogan, 2:674–75. The version of 1786 is in *Farces and Entertainments Performed on the British Stage* (Edinburgh: C. Elliot, 1786), 1:87–103. Garrick's version, which draws upon Morgan's, was called *Florizel and Perdita: A Dramatic Pastoral in Three Acts* (London, 1756, 1758, 1762), and it was presented at Drury Lane in 1756. Marsh's version is *The Winter's Tale: A Play Alter'd from Shakespear* (London: privately printed, 1756). The various redactions are discussed by Joseph Knight in *The Works of William Shakespeare*, ed. Henry Irving and Frank A. Marshall (New York: Scribner and Welford, 1890), 7:313–15; Frederick W. Kilbourne, *Alterations and Adaptations of Shakespeare* (Boston: The Poet Lore Co., 1906), pp. 84–90; Hans Krause, *Umarbeitungen und Bühneneinrichtungen von Shakespeare's The Winter's Tale* (Bern: Buchdruckerei Büchler & Co., 1913), pp. 6–25; Odell, 1:357–61, and 2:15–17; Harold Child, "The Stage History," pp. 186–89; and Pafford, pp. 176–78. Alterations made in the play by Thomas Hull (1771) and George Coleman, the elder (1777), are outlined by Hogan, 2:675–76.

29. Garrick, *Florizel and Perdita*, in the version of 1762, at p. 63.

sicism began to have practical results. Anachronisms, improb-
abilites, and violations of prescribed unities slowly faded as
subjects of concern. When John Philip Kemble revived the play
in 1802, the geographically unimpeachable "Bithynia" of
Hanmer and other redactors was excised and Bohemia was
restored, seacoast and all.

The legacy of the age, however, was not destined to be easily
broken. Onstage the play had been altered to make it conventionally acceptable. The seriousness found in Forman's account and the strangeness gleaned from Jonson could only be
rediscovered and combined through new critical acumen and
daring theatrical experiment.

VI

The romantic *Winter's Tale* was bigger and better than that of
the preceding age: bigger in the sense of being more complete if
also more spectacular; better in the sense, chiefly, of having its
characters more finely drawn. An increasing appreciation of
complexity in Shakespearean characterization, reflected in
Maurice Morgann's *Essay on the Dramatic Character of Sir John
Falstaff* (1777) and the essays of his contemporaries, eventually
reached *The Winter's Tale*. Coleridge, in 1813, described certain
"effects and concomitants" of Leontes' jealousy:

> Excitability by the most inadequate causes.... Eagerness to
> snatch at proofs.... Grossness of conception, and a disposition to
> degrade the object of it. Sensual fancies and images.... Shame of
> his own feelings exhibited in moodiness and soliloquy.... And yet
> from the violence of the passion forced to *utter* itself, and, there-
> fore, catching occasion to ease the mind by ambiguities,
> equivoques, talking to those who cannot and who are known not
> to be able to understand what is said—a soliloquy in the mask of
> dialogue. Hence confused, broken manner, fragmentary.... The
> dread of vulgar ridicule, as distinct from the high sense of honor
> ... and out of this, selfish vindictiveness.[30]

William Hazlitt in 1817 remarked upon "the crabbed and tortu-
ous style of the speeches of Leontes, reasoning on his own
jealousy, beset with doubts and fears, and entangled more and
more in the thorny labyrinth...."[31] Such particularistic

---

30. *Samuel Taylor Coleridge: Shakespearean Criticism*, ed. Thomas Middleton Raysor, 2d edn. (London: Dent, 1960), 1:110−11.
31. *Characters of Shakespear's Plays* (London: C. H. Reynell, 1817), p. 278.

analyses of character set the tone for literary critics through most of the nineteenth century. Thus the power of its characterizations and a measure of its overall seriousness were rediscovered.

Onstage, between complementary accentuations of character and spectacle, the play became more impressive, but its sinuous intricacy was lost. Hazlitt said, *"The Winter's Tale* is one of the best-acting of our author's plays" (280). He had seen and probably was thinking of Kemble's staging, described as elaborate and stately, in which Kemble as Leontes and Sarah Siddons as Hermione repeatedly stirred the spectators.[32] Garrick's expansions of the statue scene were, however, only slightly pruned, and Kemble added spectacular touches of his own. When Paulina asks Leontes if she should draw the curtain, Leontes replies (in the Folio), "No: not these twenty years." Kemble could not resist changing "twenty" to "thousand." And in his version, Hermione, once wakened, turns to Perdita and "catches her in her arms."[33] Hermione than blesses both Perdita and Florizel who kneel before her as a couple before the altar. The whole overdramatic, almost melodramatic, effect quite misses the charged quiet of Shakespeare's ending.

The statue scene, nonetheless, proved sensationally effective in the theater and probably contributed more than anything else in the play to sustaining the regard of actors and audiences. Elizabeth Inchbald criticized the piece generally but called the last scene "an exception to the rest, in being far more grand in exhibition than the reader will possibly behold in idea."[34] In one of William Macready's versions, using a text similar to Kemble's, Paulina drew back "a scarlet Curtain" to discover Hermione in a white Grecian dress, as well framed as a lily by roses.[35] In 1837, Macready and Helena Faucit performed the statue scene to "a tumult of applause that sounded like a

32. See Joseph Knight, in the Irving *Shakespeare*, 7:315−16, and Harold Child, "The Stage History," p. 190.

33. *Shakespeare's Winter's Tale: A Play Adapted to the Stage*, by J. P. Kemble (London: privately printed, 1811), p. 78. Kemble stylized Shakespearean texts by mixing the original with various adaptations. See Harold Child, *The Shakespearean Productions of John Philip Kemble* (London: Oxford University Press, 1935), pp. 7−19.

34. "Remarks" on *The Winter's Tale*, collected in *The British Theatre* (London: Longman, 1808), 3:6.

35. See *Cumberland's British Theatre* (London: John Cumberland, 1826), 5:1−72 (first play in volume, others not serially paged), containing a so-called acting copy of the play and giving costumes, cast lists, and stage directions.

storm of hail."[36] Reviewers of Faucit's performances of the statue scene rhapsodized in terms worth quoting:

> When amidst the melody of music, she turned her head towards the king, the whole house started as if struck by an electric shock, or as if they had seen the dead arise.

> It was something supernatural almost; and till the descent was fully accomplished, and the stone turned to palpable woman again, something of a fine fear sat upon us like a light chilliness.

> Once seen, it is engraven on the memory for the whole of life.[37]

Once we eschew a condescending attitude toward these spectators, we may suspect that they, together with the performers, unlocked a secret of the play that current directors might well ponder. Their success lay partly in the new seriousness with which they treated the reunion and in their empathetic regard for the spirit of bereaved reconciliation that simplifies and chastens the quiet ending. In Macready's and later in Phelps's productions,[38] character had not yet given way to spectacle.[39] The action advanced more swiftly and clearly

36. Helena Faucit, Lady Martin, *On Some of Shakespeare's Female Characters* (Edinburgh: Wm. Blackwood & Sons, 1891), p. 390. Miss Faucit there reports an occasion in which the audience, in response to her waking as Hermione, rose up in collective surprise and awe. She alludes to Donne's comment on Elizabeth Drury's capacity for corporal speech, "The Second Anniversary," l. 246: "One might almost say, her body thought." To allow for a degree of extravagance here may be insufficient still to overcome a measure of wonder at how often the play has evoked a special bond between actors and spectators, one essentially mysterious, corresponding perhaps to what Robert Graves has identified as "duende": "at times, something gets into the performer which corresponds to something that gets into the audience . . . and things happen there which nobody can explain." Quoted from a recorded discussion of Graves with Howard Nemerov, Stanley Kunitz, and Marianne Moore in *The Writer's World*, ed. Elizabeth Janeway (New York: McGraw-Hill, 1969), p. 319.

37. The first two quotations are from the *Glasgow Herald*, 14 March 1848, and the *Glasgow Citizen*, April 1848, respectively, and appear in *The Winter's Tale*, ed. Horace Howard Furness (1898; Reprinted, New York: Dover, 1964), pp. 392–95. The third quotation is from the *Glasgow Herald*, 14 March 1848, and appears in Sir Theodore Martin, *Helena Faucit (Lady Martin)*, 2d ed. (Edinburgh: Wm. Blackwood & Sons, 1900), p. 183 n.1.

38. See Odell, 2:273, 318, and Merchant, p. 210; Phelps' productions at Sadler's Wells were particularly restrained, and his relative faithfulness to the text arguably made Phelps father to the Elizabethan revival that followed later in the century.

39. See Dennis Bartholomeusz, *Macbeth and the Players* (Cambridge: Cambridge University Press, 1969), p. 180, citing Macready's disdain for a production-oriented as opposed to acting-oriented review of a performance of *The Winter's Tale* and arguing: "Macready maintained a just balance

toward its human resolution than it would in succeeding productions where time, instead of triumphing, would nearly go under.

The new seriousness, on the other hand, with which Hermione and Leontes came to be played and regarded, partly as a result of romantic character criticism, threw the play out of balance almost as much as did the pastoralizing redactions of the mid-eighteenth century. In the criticism and productions of the day, character was king as actors strove to realize the passions of the protagonists. But *The Winter's Tale* often subordinates character to situation, as in the brusque appearance of Leontes' jealousy or the unlikely silence of Hermione, so near to her grieving husband, for sixteen years. The psychological criticism of Coleridge and succeeding character analysts, moreover, could transmit little real authority and confidence to actors of Leontes' part. They could not separate the King from the action and project him as a complete, rounded, and realistic figure. Nor were they willing to merge him with the other characters to produce a single buildup of interlocking forces. The actors, understandably, either lacked the skill or lacked the perspicacity needed to portray the shifting enigmatic figure suggested by the text: now a pasteboard mask ("an instrument / To vice you" [1. 2. 415]) and now a hurt father ("How does the boy?" [2. 3. 9]), now almost a morality figure of penitence ("Apollo, pardon.... I'll reconcile me to Polixenes, / New woo my queen, recall the good Camillo" [3. 2. 153]) and now a mere man, touching and amazed ("O, she's warm!" [5. 3. 109]). If the critics and actors of the time saw how the crucial but evasive part of Leontes was central to an adequate representation of the whole play, they failed, nonetheless, to make that part fit the play and to avoid the excessive individualizing that tends, as in the case of Shylock, to pull the play apart.

Post-Jacobean critics and performers, then, had yet to come to grips with the whole play. Each successive distortion represented an attempt to find the easy way out, to account for too

---

between the needs of the actor and the needs of the production as a whole." A promptbook of Macready's production of 1837 suggests ways in which he downplayed spectacle while at the same time he directed minutiae of gesture and movement. The Bear, for example, was eliminated. The actor playing Mamillius was directed to catch Leontes by the robe just before Leontes said, "How now, boy?" (1. 2. 207). *Promptbook 2* of *The Winter's Tale* promptbooks in the Folger Shakespeare Library.

much with too little. A return to the complete text and a truly balanced performance was destined to occur, however, only in reaction to still further excesses.

From Victorian Spectacle to Victorious Simplicity

VII

If one wished to account for the taste displayed in mid-Victorian productions of *The Winter's Tale*, one would have to consider certain interanimating causes and effects: a penchant for sensational effects, ability to produce spectacle through a vastly increased command over the visual apparatus of production, spreading antiquarianism, intense regard for pictorial realism and elaborations of detail, together with a combined religious, economic, political, social, and aesthetic vision that often overvalued and excessively promoted the sentimental, safe, substantial, and ritually correct elements in popular culture.[40] Innumerable exceptions and qualifications would suggest themselves. But we are not seeking to define Victorian taste through its stagings of *The Winter's Tale*; we are asking whether that taste, embodied in its stagings, tells us something about the underlying stable or resistant form and pressure of the play. That the play (in Kean's version of 1856), severely cut toward a bravura score, staged with elaborate archaeological display, and larded with hundreds of extra actors, could be used to yield a magnificent spectacle is much less important for our purposes than the tentative protest, the incipient reaction, thereby provoked. Kean's production[41] received only guarded praise from a reviewer from the *Times* who had the temerity to observe: "In the play itself, as everyone knows, there is nothing to suggest excessive splendour of decoration."[42] What Kean's and the major productions of the next fifty years demonstrated was that the play itself could more easily be hidden than enhanced by splendid decoration.[43] Even the relatively restrained

40. A survey is George Rowell's, *The Victorian Theatre* (Oxford: Clarendon Press, 1967).
41. A stage edition was published in London by John K. Chapman & Co., 1856. The production is discussed by Merchant, pp. 210−20.
42. 1 May 1856, as quoted by Merchant, p. 219. Other critics raised similar objections (218−20).
43. Kean's production and the misguided Shakespearean idolatry it fed upon provoked a burlesque in the same year, William Brough's *Perdita or the Royal Milkmaid*. See Stanley Wells, "Shakespearean Burlesques," *SQ* 16

realism of the production by Mary Anderson (1887) presented, finally, a *Winter's Tale* less humanly proportioned and less carefully developed than the text demands.

Loss of proportion characterized even the most successful productions. Anderson's revival at the Lyceum in 1887 ran for hundreds of performances, over seven months, and drew ecstatic praise. But essentially it was a series of arias and tableaux designed to show Anderson to her best advantage. A typical photo shows the trial scene with the actress occupying all of stage center, there being a cleared area of at least ten feet on all sides of her. Not only do the positioning and lighting rivet attention upon the area where she stands but a questionable property, a huge tiger skin draped near her, also draws one's gaze, while Leontes must be picked out, if at all, from the shadow. (Was the skin meant to symbolize the threat of the leonine king?) I have counted some fifty-three persons onstage. This is more than three times the number necessary to stage any play of Shakespeare's. The enormous cast, the grandeur of background, the elaborately formal balance, the historical detail all aim away from the text that insistently directs the audience toward active engagement with the dreamlike debate between King and Queen, a debate that circles always back to the insubstantial yet invaluable virtue of honor. Isolated and remote in a high Greek palace, Anderson's Hermione could not convincingly include the audience in her references to "spectators," "all that hear," and "Your honours all." Hermione, moreover, is supposed to say to Leontes, "My life stands in the level of your dreams" (3. 2. 81), but the heavy, realistic detail evident at the Lyceum encourages no such projection of the King's dementia. "Life" echoes through Hermione's speeches to weigh out in her judgment as a value lighter than honor (see 3. 2. 42, 93, 109) while, for a moment, she and Leontes represent psychomachic forces of faith and unfaith rising in debate far above the particular circumstance. At the Lyceum, however, "life" in all its visual and aural obtrusiveness, the magnificent set, the fifty-three almost unmoving bodies (imagine the clink-

---

(1965):56–58. Kean's spectacular interpolations, such as the "Pyrrhic dance" in 1. 2 and allegorical tableau of sinking moon and rising sun (4. 1) prompted the unintended burlesque of W. E. Burton's New York production of 1857 in which Time, first discovered on the back of a Republican eagle, came forward "with an American flag in his hands delicately hinting at manifest destiny which will enable Time to carry the Stars and Stripes all over the Earth and adjacent planets." Folger Library, *Winter's Tale Promptbook 10.*

ing shields and creaking leather), must have counted most heavily of all.

"The next great effect of the play was in the rustic festival, a built-up scene with flowery banks and shady trees; down the incline dashed the dancers, led by Miss Anderson as Perdita."[44] The actress doubled as Hermione and Perdita, a practice that required a stand-in for the final scene. Perhaps the new Perdita then faced away from the audience, as is indicated by the reported staging: "For the statue scene Miss Anderson arranged a high flight of marble steps, at the top of which the statue was placed. As red velvet curtains were drawn, displaying the image, one had an impression of almost illimitable space, white marble steps leading up and up and up, the vista terminated by the statue" (437). Such an effect necessitated many changes in the Folio text, where Leontes refers to Hermione's wrinkles and all present are close enough to touch the statue easily. The greatly built-up scenes aimed, obviously, at isolated moments of charm or grandeur rather than the more intimate, fast-driving drama of the text. The twelve changes of sets indicated by Odell (438), even after allowing some scenes to be played forward of a drop curtain, must have repeatedly disrupted the flow of the action.

Anderson's method of acting, like the cumbersome staging, consumed a distracting amount of time and attention. At the trial scene, she struck a dozen tableaux poses—crouching at the altar during the thunderstorm that was manufactured to accompany the Oracle's verdict, receiving the news of Mamillius's death in stricken anguish, and falling to the stage in an elaborate faint. Such acting inevitably lengthened the play, and accordingly, like all Victorian producers, Anderson cut the text, elevating its tone and emasculating its vigor by concentrating her excisions upon scenes involving Autolycus (though she also omitted the delicate and poetic scene between Cleomenes and Dion, [3.1.]). At the same time, she transposed and interpolated:

44. Odell, 2:437; Odell is the source of much of the information that follows. The Folger Library *Winter's Tale Promptbook 3* supplies interesting stage business employed in the production by Mary Anderson. For example, the many Lords and Ladies attendant at the opening of l. 2 are listening to Hermione persuade Polixenes to stay. At his remark, "Your guest then, madam" (1.2.56), the *Promptbook* directs a "Movement of Satisfaction from all." After Hermione declares herself the "kind hostess" of Polixenes (1.2.60), the attendants and extras leave, thus accentuating the focus upon the principals. Florizel's decision to disobey Polixenes (4.4.485) calls for a dramatic shift in lighting to the "pink limes."

she closed the fourth scene of the fourth act with a speech by Florizel from earlier in the scene, and she ended the play with a couplet from *All's Well that Ends Well*. In her stage edition (1887), Anderson explained that no audience would care to sit through the entire play as written, and, further, "A literal adhesion to the text as it has been handed down to us would in any case savour of superstition."[45]

Anderson's reference to the text "as it has been handed down" is intended to suggest that the text in most editions was somehow corrupt. Reasons for such a belief had long since disappeared, however, as students of the Folio had recognized both the relatively good condition of the text of *The Winter's Tale* and its authenticity. What Victorian actors and producers were really intent upon was the achievement of spectacle and the purification of character. If, to achieve these ends, it was necessary to apotheosize Hermione, then that was accomplished by declaring that she represented "love without passion," by bowdlerizing suspected innuendo in her solicitation of Polixenes, and by removing references to sex from her speeches at the trial.[46] These were attempts to challenge and change the play, not to accept or enhance it.

VIII

Reaction inevitably set in. The last two decades of the century saw the now-famous Elizabethan revival, championed by Frank

---

45. Odell, 2:438, quoting from the stage edition. The Folger Library *Winter's Tale Promptbook 3* indicates a playing time for the Anderson production of just two hours and eight minutes. Among the excisions: the Bear, the Clown's description of the storm, the Shepherd's mention of things dying and newborn, and the meeting of Autolycus, Shepherd, and Clown at the end of 4.4.

46. See the acting version of Charles Kean (London: John K. Chapman & Co., 1856), p. 15, and the Irving Shakespeare, 7:339–40. The atmosphere of Bardolatry and moral didacticism surrounding Anderson's production may be noted from contemporary pamphlets such as that of H. Kate Richmond-West, *Interpretation of "A Winter's Tale"* (Chicago: Knight & Leonard, 1882), which said of Hermione (at p. 10): "Would your spirit could be spread abroad, that every mother, wife, and daughter might catch but a breath, and rejoice to claim you as their own"; and of Paulina (p. 16): "Should not humanity be enriched by the knowledge of this ennobling spirit?" Dinah Maria Craik (who also wrote *The Adventures of a Brownie*) opined in "Miss Anderson in the 'Winter's Tale,'" *Concerning Men, and Other Papers* (London: MacMillan, 1888), p. 192: "It is this view of the stage as a great teacher, better than most books and many sermons, which has evoked the present notice of the *Winter's Tale* at the Lyceum."

Benson, Ben Greet, and, particularly, William Poel. Largely outside the commercial theater of London, their productions
demonstrated that Shakespeare could be popular though relatively plain. Simplified sets, a rapid, tuned delivery, continous
staging, and experiments with a platform became hallmarks of
Poel's Shakespearean productions.[47]

The Winter's Tale first benefited from the Britishers'
Elizabethan revival, strangely enough, in an American production. In 1910, at the New Theater in New York, a privately
endowed repertory venture, under the direction of Winthrop
Ames, the play was put on in the manner of Poel's productions.
Instead of elaborately realistic sets, curtains, painted canvas,
and rich tapestries were used as backdrops. Central and upstage areas were employed for major scenes of definite locale
such as in the palace or at the shearing feast. The platform was
extended out over the orchestra pit, and smaller, interstitial
scenes were brought forward of a curtain drawn across the
main stage. Only one intermission was taken. The acting and
delivery were given in a swift, unbroken flow.

The New Theater production was deemed "strikingly successful."[48] Perhaps part of its success should be attributed to
the definite shift in taste away from pictorial realism. Program
notes of the production argued that the "play itself" seemed "to
forbid a realistic scenic background." The entire style of presentation with rapid, continuous delivery of the lines was destined to be much more than a passing fancy.

Two years later in September of 1912, Granville-Barker made
theater history in London with his staging of *The Winter's Tale*
at the Savoy. This production, generally accepted as the first
post-Jacobean use in commercial theater of the original text,
staged continuously with rapid delivery,[49] featured a forestage

47. See, for example, William Poel, *Shakespeare in the Theatre* (London:
Sidgwick & Jackson, 1913), and Robert Speaight, *William Poel and the
Elizabethan Revival* (London: Society for Theatre Research and William
Heinemann, 1954).

48. *The Outlook* (N. Y.) 94 (1910):785. For reviews of this neglected piece of
pioneering, see Albert Ellery Bergh, "The Winter's Tale," *The Columbian* 2
(1910):1295—1311; Matthew White, Jr., "The Stage," *Mumsey's Magazine* 43
(1910):421—22; Montrose J. Moses, "A Year of the New Theatre," *The Independent* 68 (1910):1030—35; *The Theatre Magazine* 11 (1910):133. Promptbooks of the production, preserved at the New York Public Library, are
described in Charles H. Shattuck's *The Shakespeare Promptbooks: A Descrip-
tive Catalogue* (Urbana: University of Illinois Press, 1965), p. 503.

49. See Norman Marshall, *The Producer and the Play*, 2d ed. (London:
Macdonald, 1962), pp. 149—58; Muriel St. Clare Byrne, "Fifty Years of Shake-

built out over the footlights and a foreshortened rear stage to bring the play closer to the audience. Décor (there was no scenery other than painted walls, backdrops, and curtains) and costumes were ahistorical, variously described as Post-impressionist and Renaissance-classic. Styles and colors (such as magenta and lemon) were designed to startle. The whole play was acted in three hours with one brief intermission. Conventional characterizations and staging traditions were ignored. The actors were specially trained to speak rapidly but naturally, using far fewer dramatic pauses than audiences were accustomed to. It was evidently a new *Winter's Tale*.

Critics, as usual, varied in their enthusiasms and paid more attention to physical aspects of the production[50] and its actors than to the overall progress of the play and the question of whether full possibilities of its text had been realized. Still, they seem to have felt challenged by the unaltered text and the nonrealistic décor to consider meanings of the cumulative development through pulsations of action—rapid and slow— and style—realistic and symbolic. One critic said:

> The tempo of dialogue and of action was throughout admirable, especially in the first act. It varied dramatically with the play's rhythm—a rhythm not alone of the verse, but of the play's procedure and emotion. Some contrasts of style between the various players were also well arranged.[51]

John Masefield thought that Granville-Barker put forward the play "as Shakespeare meant it to be presented, as a continuous stream of human fate."[52] Then he added:

> The performance, besides giving me intense pleasure, gave me (for the first time in any English theatre) a sense of Shakespeare's power and art, of his mind at work shaping and directing, and of his dramatic intention. The performance seemed to me to be a riper and juster piece of Shakespearian criticism, a clearer per-

_____

spearian Production: 1898–1948," *ShS* 2 (1949):8; G. Wilson Knight, *Shakespearian Production* (London: Faber and Faber, 1964), pp. 224–27; *The Oxford Companion to the Theatre*, ed. Phyllis Hartnoll, 3d ed. (London: Oxford University Press, 1967), p. 80.

50. "Most of the critics, accustomed to the historical exactitude of Irving and Tree, were much bothered by the absence of any recognizable 'period atmosphere' in the production." Marshall, p. 151.

51. John Palmer, "Shakespeare's 'The Winter's Tale,' " *The Saturday Review* 94 (1912):391.

52. Letter to *The Times*, 27 September 1912, p. 7. Masefield had already written trenchantly on Shakespeare's art in *The Winter's Tale*. "In this play, he

ception and grasping of the Shakespearian idea, than I have
hitherto seen in print or on the stage here; in fact, a big and new
achievement, to be valued as a step forward.[53]

Few critics ventured new thoughts as to what the play was
about, but the economy[54] and speed of the production let them
grasp, for the first time, its wholeness. Such comment as that
above on the rhythm of the play's "procedure and emotion" and
its presenting "a continuous stream of human fate" hinted,
though perhaps no more than hinted, that the play itself
worked partly in terms of semiformal or musical content, that
its subject was as elemental as the rhythms of renewal in the
seasons and in human generations.

Granville-Barker, too, described the action in terms of its
motion, changes, and contrasts, rather than its cognitive density, as in this account of the final scene:

> From the moment the statue is disclosed, every device of chang-
> ing colour and time, every minor contrast of voice and mood that
> can give the scene modelling and beauty of form, is brought into
> easy use. Then the final effect of the music, of the brisk stirring
> trumpet sentences in Paulina's speech, of the simplicity of
> Leontes' "let it be an art lawful as eating." Then the swift contrast
> of the alarmed and sceptical Polixenes and Camillo, then Paulina's
> happiness breaking almost into chatter. And then the perfect
> sufficiency of Hermione's eight lines (oh, how a lesser dramatist
> might have overdone it with Noble Forgiveness and what not!) — it
> all really is a wonderful bit of work.[55]

The critics often followed a similar line, saying how it was done
but not much about what meaning it had. Various particulars
were pointed to but rarely related to the whole. Only occasional
comments sought the main virtue of the changes. One reviewer
remarked:

---

followed his usual practice of showing the results of a human blindness
upon human destiny. The greater plays are studies of treachery and self-
betrayal. This play is a study of deceit and self-deception. Leontes is deceived
by his obsession, Polixenes by his son, the countryman by Autolycus, life,
throughout, by art." *William Shakespeare* (New York: Holt, 1911), p. 228.

53. This letter is quoted in part by Pafford, p. 180.

54. Granville-Barker observed a "ruthless excision of bits of traditional
business and clowning." Byrne, "Fifty Years," p. 8.

55. "Preface" to *The Winter's Tale by William Shakespeare: An Acting Edi-
tion* (London: William Heinemann, 1912), p. vii, Reprinted in Harley
Granville-Barker, *More Prefaces to Shakespeare*, ed. Edward M. Moore
(Princeton: Princeton University Press, 1974), p. 22.

The built-up scenes with the real trees in tubs and the real rabbits and the trickly fountains which you have come to associate with Shakespeare, take time; and, if you think it over, they are not really natural, only customary—not so natural, you must admit, as the beautiful language of Shakespeare, what is left of which you cannot hear for the banging of Sir Herbert Tree's carpenters. Then why not give Mr. Barker's way a trial?[56]

Others found signal value in the use of the apron. "Most of the action was placed well forward."[57] Intimacy with the audience being increased, the "resistless verse" and the asides and soliloquies, both vehement and secretive, made a profound impression.[58] Perhaps as a result of forward placement, certain scenes became instantly more effective. Two critics, for instance, each writing many years after the event, recall the unexpected humor and charm of the second scene in the fifth act, where three Gentlemen relate to each other and to Autolycus the story of Leontes' recognition of Perdita.[59] Finally, the delivery by the actors, discounted by some critics as too staccato, was identified by others as a virtue. One said:

> Mr. Barker has struck at the root difficulty, and has to a great extent abandoned the conventional blank-verse delivery. He has endeavored (not always with success) to make his actors bring out the *meaning* of their sentences, to make them speak in voices approximately human, and at a pace rapid enough to hold the interest of the audience.[60]

Granville-Barker also worked to eliminate the earlier focus upon Hermione's heroism. Henry Ainley played Leontes as a person in whose reality one could believe and for whom one could have sympathy; his passion became more infectious and his part more equal to Hermione's in power.

56. Unsigned review, *The Outlook* 30 (1912):452.

57. C. B. Purdom, *Producing Shakespeare* (London: Pitman, 1950), p. 96. "Actors delivered their set speeches from the very edge of the apron." J. C. Trewin, *The Theatre Since 1900* (London: A. Dakers, 1951), p. 100.

58. See Palmer, *Saturday Review* 114 (1912):391; and see unsigned review in *The Athenaeum*, 28 September 1912, p. 351, and *The Outlook* 30 (1912):453.

59. Gordon Crosse, *Shakespearean Playgoing: 1890–1952* (London: Mowbray, 1953), p. 47, was "delighted to find how amusing V. ii (which Tree omitted altogether) proved on the stage," and J. C. Trewin, *Shakespeare on the English Stage: 1900–1964* (London. Barrie & Rockliff, 1964), p. 54, "heard with a shock of discovery, the [scene] with its little bravura part of Paulina's steward."

60. Unsigned review, *The Spectator* 109 (1912):451.

Years later, Granville-Barker's achievement was summarized judiciously: "Itemize his reforms, analyse his methods, they all add up to the one supremely important aim—the theatre in search of authenticity, learning to come to terms with the author's text, and unlearning a great many bad habits in the process."[61] What *authenticity* means, of course, is neither imitation of Shakespearean staging nor flattery of contemporary taste. It requires unflagging attention to the meanings that build slowly through the complete text like a shelf of coral and staging that is faithful to these meanings. The Savoy production is memorable because, in it, the aim and the flow of the play were sensitively reconsidered from first to last. Unfortunately, while it improved Shakespearean staging, it failed to provoke many new insights into *The Winter's Tale.* In this sense, the play suffered from the regrettable though fully understandable reluctance of reviewers and critics to analyze in detail meanings implicit in the experience they had had.

After 1912: An Old Play Dawning?

IX

The Winter's Tale has in our time continued to suffer from failures of criticism and production to enter a cooperative relationship. Criticism, particularly, has explored new perspectives upon the play without questioning, until recently, how those perspectives connect, if at all, to direct experience.

Instead of mediating between the school of Dowden that found the play part of Shakespeare's late charming glow and the school of Strachey that pronounced it a careless bore, a few English critics in the late 1930s took an entirely new approach. They argued that the text, properly considered, revealed a maturity and significance far beyond the fairy-tale surface of its action. One examined Shakespeare's skillful exploitation of stylistic resources in an attempt to get at the "range and scale of experience behind the words."[62] He found hints of vegetation myths, of a Waste Land made fertile, and he traced out relationships in the play between the individual and the state, youth and age, court and country, dream and reality. Throughout he

61. Byrne, "Fifty Years," 8. See also her "Introduction" to Harley Granville-Barker, *Prefaces to Shakespeare* (1930; Reprinted, London: B. T. Batsford, 1963), 1:vii-xxii.
62. F. C. Tinkler, "The Winter's Tale," *Scrutiny* 5 (1937):344.

saw a persistent irony in the play, a "savage humour," working
to achieve a conservative synthesis of disparate attitudes in
Elizabethan culture. Another critic discussed Shakespeare's
"symbolic technique" and saw the play, in part, as "a profound
and highly individual effort to bring the *impasse* suggested by
the exploration of the part played by 'blood' in human
personality—a part which is at once fulfillment and destruction—into relation with feelings which imply understanding of a great religious tradition."[63]

Not long after these and related studies came out,[64] a
cautionary note was sounded. Praising *The Winter's Tale* as a
masterpiece of broader perfection than *The Tempest* and con-
ceding that Shakespeare exploited symbolic effects, F. R. Leavis
warned that, in the criticism of Shakespeare's late plays, "we
may err by insisting on finding a 'significance' that we assume
to be necessarily there."[65] *Cymbeline*, he suggested, may have
no particularly "profound significance." And, while he agreed
that *The Winter's Tale* might have a significance beyond its
plot,[66] he carefully avoided distilling that significance into any
form of summary or statement. Instead, he stayed close to the
affective surface, praising the play for "the concrete presence of
time in its rhythmic processes" and its "effect as of the sap
rising from the root" (345).

Leavis's warnings were largely ignored. The major criticism
that followed tended to treat the play as a philosophical poem.
In a suggestive essay, not susceptible to summary, G. Wilson
Knight worked through the text, playing off shrewd analyses of
individual psychology against larger patterns of natural
metamorphosis.[67] Each psychic detail, he argued, fits into a
cycloramic movement. Within Leontes' outbursts, for example,
resides a "final, icy reserve" (81):

63. D. A. Traversi, *Approach to Shakespeare* (London: Sands, 1938), p. 135.
64. See, for example, E. M. W. Tillyard, *Shakespeare's Last Plays* (London:
Chatto & Windus, 1938), pp. 40–48, 76–78, 81–85.
65. "The Criticism of Shakespeare's Late Plays: A Caveat," *Scrutiny* 10
(1942):340.
66. "The relations between character, speech and the main themes of the
drama are not such as to invite a psychologizing approach; the treatment of
life is too generalizing (we may say, if we haste to add 'and intensifying'); so
large a part of the function of the words spoken by the characters is so plainly
something other than to 'create' the speakers or to advance an action that we
can profitably consider in terms of the interacting of individuals" (341).
67. " 'Great Creating Nature': An Essay on *The Winter's Tale*," in *The Crown
of Life* (London: Methuen, 1947), pp. 76–128.

Indeed, Leontes' most vitriolic spasms get themselves out with a certain underemphasis, not unlike Swift's general expression of nausea through *meiosis*; as though the extreme of satiric bitterness were always loath to risk suicide in the katharsis of luxuriant expression (81).

Struggling with his own mental web of suspicion, Leontes is suitably bound up with a figure of confidence and counsel like Camillo. Leontes endures a long, blank, pre-cathartic winter of penance (95) before the final life-giving release of Hermione's restoration. In Knight's words, the drama moves to show "Leontes, under the tutelage of the Oracle, as painfully working himself from the bondage of sin and remorse into the freedom of nature, with the patly-named Paulina as conscience, guide, and priestess" (127).

The critics of the time were mainly content to argue that *The Winter's Tale* contains a supercharged meaning; they saw no necessity to reveal how Shakespeare made that meaning accessible to his audience. One critic did argue that Shakespearean dramatic techniques became purposefully antiquated and unreal so as to force the audience "to seek for 'inner meanings,' to observe the subtle interplay of a whole world of interrelated ideas."[68] Though it would be wrong to allegorize or mythify the action, it is nonetheless full of symbols and best seen as "an acted parable of social regeneration" (94), a "literary expression of Christian humanism." The question of whether or how symbols, parable, and humanism could become part of the dramatic experience remained unanswered.

Onstage, regard for the play also increased. Granville-Barker's innovations, at least some of them, filtered into general use, and one or two productions reached white heat for critics whose negative preconceptions did not block out the play. Thus one viewer found a production at the Cort of New York in 1946 "a thing of utter magnificence."[69] He singled out the "no star" teamwork of the cast, praised the credibility of Leontes as slightly underplayed, and concluded: "In spite of 300 years of criticism that it is a minor tour-de-force which doesn't quite come off, this Theater Guild production of 'The Winter's Tale'

68. S. L. Bethell, *The Winter's Tale: A Study* (London: Staples, 1947), p. 55. And see, S. L. Bethell, ed., *The Winter's Tale*, New Clarendon ed. (Oxford: Clarendon Press, 1956), pp. 7–40.

69. Burton Rascoe, review of Theater Guild performance, 15 January 1946, in the *New York World-Telegram*, 16 January 1946, as quoted in *New York Theatre Critics Review* 7 (1947):487.

shows me that it is one of the Bard's great theatrical master-pieces." (487). Reviewers who were critical of the production fell back upon the widely held notion, a legacy of centuries, of redaction, that *The Winter's Tale* is "not one of the Bard's best plays."[70] Those who were impressed by it concentrated upon the experience itself.[71]

A breach in the wall between study and stage may have been opened in 1951 with the production by Peter Brook at the London Phoenix, which was acclaimed as the "best all-round performance of that play since Granville-Barker's."[72] Brook divided the play into tragedy, pastoral, and resurrection as had been suggested by Knight, and the "underemphasis" and "reserve" of Leontes, also noted by Knight, became the central strength of Gielgud's interpretation. Many reviewers commented. Gielgud began quietly, and the jealousy stole upon him almost unaware.[73] When Leontes tells Hermione she never spoke to better purpose than in persuading Polixenes to stay, the Queen asks, "Never?" (1. 2. 89). Leontes replies, "Never, but once."[74] In separating the two parts of the reply and changing the tone of "but once," Gielgud daringly suggested the first breath of jealousy, and after the words "Too hot, too hot!" (1. 2. 108), he showed the King caught in a seething, agonizing onrush.[75] Pondering the universal cuckolder, "Sir Smile," "he boldy addressed the audience" while standing "far downstage."[76] His fevered speech swelled to a "trumpet music" (164)

70. Lewis Nichols, *New York Times*, 16 January 1946, in *N. Y. T. C. R.* 7 (1947):486.

71. Robert Garland, *New York Journal American*, 16 January 1946, in *N. Y. T. C. R.* 7 (1947):486, for example, praised the swift pace of the production—"it gets a truly Elizabethan move on"—and wrote "a rave review of a great play."

72. Gordon Crosse, *Shakespearean Playgoing*, p. 144. J. C. Trewin called it "a triumph both of performance . . . and of dignified and imaginative direction." *World Theatre* 1 (1951):71.

73. Knight, interestingly enough, thought Gielgud's interpretation too "reserved." *Shakespearian Production*, p. 259.

74. Some editors (including Pafford) unwisely remove the comma that is in the Folio between "Never" and "but once."

75. These tonal shifts are beautifully clear in the company's recording of the play for the Shakespeare Recording Society, *SRS* 214.

76. Arthur Colby Sprague, *Shakespearian Players and Peformances* (Cambridge, Mass.: Harvard University Press, 1953), p. 164. Arthur Colby Sprague and J. C. Trewin, *Shakespeare's Plays Today* (Columbia, S. C.: University of South Carolina Press, 1971), p. 115, note that Peter Brook consistently moved the actors as far forward as possible and encouraged them to employ as much direct address as they could.

in saying "My wife is nothing, nor nothing have these nothings,/ If this be nothing" (1. 2. 295). Yet he betrayed a strange under-current of "warmth" and "humanity" in his affection for Mamillius, an achievement essential for the believability and emotional pull of the later penance and reconciliation.[77] Even his melodramatic reaction to the oracle eventuated in an affecting remorse. "He seemed at first stunned, then staggered across the stage (the boards sounded), then sank upon the throne and groaned once."[78] After the announcements of Mamillius's and Hermione's deaths, he shed tears "easy to share."[79] Trying to sum up an audience's perception of Gielgud's Leontes, one reviewer wrote:

> They are sorry for Leontes by the end of the evening, regarding him, like Lear, as a great man with a mistaken passion for violence against those who love him. He repents after great suffering and his wife is restored to him in a deeply moving scene of reconciliation, touched with sublime forgiveness. Although Leontes is not as well known to us as Falstaff, Shylock, or Malvolio, he is no less human than they are, and when a Gielgud decides to bring him to life we are left wondering why the play is so rarely performed.[80]

The final scene, simply staged in tones of gray and white, was particularly well received and was termed "moving," "gripping," "natural," and surrounded "with stillness of beauty." Reviewers commented upon the special pathos of Leontes' childlike cry, "O, she's warm" (a cry too daringly simple for Garrick and other redactors).[81] And once again, as in Granville-Barker's production, the little-played second scene of the fifth act with its foppish gentlemen's chatter was found "extremely diverting."[82]

"The tempest which flap-dragon'd the vessel of Antigonus turned into a whirl of snow through whose flakes Father Time

77. Alice Venezky, "Current Shakespearian Productions in England and France," *SQ* 2 (1951):338. Referring to the parts of Leontes and Angelo, Gielgud himself said: "it is no use trying to act these parts if one imagines them to be melodramatic monsters without a shred of humanity." *Stage Directions:* (New York: Random House 1963), p. 44.

78. Sprague, p. 165.

79. Unsigned review, *The Times*, 28 June 1951, p. 8.

80. Eric Johns, "Gielgud in a New Role," *Theatre World* 47:319 (1951):7.

81. See Sprague, p. 174, and J. C. Trewin, *Shakespeare on the English Stage*, p. 53.

82. George Rylands, "Festival Shakespeare in the West End," *ShS* 6 (1953):143. And see Kenneth Muir, "The Conclusion of *The Winter's Tale*," in *The Morality of Art*, ed. D. W. Jefferson (New York: Barnes & Noble, 1969), p. 98.

materialized—and melted away. The skies cleared to an open stage dressed with sunburnt rustics."[83] Despite this magical transition to them, the pastoral scenes in the Phoenix production were the least successful. Perdita and Florizel were considered relatively weak,[84] and the festival for at least one critic was "raucous" and "confused." The pastoral scenes and characters had been, since the eighteenth century, both over-promoted and overpowered by scenery, dancing, and tricks. No students of the play were concerned enough with its continuity, with its funding of typical but progressively more complex and moving patterns of action. Knight's essay, after proceeding chronologically over the drama, stressed only a final impression of enigma, "a vague, numinous sense of mighty powers, working through both the natural order and man's religious consciousness, that preserve, in spite of all appearance, the good."[85]

In 1951, therefore, at the time of the Phoenix production, no critical insights of stage or study had illumined, in Leavis's phrase, "the concrete presence of time in its rhythmic processes" through the play. No tradition of thought about the play persuasively related its pastoral scenes to the disruptive and restorative ones that preceded and followed them. Before Leavis's truly sensed "effect as of sap rising from the root" could be translated into theatrical terms, critics would have to turn away from philosophical criticism and work out instead the correspondence between "inner meaning" and outer process in the play. It was not yet understood that the same rhythmic pattern, the same multiplex commentary upon human and natural artifice, developed itself through all portions of the play and that the precarious tension associated with the gathering of human purpose into rituals of kingly entertainment, marriage vow, trial, or artwork must be as present in the pastoral scenes as elsewhere. Brook and Gielgud had no rationale whereby they could achieve as sophisticated and tonally consistent a staging for the pastoral scenes as for the rest. The problem remains largely unsolved by criticism or production, and I will discuss it in the final chapter.

83. Rylands, 145.
84. Rylands, 143, and Venezky, 337.
85. *Crown of Life*, p. 128

X

It is possible that the critics of *The Winter's Tale* have begun to use the play as a model, in recent years, in their search for "a critical language capable of interpreting the Romances."[86] The search, insofar as profitable, has avoided "taking shortcuts into Shakespeare's vision" (18) and has moved closer to the twistings and turnings of the immediate dramatic encounter. Unafraid of naive inquiry, the searchers seem to be asking, What sequence of thoughts and "what kind of emotional response were the Romances designed to arouse?" (17).

As an example of such inquiry consider the comments in a series of recent articles, all of which have something to say about the first hundred lines of the second scene in the play. Ever since the complaints of Charlotte Lennox in the mid-eighteenth century, critics have discussed the seemingly inadequate motivation of Leontes. An editor of the New Cambridge edition suggested that Leontes should be played as if jealous "from the very outset."[87] More recently, a critic supported the argument, pointing out that Hermione, at the opening of the second scene, is "visibly pregnant." Considering that Polixenes, standing beside her, refers to nine months and to "standing in rich place," "Who can fail to wonder whether the man so amicably addressing this expectant mother may not be the father of her child?"[88]

A few years later, it was argued that the banter between Polixenes and Hermione is full of "sexual overtones" in such

86. Philip Edwards, "Shakespeare's Romances: 1900−1957," *ShS* 11 (1958):18.

87. *The Winter's Tale* (1931, Reprinted, Cambridge: Cambridge University Press, 1968), p. 131. J. D. Wilson pointed to the implied threat that could be found in Leontes' remark, "Stay your thanks a while, / And pay them when you part" (1. 2. 9).

88. Nevill Coghill, "Six Points of Stage-Craft in *The Winter's Tale*," *ShS* 11 (1958):33. Roger J. Trienens, "The Inception of Leontes' Jealousy in *The Winter's Tale*," *SQ* 4 (1953):321−26, also agreed with the New Cambridge editor and stressed the curtness of Leontes and his remark after Hermione's persuasion of Polixenes, "At my request he would not" (1. 2. 87). M. M. Mahood, *Shakespeare's Wordplay* (London: Methuen, 1957), p. 147, argued that Polixenes' references to the Moon's "nine changes" and to a "burden" imply a theme of pregnancy. John Russell Brown, *Shakespeare and his Comedies*, 2d ed. (London: Methuen, 1962), p. 217, while favoring an initially unsuspecting Leontes, noted the "uneasy sophistication" of the conversation between Camillo and Archidamus and between Hermione and Polixenes.

words as *multiply*, *breed*, and *charge* that Camillo continues
the innuendo in describing Polixenes' "anchor" coming
"home," his "business more material," and his desire to "satisfy" Hermione, so that Leontes, far from being unmotivated, is
given "the *ne plus ultra* in motivation."[89] It was next suggested
that double entendre and hence motivation arise from Hermione's use of such words as *hostess* and from her lines:

> Th' offences we have made you do, we'll answer,
> If you first sinn'd with us, and that with us
> You did continue fault, and that you slipp'd not
> With any but with us.[90] (1. 2. 83)

Another critic then argued:

> Hermione's use of elaborate metaphor for its own sake, separate
> from meaning, evokes the initial unpleasant suggestions in
> Leontes' imagination. Trying to determine when she spoke to best
> "purpose," she uses images which are unsavory in context. . . . Her
> unfortunate choice of the two-sided word "friend" finally pro-
> vokes Leontes to respond.[91]

A later critic points to over a dozen new parts of the conversation between Hermione and Polixenes that could contain
sexual innuendos.[92] He argues (perhaps overargues): "We, as
audience, are thus led into the trap of reading a guilty meaning
into all that we hear" (97). He goes on to say:

> It is sometimes assumed that there has been a relaxation of
> dramatic intensity in the late romances. I would not think that the
> scene we have been considering suggests any such relaxation. If
> there is anything new here, it is that Shakespeare is working more

89. Edward L. Hart, "A Mixed Consort: Leontes, Angelo, Helena," *SQ* 15
(1964):79.

90. Norman Nathan, "Leontes' Provocation," *SQ* 19 (1968):22. See also the
finely balanced discussion of A. D. Nuttall, *William Shakespeare: The Winter's
Tale* (London: Edward Arnold, 1966), pp. 18–24.

91. Mary L. Livingston, "The Natural Art of *The Winter's Tale*," *MLQ* 30
(1969):342–43. That the Elizabethans were supersensitive to ambiguities
often implanted in courtly compliment could easily have been shown.
Spenser, for example, makes the host Malbecco a victim of his guest Paridell's
conversation with Hellenore, Malbecco's wife: "He courted her, yet bayted
every word, / That his ungentle hoste n'ote him appeach / Of vile un-
gentlenesse, or hospitages breach." *F.Q.* 3. 10. 6. 7. *The Works of Edmund
Spenser*, ed. Edwin Greenlaw et al., (Baltimore: Johns Hopkins Press, 1934),
3:139.

92. William H. Matchett, "Dramatic Techniques in 'The Winter's Tale,' "
ShS 22 (1969):95–97. See also, A. L. French, *Shakespeare and the Critics*
(Cambridge: Cambridge University Press, 1972), pp. 135–43.

directly than ever with audience response, not merely presenting an action for our consideration, but directly manipulating our response in order to bring us out where he wants us. (98)

This series of investigations plainly clarifies earlier suggestions that criticism of the romances might now profit from less concern with ultimate significance and more concern with the immediate working of individual scene and episode. One notices that the questions as to when Leontes first becomes jealous and whether or not he is motivated are not solved. They become largely irrelevant. The King has his being in a world where the certainty of knowledge and the rationality implied as tests for adequate motivation are themselves brought into question. It is a world where words mean many things and where "mixtures of tone" refuse "to guide us to a particular response" (99−100).

By according first respect to the text and to dramatic relations between characters and between characters and audience, these critics have begun to open up an infinitely subtle and an essentially new (or authentically old) play, a play not well grasped by most critics who were interested chiefly in mythical and allegorical meanings.[93] The new play is one that lives temporally in the theater or in the immediate experience of a reader.[94]

Directors can and will respond to criticism of the sort mentioned. At the 1969 Stratford-upon-Avon production, the play opened to the view of a person tumbled in a revolving glass box. One reviewer took it to be an "image of Renaissance man changed to a helpless figure."[95] Then, "he, symbol of self-pity, is swiftly changed into a toy,"[96] and all the first part of the action takes place in Mamillius's nursery "equipped with bleak white toys." With the onset of Leontes' jealousy, "Suddenly the light changes to an eerie hue and—as we are inside Leontes'

93. Compare F. David Hoeniger, "The Meaning of *The Winter's Tale*," UTQ 20 (1950):11−26, and J. A. Bryant, "Shakespeare's Allegory: *The Winter's Tale*," *SR* 73 (1955):202−22.

94. Notice that the possibility of finding innuendo in the conversation of Polixenes and Hermione does not come so much from the inherent ambiguity of the words they use as from a visualization of their physical condition and proximity and a new flexible conception of "character" that allows into their banter the hints of innuendo so overblown by Leontes. Not close reading of the words alone but imaginative projection into the dramatic situation accounts for the increased understanding of the scene.

95. *The Times*, 17 May 1969, p. 19, a review by Irving Wardle.

96. *The Sunday Times*, 18 May 1969, p. 57, review by J. W. Lambert.

mind—the movement of his wife and friend goes into slow motion so that their gestures become hideously, exaggeratedly obscene and lustful."[97] Here is one of several suggestive and coherent stagings that might be imagined.

No doubt certain insights are appropriate to each age. In some respects, the Victorians pursued character because they had it; at least they sometimes advanced nobility of self as a defense against attacking relativisms, as if integrity could ward off chaos. Personality was then often conceived in terms more monolithic than ours, and in this sense the heroes and heroines recognized in Shakespeare's plays were truly more heroic than we today readily recognize or grant.[98] Partly it is our loss. Certainly in some sense the tragic and the heroic have become for us more elusive than they were for our grandfathers and great-grandfathers. Perhaps as a consequence, in several of the many recent productions of *The Winter's Tale*, character has remained firmly subordinated to overall design.[99]

97. *The New York Times*, 1 June 1969, 2:4, 19. See also the generally approving comments of Gareth Lloyd Evans, "Interpretation or Experience? Shakespeare at Stratford," *ShS* 23 (1970):133–34. Partly because of limited total length and the need for reasonable proportions, I eschew detailed analysis of the more recent productions. They are numerous, and few, if any, stand out for selective treatment. An overview of evolving trends in staging may be obtained from spring issues of *Shakespeare Quarterly*. See note 99.

98. "One reason why nineteenth-century criticism differs strikingly from our own is that it could use words like 'character,' 'individual,' and 'soul' much more confidently than we can." J. P. Brockbank, "Shakespeare and the Fashion of these Times," *ShS* 16 (1963):35.

99. At Oregon and Alabama productions in 1975, which I saw, such subordination was clearly in evidence, and reviewers so noted. Alan C. Dessen, "The Oregon Shakespearean Festival, 1975," *SQ* 27 (1976):91–93, stressed the director's charting of sequentially presented worlds in the play, the impressive coordination of effects, the visual patterns, as of joined hands, and the careful orchestration of all details. Carol McGinnis Kay, "Alabama Shakespeare Festival," *SQ* (1977):221, described the actor's Leontes as a man trying "to keep his emotions under some control," and she stressed the "progress of the play" and its "rapid and smooth pacing." Again, at Stratford, Connecticut, where the play was presented in 1975 and 1976, I noted the same emphasis upon "a governing idea" "expressed . . . through all available means" as described by Peter Saccio in reviewing the production, "The 1975 Season at Stratford, Connecticut," *SQ* 27 (1976):49–51: "The pattern of loss and restoration, of passion and repentance, of destruction and renewal emerged visually as a circle. Human action, under divine guidance, curved back upon itself to close where it had begun." At the trial scene, "even this truly surprising fury was within the pattern of the whole," and the "costumes, like Time's branch, emphasized the growth within the pattern." Compare a reviewer's comment upon the director's achievement of unity in a 1976 production at the Tyrone Guthrie theater: "He does it by keeping his characters human, by orchestrating them into chamber music rather than grand opera." Quoted in "Theatre

Future production and criticism will experiment, quite properly, with a variety of views upon the play. No one conception of it can ever be final. For some, the tender and pastoralized story of reconciliation will always be paramount. For others, the intricate questioning and upholding of art in its many forms will take precedence. And yet, not all ages and individuals can be said to respond with equal fullness to the play. The history of man's encounter with *The Winter's Tale* translates into a hope the assertion that "Shakespeare has more meaning and value now than he had in his own day."[100] Our age may discover at least momentarily, a new and dramatic yield from what has so long lain fallow.[101]

Because a knowledge of the play's history is partly negative, that is, a knowledge of distortions foisted upon it, one cannot build a positive account out of that knowledge alone. There must be provided first at least a partial answer to the questions raised by Jonson and plaguing us to this day: What, basically, was Shakespeare trying to do in *The Winter's Tale*? Why did he alter his source as he did? In what sense did the progression of Shakespeare's works lead toward this play? What ideas and procedures in contemporary works were developed by Shakespeare in *The Winter's Tale*? All of these questions coalesce in the question of how an informed spectator or reader may appropriately respond to the unfolding play. With an engaging, if provisional, "answer" to this question as the eventual goal of the last chapter and of the book as a whole, I undertake in the next chapter a study of questions leading toward it.

Reviews," *SQ* 28 (1977):224. Another reviewer of the production found Leontes' last gesture in the statue scene "the final turn in a ritual dance" (225). The dangers of too great emphasis upon directorial "interpretation" of the grand design should also be noted, however, for, as Robert Speaight complained of the 1976-1977 production of *The Winter's Tale* at Stratford-upon-Avon, it may take superb individual acting to overcome a director's fondness for "Nordic nonsense" or other mishandled contexts. "Shakespeare in Britain," *SQ* 28 (1977):189. See, in this connection, John Russell Brown's "Free Shakespeare," *ShS* 24 (1971):127−35, arguing for more "freedom from a director's limiting conception and guidance to actors."

100. A remark made, to illustrate the fallacy and futility of intentionalist criticism, by W. K. Wimsatt, "Genesis: A Fallacy Revisited," in *The Disciplines of Criticism*, ed. Peter Demetz, Thomas Greene, and Lowry Nelson, Jr. (New Haven: Yale University Press, 1968), p. 225.

101. In addition to studies of *The Winter's Tale* in performance, studies of ways in which both its rhetoric and its family romance psychology contribute to the overall effect and significance appear particularly promising now.

After certain perhaps disappointingly familiar and predictable books such as those of A. D. Nuttall, *William Shakespeare: The Winter's Tale* (London: Eduard Arnold, 1966), Kenneth Muir, ed. *Shakespeare: The Winter's Tale* (London: MacMillan, 1968); and Fitzroy Pyle, *The Winter's Tale: A Commentary on the Structure* (London: Routledge & Kegan Paul, 1969), what is needed is renewed attention to still largely unmapped resources of Shakespeare's late style as evidenced in the play. The new stylistics should generate important new readings. Recent interest, moreover, in psychological tensions and growth within Shakespeare's dramatic families and other kinship groups— witness, for example, papers at recent meetings of the Shakespeare Association of America, Marjorie Garber, "Coming of Age in Shakespeare," *YR* 66 (1977):517–33, and the MLA Special Sessions on Marriage and the Family in Shakespeare and on Feminist Criticism of Shakespeare—should also be brought to bear upon *The Winter's Tale*. See also my article, "Shakespeare's Imperiled and Chastening Daughters of Romance," *South Atlantic Bulletin* 43 (1978):125–40.

Chapter III.

Backgrounds

I have argued in the first chapter that criticism can and should meet *The Winter's Tale* as a dramatic whole. Criticism need not work exclusively in terms of intellectual content nor of remembered emotion. It may also work in terms of our temporal encounter with the play, centering in the middle range between feeling and thought, and between engagement and detachment. Successful criticism in this vein, however, while striving to explain the play, to answer especially the questions that precede or accompany rather than follow it, paradoxically intensifies our need for the irreplaceable experience of the play itself. Thus the best dramatic criticism, in my view, will be satisfied with—in fact, will aim at—nothing less than a kind of failure, a conviction of having brought the reader or spectator not to the completion of the journey but only to its beginning.

The preceding chapter presents a view of the staged and printed reality of *The Winter's Tale* through a history that has both discouraged and promoted its vigor. Implicit in the chapter is a conviction that we can learn from critical and theatrical misses as well as from hits. It attempts to bring into relief the action of the play, its theatrical impressiveness and intellectual respectability, and to provoke curiosity about ways for the spectator or reader to realize a more full meaning of the dramatic object before his eyes. I turn from this now to apply another perspective, to ask: What backgrounds inform the inner development of the play? What sources and what analogues help illumine the three-hour traffic with the text we all experience onstage or in an armchair? Here must be considered what Shakespeare borrowed from, altered, and added to his primary source; What in his own development contributed to the play; and what in the literary world around and preceding him helped illuminate at least a few of our more problematic responses. Let us look, then, first at the source.

Pandosto

I

"Shakespeare's plays are, of course, something utterly differ-ent from their sources however carefully these may have been used. He does not simply 'turn' *Rosalynde* or *Pandosto* into a play."[1] A truism, we say. Still, comparisons of *Pandosto* and *The Winter's Tale* have regularly assumed some similarity between them. According to Charlotte Lennox, "If we compare the Con-duct of the Incidents in the Play with the paltry Story on which it is founded, we shall find the Original much less absurd and ridiculous."[2] Later commentators, while striving to correct this judgment, have succeeded mainly in uncovering disparate bor-rowings and changes of incident, phrasing, and attitude.[3]

How, then, can *The Winter's Tale* as a whole be "utterly different" from its source? So long as a critic attends chiefly to

1. J. H. P. Pafford, ed., *The Winter's Tale*, Arden ed. (London: Methuen, 1963), p. xxx n.1.
2. *Shakespear Illustrated* (London: A. Millar, 1753), 2:75. I have mod-ernized the text.
3. Pafford, despite the comment quoted in the text, conducts his discus-sion mainly in terms of similarities and differences among characters and scenes of Greene's novel and Shakespeare's play and the resulting changes in credibility. "He gives life to his characters and does everything possible to give credibility to the plot" (p. xxxi). Pafford concludes that *Pandosto* lacks the "vigour, beauty, and humanity of *The Winter's Tale*" (p. xxxiii). Geoffrey Bullough, *Narrative and Dramatic Sources of Shakespeare* (London: Rout-ledge and Kegan Paul, 1975), 8: 115 – 55, details many changes by Shakespeare of Greene's settings, names, action, and theme, and he mentions, contrary to Pafford, that some of the changes lead to loss of probability. Neither Pafford nor Bullough devotes much attention to the differing effects (and their causes) of reading Greene's prose narrative versus seeing Shakespeare's verse drama. See also, F. W. Moorman, ed., *The Winter's Tale*, Arden ed., 2d ed. (London: Methuen, 1922,) pp. xxii – xxi; Kenneth Muir, *Shakespeare's Sources* (London, 1957), 1: 240 – 47; and see Samuel Lee Wolff, *The Greek Romances in Elizabethan Prose Fiction* (New York: Columbia University Press, 1912), pp. 451 – 55; Arthur Quiller-Couch, Introduction to *The Winter's Tale*, New Cam-bridge ed. (1931; Reprinted, Cambridge: Cambridge University Press, 1968), pp. xiii – xviii; Frederick E. Pierce, ed., *The Yale Shakespeare Winter's Tale* (New Haven: Yale University Press, 1918), pp. 128 – 30; Fitzroy Pyle, *The Win-ter's Tale* (London: Routledge and Kegan Paul, 1969), pp. 155 – 57; Hallet Smith, *Shakespeare's Romances* (San Marino, Calif.: Huntington Library, 1972), pp. 95 – 120. A more comprehensive analysis of Greene's influence upon Shakespeare is that of Norman Sanders, "The Comedy of Greene and Shakespeare," *Early Shakespeare*, Stratford-Upon-Avon Studies 3, ed. John Russell Brown and Bernard Harris (London: Arnold, 1961), pp. 35 – 53, who makes the intriguing suggestion, *inter alia*, that Greene, in progressing from *Friar Bacon* to *James IV*, prefigured Shakespeare's development from roman-tic comedy to dramatic romance. See also Walter R. Davis, *Idea and Act in Elizabethan Fiction* (Princeton: Princeton University Press, 1969), pp. 167 – 70.

changes in the story line, he can only conclude that Shakespeare worked upon his source to "intensify its essentially romantic character,"[4] or to improve its credibility at this point and that, or to increase its "dramatic effectiveness"[5] whatever, precisely, that means. Even less convincing is the critic who asserts that Shakespeare changed Greene's story in order to advance a certain set of beliefs. To argue, for example, as has been done,[6] that Shakespeare purposefully altered *Pandosto* to contrast Senecan fatalism (in the first three acts) with Christian grace (in the last two acts) is to ignore the moment-by-moment affective impact. Neither Greene nor Shakespeare was a priest, and it seems as mistaken to relate the source to the play simply in terms of message as it is to relate the two simply in terms of plot. For a Shakespearean play, considered affectively, as I am doing here, represents a vicarious moment of experience intervening somewhere between our perception of its plot and our reflection upon its message, a moment in which the successive intellectual and emotional states the play has generated in us are felt as an aesthetically satisfying shape of time. The time spent seeing *The Winter's Tale* makes clear from the beginning that it will profit a quicker, more subtle and serious intellect and a wider range of sensibility than will the time spent reading *Pandosto*. The play, through its stimulation and enlargement of these faculties, offers its audience a life-enhancing, world-accepting confidence foreign to Greene's narrative.[7]

4. Moorman, p. xxv.

5. Muir, 1: 234, 235.

6. See S. R. Maveety, "What Shakespeare Did with *Pandosto*: An Interpretation of *The Winter's Tale*," in *Pacific Coast Studies in Shakespeare*, ed. Waldo F. McNeir and Thelma N. Greenfield (Eugene: University of Oregon Press, 1966), pp. 263–79.

7. That is, in the case of Greene at least, those aspects of style that help define the sort of perceiver and believer sought by the work appear much more important, finally, in showing relations of source to play, than do other matters. Max Bluestone, *From Story to Stage* (The Hague: Mouton, 1974), argues that the significance of Shakespeare's dramatic adaptation should be sought primarily in the difference between silent, nonsensuous reading of a static Elizabethan prose narrative and the vivid sounds and sights of dramatically rendered moments of time and uses of space. Bluestone tends, however, to ignore readers' capacities to vivify out of their own resources fiction that fails to particularize reality. Greene, furthermore, hardly eschews all interest in details: "Shall the seas be thy harbour and the hard boat thy cradle? Shall thy tender mouth, instead of sweet kisses, be nipped with bitter storms? Shalt thou have the whistling winds for thy lullaby, and the salt sea foam instead of sweet milk?" Robert Greene, *Pandosto. The Triumph of Time* (London, 1588, 1592, 1595, 1607, and others), p. 193, as printed in a specially

II

What, basically, does *Pandosto* offer to its reader? Greene's tale rehearses the even ups and downs of mechanically capricious fortune. In an hour's sitting, the mind moves at a pleasant dogtrot through action and character all stylized with the same unchanging sprightliness. To illustrate, compare the opening to the complaint later on of Queen Bellaria in prison. Greene begins:

> In the country of Bohemia, there reigned a king called Pandosto, whose fortunate success in wars against his foes, and bountiful courtesy towards his friends in peace, made him to be greatly feared and loved of all men. This Pandosto had to wife a lady called Bellaria, by birth royal, learned by education, fair by nature, by virtues famous, so that it was hard to judge whether her beauty, fortune, or virtue won the greatest commendations.... They had not been married long, but Fortune, willing to increase their happiness, lent them a son, so adorned with the gifts of nature, as the perfection of the child greatly augmented the love of the parents and the joy of their commons....
>
> Fortune envious of such happy success, willing to shew some sign of her inconstancy, turned her wheel, and darkened their bright sun of prosperity with the misty clouds of mishap and misery. (184)

Later, jailed by the jealous King, the Queen exclaims:

> "Alas, Bellaria, how unfortunate art thou, because fortunate! Better hadst thou been born a beggar than a prince, so shouldest thou have bridled fortune with want, where now she sporteth herself with thy plenty. Ah, happy life, where poor thoughts and mean desires live in secure content, not fearing fortune because too low for fortune! Thou seest now, Bellaria, that care is a companion to honour, not to poverty; that high cedars are crushed with tempests, when low shrubs are not touched with the wind; precious diamonds are cut with the file, when despised pebbles lie safe in the sand. Delphos is sought to by princes, not beggars, and Fortune's altars smoke with kings' presents, not with poor men's gifts." (191−92)

Whether happy or sad, whether the narrator's or a character's, all voices sound and mean alike. Here and everywhere in

---

collated text by Pafford, pp. 184−85. I omit variants. Even if, finally, *The Winter's Tale* is more vivid than *Pandosto*, surely that relation is less important than others noted below.

the story, each marionette of fortune is made to speak through euphuistic aphorisms expressing age-old sentiments, trite and true. The tendency to summarize, to use familiar gestures and sentiments, to manipulate the story line capriciously, to avoid individualized scenes, costumes, physiognomies, and all particularizing complication shows Greene's sense of the romance mode as well as his debt to oral tradition, the art of ancient storytellers. And since the world view invoked is a child-wise one in which marvels and defeats, wonders and woes, inevitably balance, it is not surprising that, offsetting the early bliss of the young lovers, Bellaria is later made to die and Pandosto to slay himself. As fortune's wheel brings some to the zenith, it plunges others to the nadir.[8]

The strength and charm of *Pandosto* lie mainly in its solid conventional wisdom mediated by an ebullient prose rather than in its power to involve the reader in sustained dramatic suspense. Pandosto's nobles, for example, entreat his mercy upon his wife and daughter, saying:

> If she had faulted, yet it were more honourable to pardon with mercy than to punish with extremity, and more kingly to be commended of pity than accused of rigour. And as for the child, if he should punish it for the mother's offence, it were to strive against nature and justice; and that *unnatural actions do more offend the Gods than men*. (193 [my emphasis])

The seriousness of the subject is reduced and contained by the detachment and confidence of the style, by its energetic tidi-

8. For purposes of generic analysis, both *Pandosto* and *The Winter's Tale* lie squarely in the tradition of pastoral romance, and many critics have helped to trace the relation of Greene's work to Shakespeare's in the contexts of pastoral and romance. See, for example, W. W. Greg, *Pastoral Poetry and Pastoral Drama* (London: A. H. Bullen, 1906); Edwin Greenlaw, "Shakespeare's Pastoral," *SP* 13 (1916): 122−54; E. C. Pettet, *Shakespeare and the Romance Tradition* (London: Staples Press, 1949), pp. 54-66; John Lawler, "Pandosto and the Nature of Dramatic Romance," *PQ* 41 (1962): 96−113; Walter R. Davis, "Robert Greene and Greek Romance," ch. 5 of *Idea and Act in Elizabethan Fiction*, pp. 183−88; Carol Gesner, *Shakespeare and the Greek Romance* (Lexington: University Press of Kentucky, 1970); Howard Felperin, *Shakespearean Romance* (Princeton: Princeton University Press, 1972); Hallet Smith, *Shakespeare's Romances*; David Young, *The Heart's Forest: A Study of Shakespeare's Pastoral Plays* (New Haven: Yale University Press, 1972). In this chapter, I minimize analysis of genre for reasons given above and because of the many earlier studies. See also studies by Jordan, Parrott, Bradbrook, Sanders, and others listed in Tetsumaro Hayashi, comp., *Robert Greene Criticism* (Metuchen, N. J.: Scarecrow, 1971). And see works listed in note 3 above.

ness. The effect is emphasized in Pandosto's reaction to the deaths of his wife and son:

> "O miserable Pandosto! what surer witness than conscience! what thoughts more sour than suspicion! what plague more bad than jealousy! *unnatural actions offend the gods more than men*, and causeless cruelty never scapes without revenge. I have committed such a bloody fact, as repent I may, but recall I cannot. Ah, jealousy! a hell to the mind, and a horror to the conscience, suppressing reason, and inciting rage; a worse passion than frenzy, a greater plague than madness." (198 [my emphasis])

Here it is appropriate but also automatic for Pandosto to repeat the nobles' warning concerning "unnatural action"; thus, Greene builds up an effect of ritual wisdom.

The conventionality of Greene's tale makes it pleasing. Though individual turns in the plot may be barely predictable, our general attitude toward the whole remains confident and secure. Since the style is as stable as the characters it describes, the only agency of change is external fortune, and no challenge confronts the reader either to participate in the psychic growth of the characters or to reorganize his apprehension of the story world. The prose is lively but commonplace; there is not much imagery that asks one to work hard, to assimilate unimagined correspondences, to edge out toward a region unknown. Instead of leading the reader through descriptions or the thought of characters toward some haunting inexpressible intricacy and beauty, Greene habitually moves in the other direction, reducing the potentially subtle to a single, familiar phrase, shunning the rarer vision for the common underview. Bellaria's attitudes, for instance, are defined by standardizing clichés (197), and in Dorastus (Florizel) personality is a conduit for stereotyped reflections (205). Greene tends to conceive of character as simply a staging area for incoming forces and plot as a sort of papier mâché strung up to contain them, assuming on the part of his audience an eager complicity in self-conscious authorial turns. When Dorastus and Fawnia set sail from Sicilia, "we leave them to the favour of the wind and seas, and return to Egistus" (Polixenes) (216). When Pandosto commits suicide it is "to close up the comedy with a tragical stratagem" (225). Greene's dedication refers to the work itself as a "triumph of time, so rudely finished"; here time and fortune are baldly at one with the author's design.

Shakespeare's source, then, is characterized by the unmistakable presence of the narrator throughout, lending his euphuistic confidence to each speaker and description and employing a familiar romance style of lively ease that consistently pleases through its aphoristic balance, predictable surprise, and journalistic pace. The short sentences, predictable sentiments, even and clear syntax, and shallow comparisons all keep us in a common colloquial world where an unvarying folksy shrewdness is the proper antidote to the inevitable upsets of fortune.

III

With the general tenor of Greene's narrative in mind, it should be possible to discuss Shakespeare's indebtedness to it and departures from it. His borrowings and semi-borrowings of plot details and bits of dialogue and description converted into dialogue have been traced thoroughly by Pafford, Bullough, and others. More difficult to analyze is the way in which here and there he develops and subtilizes the germ of a suggestion found in Greene.

In his introduction, Greene somewhat archly asks his reader to excuse the "rude and homely" character of his art, expressing the hope that "my willing mind shall excuse my slender skill" (183). Shakespeare echoes this opposition of imperfect success to ideal intention in his prologue-like first scene. The lines not only forecast the action but also focus attention upon the opposition that is and will be at issue. "If you shall chance, Camillo," says Archidamus, "to visit Bohemia on the like occasion whereon my services are now on foot, you shall see, as I have said, great difference betwixt our Bohemia and your Sicilia." The "difference" is that between the magnificent entertainment of Sicilia and the rude and homely hospitality of Bohemia. But, says Archidamus, "Wherein our entertainment shall shame us,[9] we will be justified in our loves" (1.1.7). And he proceeds to enact a kind of hesitant groping down through the surface of courtly compliment to the fount of integrity and clear will: "Verily I speak it in the freedom of my knowledge: we cannot with such magnificence—in so rare—I know not what to say—(1. 1. 11)/Believe me, I speak as my understanding

9. I have changed to a comma the colon employed by Pafford, who follows the Folio.

instructs me, and as mine honesty puts it to utterance" (1.1.19).
When Camillo then describes the mature affection of the two
kings, "not personal" but "royally attorneyed with interchange
of gifts, letters, loving embassies," Archidamus responds by
turning to the "unspeakable" comfort of Mamillius. And when
Camillo says that Mamillius provides an "excuse" for those on
crutches to desire life, Archidamus replies, "If the king had no
son, they would desire to live on crutches till he had one" (1.1.
44). Greene's faintly disingenuous defense of his rude work
excused on account of his "willing mind" thus grows, in the
playwright's hands, to an epitome of the play to come. Shakespeare shows minds groping past flawed performance, magnificent but impersonal entertainment, persons and actions
maimed and on crutches, toward the truest and freshest
sources of social harmony—justifying love, honesty, the comfort of youth.

If we remember that Shakespeare, writing probably in 1610 or
1611, was dramatizing a popular novel first published some
twenty-three years before, we can appreciate why he may have
wished to stress at the outset a new approach to Greene's
subject and a more responsive style. We do not know whether
the play was advertised as a dramatization of *Pandosto*, but
Shakespeare must have anticipated that, after the first performance, many in his audience would know that it was and would
adjust their expectations accordingly. In his dedicatory letter,
Greene had written: "The mind is sometimes delighted as
much with small trifles as with sumptuous triumphs; and as
well pleased with hearing of Pan's homely fancies, as of Her-
cules' renowned labours" (183). In his title for the play, Shakespeare, too, adverts to the fanciful and seemingly trifling as
opposed to the Herculean.[10] His first scene plainly suggests
that his subject is the "malice or matter to alter" the friendship
of age and the comfort of youth that cures and restores. Here is,
in other words, no heroic theme, at least as conventionally
defined. But, whereas Greene couches his opening in euphuistic terms and suggests slyly that his potential critics are "oftentimes most unlearned of all," Shakespeare seconds no such
attitude, choosing instead to develop through Archidamus,

10. "Tales" in Shakespeare are often made light of. See, for example, *WT*
5.2.62 and 5.3.117. See also Pafford, p. liii, where associations of tales and
triviality are developed. *Winter's* tales, however, may concern malign
phatoms. Compare *Mac*. 3.4.63−66.

who represents pastoral Bohemia, the hints in his source about the superiority of rude but willing minds and art.

A second example of the way in which Shakespeare develops the embryonic suggestions he finds in Greene's narrative is provided by the respective Messenger scenes in the two works. In *Pandosto*, the Messengers

> arrived at Delphos, where they were no sooner set on land but with *great devotion* they went to the *temple* of Apollo, and there *offering sacrifice* to the God and gifts to the priest, as the custom was, they humbly craved an answer of their demand. They had not long kneeled at the altar, but Apollo with a *loud voice* said: "Bohemians, what you find behind the altar take and depart." (196 [my emphasis])

The Messengers find the Oracle and take their leave "with great *reverence*" [my emphasis].

Shakespeare places his equivalent scene just after the long, thunderous argument between Leontes and Paulina who has pronounced the King "mad" in his "weak-hing'd fancy" and who has prayed for the infant Perdita whom she sets at the King's feet: "Jove send her / A better guiding spirit!" (2. 3. 125). Leontes, nonetheless, commands Antigonus to cast away Perdita in "some strange place / Where chance may nurse or end it" (2. 3. 181). The imminent arrival of the Messengers is then announced, and all who are present exit to prepare for the reading of the Oracle. Cleomenes and Dion enter:

> *Cleo*. The climate's delicate, the air most sweet,
> Fertile the isle, the *temple* much surpassing
> The common praise it bears.
> *Dion*.   I shall report,
> For most it caught me, the celestial habits
> (Methinks I so should term them), and the *reverence*
> Of the grave wearers. O, the *sacrifice*!
> How ceremonious, solemn and unearthly
> It was i' th' *offering*!
> *Cleo*.   ·   But of all, the burst
> And the *ear-deaf'ning voice* o' th' Oracle,
> Kin to Jove's thunder, so surpris'd my sense,
> That I was nothing. (3. 1. 1 [my emphasis])

Shakespeare incorporates Greene's mention of the "temple," "offering," "sacrifice," Apollo's "voice," and the "great devotion" or "reverence" of the Messengers, but here with a new, "curiously impressive" effect (Pafford, p. xxx). Leontes, caught in dream and nothingness (see 1. 2. 142, 295), has just attempted, with his own ear-deafening passion, to sacrifice his infant daughter. His madness is nearly complete. The obverse, out of which health will eventually spring, is the Delphic ceremony, with its corresponding unearthliness and the nothingness to which it reduces the observer, a creative nothingness. For in this ceremony the stormy voice and the extreme obliterative response it calls for lead toward new life. The Messengers make the audience sense that "something rare" will soon "rush to knowledge."

Through such juxtaposition of scenes and through such imaginative extension and interconnection of their contents, Shakespeare continually draws out surprising and challenging implications from what Greene presents in embryo.

A third instance of the way in which Shakespeare generates compelling drama out of Greene's raw materials may be found in comparing the exchanges between Dorastus and Fawnia with those between Florizel and Perdita. Greene's lovers engage in formal, and unlikely, debate:

> "Fawnia, I see thou art content with country labours, because thou knowest not courtly pleasures. I commend thy wit, and pity thy want; but wilt thou leave thy father's cottage and serve a courtly mistress?"
>
> "Sir," quoth she, "beggars ought not to strive against fortune, nor to gaze after honour, lest either their fall be greater, or they become blind. I am born to toil for the court, not in the court, my nature unfit for their nurture: better live, then, in mean degree than in high disdain."
>
> "Well said, Fawnia," quoth Dorastus: "I guess at thy thoughts; thou art in love with some country shepherd."
>
> "No, sir," quoth she: "shepherds cannot love that are so simple, and maids may not love that are so young."
>
> "Nay, therefore," quoth Dorastus, "maids must love because they are young; for Cupid is a child, and Venus, though old, is painted with fresh colours."
>
> "I grant," said she, "age may be painted with new shadows, and youth may have imperfect affections; but what art concealeth in one ignorance revealeth in the other." (208–9)

Fawnia's ready hand at repartee wins Dorastus, who promptly dresses in shepherd's clothes; this causes Fawnia to point out: "All that wear cowls are not monks: painted eagles are pictures, not eagles. Zeuxis' grapes were like grapes, yet shadows; rich clothing make not princes, nor homely attire beggars" (211).

Perdita is much less pert and pithy in her speech than is Fawnia. But Shakespeare expands upon Greene's hints to suggest her deeply instinctual commitment to the natural as opposed to the artificial way in all things. Her opening speech, addressed to Florizel, begins:

> Sir: my gracious lord,
> To chide at your extremes, it not becomes me—
> O pardon, that I name them! Your high self,
> The gracious mark o' th' land, you have obscur'd
> With a swain's wearing, and me, poor lowly maid,
> Most goddess-like prank'd up: but that our feasts
> In every mess have folly, and the feeders
> Digest it with a custom, I should blush
> To see you so attir'd; swoon, I think,
> To show myself a glass. (4. 4. 5)

She repeats her feeling of unease in "borrowed flaunts" (4.4.24). How, she says, should she, so attired, face up to Polixenes were he to pass their way "by some accident." Like Fawnia, she seems to be saying that rich clothing does not make a princess; her nature is unfit for the nurture of the court. But, when Polixenes does appear, in disguise, she finds herself arguing the inferiority of nurture, as evidenced in the art of grafting, as against the purity of "great creating nature" (4. 4. 88). Her instinct, like Fawnia's, is that art conceals with shadows; she will have nothing to do with grafting: "No more than, were I painted, I would wish / This youth should say 'twere well, and only therefore / Desire to breed by me" (4. 4. 101). Perdita purports to mistrust even the art of Florizel, for, when he praises her in an exalted lyric ("when you do dance, I wish" and so forth), she says:

> O Doricles,
> Your praises are too large: but that your youth,
> And the true blood which peeps fairly through't,
> Do plainly give you out an unstain'd shepherd,
> With wisdom I might fear, my Doricles,
> You woo'd me the false way. (4. 4. 146)

All through the scene the natural blushes of Perdita and Florizel appear as a guarantee of their chaste sincerity. But it should not escape us here that Perdita is pursuing a false way of her own in using Florizel's assumed name and saying that his blush proves him a shepherd. Through the dramatic situation

and the thought, Shakespeare greatly complicates the oppositions set up by Greene. Perdita, with the instinctive nurture of
the highborn, cannot avoid her own intense consciousness of
art in everything. She gives to each guest flowers appropriately
chosen according to an intricate symbolism. She says,
"Methinks I play as I have seen them do / In Whitsun pastorals"
(4. 4. 133). Later, she sees herself almost as the artificer of
Florizel's faith: "By th' pattern of mine own thoughts I cut out /
The purity of his" (4. 4. 383). Still later, she says, "I see the play so
lies / That I must bear a part" (4. 4. 655).

An aspect of Shakespeare's method, then, is to seize upon
certain parts of *Pandosto* —professed authorial goals, various
scenes, particular characters—and to enlarge upon them, challenging from various angles their stereotypic artfulness. Often,
he invites the spectator to consider that Nature, in its most true
and original forms, displays a wholesome, restorative order
mysteriously linked with Art. Thus in the first scene it is Archidamus, the hesitant representative of pastoral Bohemia, who
gropes below the surface of Sicilian "magnificence" that somehow accuses and shames him. His instinct leads toward a more
natural and vital civilizing principle, the magnificence of the
gallant, princely Mamillius, a gentleman of the greatest promise. Thus, too, the restorative miracle produced by the Oracle
out of costumed ceremony depends in part upon the delicate
climate, sweet air, and fertile isle of its origin. Likewise, the
extreme of natural purity that is Perdita finds its truest expression in flower codes, dancing, playacting, costume, references
to myth and to pure patterns of thought. Shakespeare, in these
ways, continually challenges his audience to draw out in
smaller details and overarching design the surprising and often
beautiful implications of Greene's ruder content.

IV

What is the affective impact of all this? "The changes," one
critic argues, "which Shakespeare introduced into Greene's
narrative are due in the main to the exigencies of dramatic
form."[11] Can this be true? Did dramatic form demand that

11. P. G. Thomas, ed., *Greene's 'Pandosto'* (New York: Duffield, 1907), p. xii.
Compare Muir's reference to the need for "dramatic tension" leading to
changes in Greene's story. *Shakespeare's Sources*, 1: 241. And see Max Bluestone, *From Story to Stage*, pp. 31–35, 74–76, 79–82.

Shakespeare change the names of the characters, or switch Bohemia and Sicilia, or alter the death of Bellaria and the suicide of Pandosto to the survival of each? Did it require the introduction of Paulina, Autolycus, and Antigonus; that Leontes' jealousy take up half the play; that there be a sheep-shearing festival; and a statue scene? Certainly if Shakespeare intended to give a straightforward dramatization of *Pandosto*, he failed. For the works differ in effect more than can be accounted for merely in terms of their basic difference in form.[12]

The names Greene has chosen for his characters, such as *Fawnia* and *Bellaria*, suggest at most some superficial attribute. Many of Shakespeare's names—*Perdita, Paulina, Antigonus, Hermione, Autolycus, Mamillius, Leontes* —not only suggest the characters' functions but also call to mind associations that deepen and universalize the story. Perdita, of course, represents "that which is lost," as the Oracle puts it. Paulina serves in some ways as Leontes' conscience, showing how the new Adam may emerge from the old. Having associations with another contest, Antigonus's name suits his opposition to the King, and his role offers possibly an analogue to that of his Sophoclean counterpart.

Hermione is a name with particular interest. Meaning pillar-like, it suits the denouement given the Queen. She is steadfast and statuesque. More than that, appearing (among other places) in the Eighth Epistle of Ovid's *Heroides*, which Shakespeare may have read,[13] she is the daughter of Helen and Menelaus. Shakespeare's Hermione, who loses a daughter for a time, may thus be associated with a more ancient figure who,

12. We need, in other words, to explore the middle ground between changes in details of form and the change in overall significance. The latter change may be neatly summarized: "The difference between Greene's *Pandosto* and *A Winter's Tale* is the difference a mature and practiced philosophy makes." J. F. Danby, *Poets on Fortune's Hill* (London: Faber and Faber, 1952). But the generalization still needs to be explained.

13. See E. E. Duncan-Jones, "Hermione in Ovid and Shakespeare," *N & Q* n. s. 13 (1966): 138–39. T. W. Baldwin, *William Shakespeare's Small Latine & Lesse Greeke* (Urbana: University of Illinois Press, 1944), 2:422–26, also maintains that Shakespeare showed an acquaintance with *Heroides*. The evidence is incomplete, however, and the name appears in other places, too. In *Remedia Amoris*, 771, Ovid writes: "*Acrius Hermionen ideo dilexit Orestes,*" suggestively translated by J. H. Mozley, *Ovid: The Art of Love and Other Poems*, rev. ed. (Cambridge, Mass.: Harvard University Press, 1939), p. 231: "The more ardently did Orestes love Hermione that she had begun to be another's." Editions of *Remedia Amoris* were printed in London during Shakespeare's lifetime.

again in the context of sexual jealousy, lost her mother for a time. Is Shakespeare, through the name, even as the play begins, hinting at separation and eventual reconciliation? And is a further mythic dimension being added by the placement of the Queen in Sicily? Association of Perdita with Proserpina whom she mentions (4. 4. 116) and who returned seasonally from the underworld to be, like Perdita, "spring to th' earth" (5. 1. 151) links Hermione with Ceres, Proserpina's mother. The Proserpina story was placed in Sicily, and, in some accounts, Ceres was considered Queen of Sicily.[14] Hermione, moreover, is a name that "occurs as a title of Demeter and Persephone,"[15] the Greek names, of course, for Ceres and Proserpina. Though Shakespeare's play forbids any explicit tracing out of correspondences with the myth, its insistence upon the likeness of Hermione and Perdita (5. 1. 226; 5. 2. 37) helps blur them, so that the figures of Helen and Hermione and of Hermione-Demeter and Hermione-Persephone rise up behind mother and daughter in the play, lending them not specific analogues so much as a special ambience, an implication of greater forces that are surfacing by means of these characters.

Such use of myth for atmospheric as opposed to allegorical purposes typifies Shakespeare's method. Autolycus, like his ancient counterpart, is the cunning descendant of thieves, but Shakespeare alludes to no exploits of his namesake. Perdita,

---

14. See E. J. A. Honigmann, "Secondary Sources of *The Winter's Tale,*" *PQ* 34 (1955): 37–38, who adds that the Jacobeans saw a vegetation myth in the Proserpina story. Leonard Digges published a translation of Claudian's *Rape of Proserpine* (1617) and attached prefatory material summarizing the "natural sense" of the story: "By the person of *Ceres* is signified *Tillage*. By *Proserpine*, the seedes which are sowed, by *Pluto*, the earth that receives them." Sig. Bl [r]. Digges identifies Pluto with "Dis" (compare *WT* 4. 4. 118) and gives as a consequence of Proserpine's loss: "*Delfo's* Oracle must silent be." Sig. F4 [v]. Apparently following Honigmann (35), Kenneth Muir, ed., *Shakespeare: The Winter's Tale* (London: Macmillan, 1968), p. 17, calls Digges, who contributed a eulogy to the First Folio, Shakespeare's "neighbour." But Leslie Hotson, in *I, William Shakespeare* (London: Jonathan Cape, 1937), cited by Honigmann (35), fails to show that Digges lived near or spoke to Shakespeare. See Hotson, pp. 209–10, 237–44. The switching of Bohemia and Sicilia could also serve as ironic commentary upon the now non-Arcadian pastoral or could have been done to place Leontes in a climate conducive to wrath. See R. A. Foakes, "The Player's Passion. Some Notes on Elizabethan Psychology and Acting," in *Essays and Studies* 7 (1954): 63, citing as an Elizabethan belief: "The hotter the climate, the more passionate, choleric and revengeful the people."

15. *Oxford Classical Dictionary*, ed. M. Cary et al. (Oxford: Clarendon Press, 1949), p. 413. The reference is to the lexicon of Hesychius, not only available to but respected by the Tudors, according to Baldwin, 1: 192.

similarly, is called Flora (4. 4. 2), and her garlands and her role of presiding over the festival invite us to summon up an image of that ancient deity.[16] But Perdita is no more specially attached to Flora than she is to Proserpina. Shakespeare allows the myths of Hermione and Ceres, and of Proserpina and Flora to blend in the observer's mind into a persistent sense of normally remote natural and supernatural powers that are represented by and working creatively through human actions.[17] His use of mythic materials parallels and perhaps feeds upon that of Golding, who also poeticizes the Proserpina myth toward dream. When, for example, Ceres finally learns where Proserpina is, Ovid characteristically describes her reaction:

> Mater ad auditas stupuit ceu saxea voces
> attonitaeque diu similis fuit. . . .[18]

Golding "translates" the lines:

> Hir mother stoode as starke as stone, when she
> these newes did heare,
> And long she was like one that in another
> world had beene.[19]

Upon learning of Perdita's survival, Hermione undergoes a remarkably similar metamorphosis.

As Shakespeare's alterations in Greene's names invite the spectator or reader to evoke around the characters a force field

16. Flora appears in, among other places, Ovid's *Fasti* 5. 183−378. Shakespeare apparently knew the *Fasti;* see A. L. Rowse, *William Shakespeare: A Biography* (New York: Harper and Row, 1963), p. 37, and Baldwin, 2: 427−28.

17. Shakespeare also converts the ancient deity Apollo from Greene's mechanically mentioned force of fortune to an all-presiding deity: the "great," "golden," "divine," Apollo; not only does Shakespeare expand the number and significance of references to Apollo, but he reduplicates the specially metamorphic sense of the divinity whom Ovid describes, *Met.* 6. 122−312, in shapes of lion and shepherd and as slayer of the sons of Niobe, herself fated to become weeping marble.

18. *Met.* 5. 509, trans. Frank Justus Miller, 2d ed. (Cambridge, Mass.: Harvard University Press, 1921), 1: 272.

19. Arthur Golding, trans., *The XV Bookes of P. Ovidius Naso, entytuled Metamorphosis* (London, 1567), 5. 632, in *Shakespeare's Ovid*, ed. W. H. D. Rouse (1904; Reprint, Carbondale: Southern Illinois University Press, 1961), p. 114. The paradox that stony contemplation may signify a special selflessness appealed strongly to the Renaissance imagination. Milton could have been describing Hermione or Demeter when he admonished Melancholy: "There held in holy passion still, / Forget thyself to Marble, till / With a sad Leaden downward cast, / Thou fix them on the earth as fast." "Il Penseroso," 42−45. Compare Milton's "On Shakespeare," 13−14.

of associations that make them at once shadowy, mysterious,
larger than life, yet also related to each other in one venerable
family out of ancient story, so his enlargement and deepening
of Leontes' wrath invites the perceiver to experience through
that figure a new and more serious questioning of human
fidelity than is found in Greene. Pandosto's jealousy arises from
the entertainment of his friend by his wife, particularly their
frequent walks in the garden:

> This custom still continuing betwixt them, a certain melancholy
> passion entering the mind of Pandosto drave him into sundry and
> doubtful thoughts. First, he called to mind the beauty of his wife,
> the comeliness and bravery of his friend Egistus, thinking that
> love was above all laws and, therefore, to be stayed with no law;
> that it was hard to put fire and flax together without burning; that
> their open pleasures might breed his secret displeasures. He
> considered with himself that Egistus was a man and must needs
> love, that his wife was a woman, and therefore, subject unto love,
> and that where fancy forced, friendship was of no force. (186)

Leontes, too, begins in a euphuistic vein—"To mingle friendship far, is mingling bloods" (1. 2. 109)—but the spectator must
soon be struck with the way his analogizing and generalizing
tendency leads not to Greene's neat and local reasons for jealousy but to huge and cloudy daydreams of doubt:

> Affection! thy intention stabs the centre:
> Thou dost make possible things no so held,
> Communicat'st with dreams;—how can this be? (1. 2. 138)
>   Physic for't there's none;
> It is a bawdy planet, that will strike
> Where 'tis predominant. (1. 2. 200)

Whereas Pandosto, "whose reason was suppressed with rage"
(190), is presented as a model of mechanical jealousy, Leontes,
whose reason stirs up and projects his rage, is presented as the
carrier of oversubtle thought, anarchic innuendo, and sweeping pseudologic. He enjoys playing with words:

> Come, captain,
> We must be neat; not neat, but cleanly, captain:
> And yet the steer, the heifer and the calf
> Are all call'd neat. (1. 2. 122)

As he loves to play with words, so he is imbued with an overwhelming sense of play in life: "Go, play, boy, play: thy mother

plays, and I / Play too" (1. 2. 186). In his asides he is "angling" (1. 2. 180). He plays upon Camillo's words *good* and *satisfy*. He displays his overweening egoism that assures him of privileged knowledge:

> Was this taken
> By any understanding pate but thine?
> For thy conceit is soaking, will draw in
> More than the common blocks: not noted, is't,
> But of the finer natures? by some severals
> Of head-piece extraordinary? lower messes
> Perchance are to this business purblind? (1. 2. 222)

His hyperactive fancy and pseudological mode of thought lead him to challenge all other reality than that manufactured in his mind:

> Is this nothing?
> Why then the world, and all that's in't, is nothing,
> The covering sky is nothing, Bohemia nothing,
> My wife is nothing, nor nothing have these nothings,
> If this be nothing. (1. 2. 292)

In Leontes, then, we witness an intellect gone awry, teaching itself to chop logic until logic dies. All that remains is, in Leontes' words, "The infection of my brains" (1. 2. 145), suspicion of all "that which seems so" (1.2.241). As the first three acts extend themselves, we see him become ever more tightly enmeshed in his own hallucinations, and, while at times his word wielding seems laughable, as when he calls Paulina a "callat / Of boundless tongue, who late hath beat her husband, / And now baits me" (2. 3. 90), we inevitably are caught up by the deep anguish of the man. For fully an hour, as much time as it takes to read Greene's entire novella, we follow the agonies to which his unfaith subjects him:

> There may be in the cup
> A spider steep'd, and one may drink, depart,
> And yet partake no venom (for his knowledge
> Is not infected); but if one present
> Th' abhorr'd ingredient to his eye, make known
> How he hath drunk, he cracks his gorge, his sides,
> With violent hefts. I have drunk, and seen the spider. (2. 1. 39)

> I
> Remain a pinch'd thing. (2. 1. 50)

> You smell this business with a sense as cold
> As is a dead man's nose: but I do see't and feel't. (2. 1. 151)

> Nor night, nor day, no rest. (2. 3. 1)

We are forced, eventually, to take the King's questioning seriously, even though we know its grounds are in one sense false. Affection does, after all, make possible things not so held. Many a man, as Leontes avers, is a cuckold. From one point of view, it is a bawdy planet. Even Polixenes laments the sexual "ill-doing" that comes with "stronger blood" and the "temptations" that cross the eyes of youth (1. 2. 70–79). Nor are Hermione's imagery and outlook always free of equivoques, whether conscious or otherwise:

> Our praises are our wages. You may ride's
> With one soft kiss a thousand furlongs ere
> With spur we heat an acre. (1. 2. 94)

When Leontes becomes jealous, though some oppose him, others are sycophants enough to "creep like shadows by him" and sigh out confirmation of "each his needless heavings" (2. 3. 34). Neither before nor after the jealous outburst is the Sicilian Court, as one critic would have it, "a world of courtesy and innocence.[20] Leontes is pained because of his supersensitivity to a corruption and deceit that are always possible.

At the same time, Shakespeare departs dramatically from Greene in raising up before us specific persons who embody self-healing forces that are called into play by the attack of Leontes' personality upon itself. Paulina argues. Antigonus saves the child. The Messengers are openly hopeful. The trial is held, Leontes defies the Oracle, learns of his son's death, and capitulates. The counterforces build up, in a manner unattempted by Greene, to an affecting crescendo. Instead of experiencing the whim of Greene's authorial fortune, externally imposed, the spectator witnesses a natural increase in the powers of conscience, mercy, and remorse that lead to a hope of cure. When Leontes says, at the end of the trial scene, that daily sorrows in the chapel will be his "recreation" (3. 2. 240), the word not only catches with irony his characteristic sense of

---

20. Frank Kermode, "Introduction" to *The Winter's Tale* (New York: New American Library, 1963), p. xxix.

play but it also hints at the larger re-creation of the King and his society toward which the drama points. Immediately following these words, we are taken through a wintry storm (3. 3) and on into the pastoral festival, re-creative in season, in dance and song, and in regenerating spirit throughout. There, as if the Bohemian scenes were Leontes' own re-creative vision of a relationship between Hermione and himself that would overcome all disruption, Florizel and Perdita shake off the duplicate wrath of Polixenes and then take the action home to Sicilia.

Shakespeare's most dramatic change from *Pandosto* is to provide for the reappearance of Hermione at the same time as he eliminates the suicide of Leontes. Like the pastoral feast, this new development suits the re-creative impulse that is established in the first moments of the play. Greene leaves us in the same world that we first entered: Pandosto lusts after his restored daughter and then in a fit of remorse slays himself. *Pandosto*, moreover, contains no sequence of seasons, no "growing" (4. 1. 16), no reference to the effects of age, no ecological wholeness nor teleological hope. Although subtitled *The Triumph of Time*, the novel does little to give time direction. In the play, on the other hand, we are quickly made aware of time forward and time backward, the first scene referring to "this coming summer," to the childhoods of the Kings, and to the "desire to live" in hopes of royal issue. In the final scene, therefore, when Hermione says to Perdita:

> I,
> Knowing by Paulina that the Oracle
> Gave hope thou wast in being, have preserv'd
> Myself to see the issue (5. 3. 125),

she becomes an enactment and vindication of the desire, expressed at the outset, to find the comfort of the next generation, which "physics the subject, makes old hearts fresh" (1. 1. 38).

The Sequence of Shakespeare's Plays

To compare the experience of reading *Pandosto* to the experience of reading or watching *The Winter's Tale* is to discover a coherence and temporal direction in the play that take us a modest distance beyond insights gained from surveying the history of its production and reception. Our encounter may be informed also by noting ways in which it builds upon and adds to patterns in the earlier plays.[21]

V

Foremost of these patterns, in my mind, is the pastoral design that takes us from court to country. Within this design, which normally includes a return to the court, Shakespeare projects similar clusters of characters, phraseology, incidents, and themes.

The Two Gentlemen of Verona works in the same way as *A Midsummer Night's Dream* and *As You Like It* to initiate its audience into a style of humorous critique toward values of court and country, art and nature. Here the curve of the action is not directly from court to country but from home to court to country, that is, as in *As You Like It, All's Well that Ends Well*, and *Cymbeline*, the protagonist trades hearth for hall only to find that intrigue abounds there. Some remnant of the same curve of action may be hinted at in *The Winter's Tale* where the opening scene of counsellors debating values of rural love versus courtly entertainment gives way to the ensnaring court.

In the opening scene of *The Two Gentlemen of Verona*, Valentine promotes his impending journey from home to Milan and castigates his friend, "loving Proteus," for being chained by affection from seeing "the wonders of the world," being instead "sluggardized at home" in "shapeless idleness" (1. 1. 1−8). But love, which has "metamorphosed" (1. 1. 66) Valentine's Protean friend and made him neglect his studies, is not so easily escaped as Valentine thinks he wishes it were. In *The Two Gentlemen of Verona*, the sons of Verona (unlike Romeo of Verona in a far different play) "seek preferment out":

21. I treat only Shakespeare's *plays* in relation to *The Winter's Tale*, but I concede that the possible relevance of his poems should be investigated further. In *Venus and Adonis*, for instance, there is the sequence of wooing, jealousy, and a woman falling like a pale statue (445−68), and there is also language reminiscent of the early portion of *The Winter's Tale*: "The honey fee or parting" (*Ven*. 538), "pay your fees / When you depart" (*WT* 1. 2. 53); "Her pleading hath deserved a greater fee" (*Ven*. 609), "Our praises are our wages" (*WT* 1. 2. 94); "love, whose leave exceeds commission. / Affection faints not" (*Ven*. 568), "where Love reigns, disturbing Jealousy / Doth call himself Affection's sentinel (*Ven*. 649); "Affection! . . . Thou may'st co-join with something; and thou dost / (And that beyond commission)" (*WT*, 1. 2. 138); talk of women being ridden, horse-fashion, by lovers (*Ven*. 419, 595; *WT* 1. 2. 94); talk of affections jealously "souring" (*Ven*. 449, 528, 655, *WT* 1. 2. 102); and so on.

> Some to the wars to try their fortune there,
> Some to discover islands far away,
> Some to the studious universities. (1. 3. 7)

Shakespeare's great theme, however, is the omnipresence and omnipotence of love. Just as Orlando in *As You Like It* and Bertram in *All's Well that Ends Well* seek heroic honor at the court but find at its center entanglements of love, so Valentine finds in Milan not manly honor but Silvia's love. He, too, is "metamorphosed with a mistress" (2. 1. 27). Silvia, like Rosalind in *As You Like It* (forest and rose), stands as the immanence of nature in the art context and nature that is at the same time an instinctive nurturing force or "influence" of feminine love beckoning the male protagonist toward his own best self:

> Unless I look on Silvia in the day,
> There is no day for me to look upon.
> She is my essence, and I leave to be,
> If I be not by her fair influence
> Fostered, illumined, cherished, kept alive. (3. 1. 180)

That immanence or impingement of uncorrupted nature in the court is too weak, nonetheless, to be effectual there. Shakespeare's pastoral comedies pull the lovers from courts to countrysides where deeper metamorphoses abide. In *The Two Gentlemen of Verona*, a love triangle that is real and not imagined like the one in *The Winter's Tale* leads to the duplicities of Proteus, and these force Valentine from Milan out into the Mantuan forest, where he finds sympathy and solitude:

> This shadowy desert, unfrequented woods,
> I better brook than flourishing peopled towns.
> Here I can sit alone, unseen of any,
> And to the nightingale's complaining notes
> Tune my distresses and record my woes. (5. 4. 2)

Nature, however, is powerless to restore his happiness unless completed by the accession of courtly and noble virtues. In the lines that follow, Valentine pleads: "Repair me with thy presence, Silvia. / Thou gentle nymph." Silvia's ability to "repair" arises from her "grace" (4. 2. 42) that Shakespeare invariably associates with noble birth and being "gentle." Perdita, in similar fashion, is first described by Time as "grown in grace" (4. 1. 24). Polixenes says of her:

> Nothing she does or seems
> But smacks of something greater than herself,
> Too noble for this place. (4. 4. 157)

Whereas Silvia only comes to the forest in the closing minutes of her play and is not shown extending much gentle influence, Perdita appears in the middle of *The Winter's Tale*, after tragedy and storm, and is presented to the audience for an extended period of time presiding over the feast as a "gentle maiden" (4. 4. 85), welcoming guests, dancing gracefully, instilling chaste desire in Florizel, proving her firm resolve to be his princess, and generally furthering the purpose of an ordered nature.

In *The Two Gentlemen of Verona*, contrasts of court and country values are explored in ways that comically challenge our assumptions about friendship, love, art, and nature. Relations, for example, among Launce, his ungentlemanly dog Crab (4. 4. 16), and his milkmaid love parody relations among the other various friends, servants, and lovers. And the "wild faction" (4. 1. 37) of forest outlaws, to take another example, is shown longing, momentarily, for a gentlemanly king and purporting to detest such "vile, base practices" (4. 1. 73) as the rape that Proteus, upon entering the woods, contemplates upon Silvia. Shakespeare's early emphasis is on the comic clash of heroic, amorous, courtly, and pastoral codes of behavior, all of which he mocks for being a bit hollow and literary. When pastoral comedy yields to pastoral romance late in Shakespeare's career, we then find less condescension and more wonder at the giddy swirl of natural forces that engender lovers' meetings and matings in patterns of minor defeats but major victory.

In *A Midsummer Night's Dream* and in *As You Like It*, the movement from court to country becomes the vehicle for more intricate and more feeling comparison of virtues and vices that are associated with each. The natural scene, however, is still viewed from an essentially comic and courtly perspective, so that, while it is prima facie a refuge and help in time of trouble, it fails to reveal the same reconstructive blending of fair season, natural goodness, and chaste regard that is achieved in *The Winter's Tale*. Most of the action in the two earlier comedies takes place in the forest, and entanglements there become worse before being resolved. In *The Winter's Tale*, the removal to Bohemia comes as a compensatory journey to a country where the "red blood reigns in the winter's pale" (4. 3. 4), to the sources of "jollity" (4. 4. 25) and "sound affection" (4. 4. 380). There the King's wrath of the first portion is repeated (without the same sexual jealousy and pervasive mistrust) as if to show how inevitably it yields to the lover's "faith" (4. 4. 478).

The audience of *A Midsummer Night's Dream* is made to view the wood near Athens in ambivalent terms. On the one hand, Hermia and Lysander, who have run afoul of the arbitrary "law of Athens" (1. 1. 119), flee into the wood and eventually win their way there. On the other hand, most of the play points to the confusion experienced by the lovers and all such "quick bright things" (1. 1. 149). Instead of being basically creative and hospitable, nature here is teasingly deceptive. The turf, seen by Hermia and Lysander as a pillowing bank, Puck describes as "dank and dirty ground" (2. 2. 75). While Lysander imagines silver Phoebe decking the grass with pearly dew, Theseus envisages the "cold fruitless moon" (1. 1. 73). "Ill met by moonlight," says Oberon to Titania (2. 1. 60). The forgeries of fairy jealousy have affected all nature:

> Therefore the moon, the governess of floods,
> Pale in her anger, washes all the air,
> That rheumatic diseases do abound.
> And thorough this distemperature we see
> The seasons alter: hoary-headed frosts
> Fall in the fresh lap of the crimson rose,
> And on old Hiems' thin and icy crown
> An odorous chaplet of sweet summer buds
> Is, as in mockery, set. The spring, the summer,
> The childing autumn, angry winter change
> Their wonted liveries; and the mazèd world
> By their increase, now knows not which is which. (2. 1. 103)

"Which is which" (or bewitched) turns into a question the play asks in many forms as Puck mistakes his mark, the lovers switch affections, Titania becomes enamored of an ass, and all the action becomes a bottomless dream concordant in its constant discord.

The audience of *As You Like It* is made to view the forest of Arden not as a mixed dream but rather as a mixed reality. A critique of the court focuses in the first act upon the familial jealousy of Oliver and the Leontes-like mistrust of the usurping duke. Frederick drives Orlando out because, as Le Beau says to the youth, "he misconsters all that you have done" (1.2.246). In the second and following acts, the audience is treated to critiques by Touchstone and by Jaques of whom it is said (with attendant complex ironies): "most invectively he pierceth through / The body of the country, city, court" (2. 1. 58). The succeeding satire often displays a dry, cosmopolitan tone—as in the second scene of the third act when Touchstone twits Corin for lacking courtly wit and Jaques and Rosalind twit Orlando for having lovesick wit.

Though something of the same tone is found in Autolycus, his play remains, for the most part, neither satiric nor comic but celebrative. True, we go from death in Sicilia (Mamillius's) to death in Bohemia (Antigonus's), from the wrath of Leontes to the wrath of Polixenes, from the flight of Camillo and Polixenes to the flight of Camillo and the lovers, and to this extent it shares, even deepens, the confusion experienced in the wood near Athens and the forest of Arden. Yet despite such complications, the principal features of the action—the finding of Perdita, the yielding of winter, the singing and dancing at the festival, the tested constancy of Perdita and Florizel— promote a far profounder sense of resolution than in the earlier plays.

That Shakespeare views the journey away from court as an emblematic search for the roots of the natural order appears as well from his use of such a journey in those tragedies where it is no necessary part of the source plot. In *King Lear*, he makes the journey out onto the stormy heath a vehicle for the most ferocious and total assault upon nature as well as upon civilization's questionable health and sanity that has ever been witnessed on the English stage:

> Blow, winds, and crack your cheeks. Rage, blow.
> You cataracts and hurricanoes, spout
> Till you have drenched our steeples, drowned the cocks.
> You sulph'rous and thought-executing fires,
> Vaunt-couriers to oak-cleaving thunderbolts,
> Singe my white head. And thou, all-shaking thunder,
> Smite flat the thick rotundity o' th' world,
> Crack Nature's moulds, all germains spill at once,
> That makes ingrateful man. (3. 2. 1)

Throughout, the images are those of waste, loss, and "uncreation." The many meanings of "nature" tend to contract toward a cold, unaccommodated nothing. Nature seems to be what lies at the end of Lear's struggle to strip off all lendings, of Edgar's search past "bog and quagmire" down the scale of living things, "the swimming frog, the toad, the todpole, the wall-newt" (3. 4. 121), to "the standing pool."

The savage pastoral of *Lear* takes its place, in my view, as part of the whole dramatic drive toward an exhausting catharsis. If Cordelia "redeems Nature from the general curse" (4. 6. 202), certainly the redemption, while in one sense at a much deeper level, produces little sense of the beauty, freshness, and hope that are inspired by Perdita. Both daughters are cast from court to play redemptive roles. But whereas Cordelia can do little to cure the great breach in abused nature (compare 4. 7. 15) and Shakespeare makes her finally go under, Perdita he lets cure the breach. The restorative faith she finds in Florizel is precisely the one lost by Lear; Florizel says of his purpose to marry Perdita;

> It cannot fail, but by
> The violation of my faith; and then
> Let nature crush the sides o' th' earth together,
> And mar the seeds within! (4. 4. 477)

Here Shakespeare seems intent to show at the pastoral center of the play a nature redeemed from both past and potential cursedness.

Plots that combine movement from court to country with redemptive suffering of a heroine seem to have fascinated Shakespeare (as well as many writers of romance). Not only, in the light vein, Silvia, Hermia, and Rosalind, but also, in a dark vein, Cordelia and even Ophelia, both reject the world of the court and bestow upon it a forgotten grace from another realm. After long and tense hours in the castle, we see Hamlet leave for England. The time that he is gone is dominated by Ophelia's madness. She sings death songs of the grass-green turf and of sweet flowers upon graves, and she dispenses "rosemary" and "rue" in a way that startlingly prefigures Perdita's gift of the same flowers for the same "grace" and "remembrance," applying again, in the eyes of the audience, to the memory of a lost father. When Gertrude describes Ophelia's death, it is with an emblematic detachment and lyricism that suddenly sweep us away from the close intrigue:

> There is a willow grows askant the brook,
> That shows his hoar leaves in the the glassy stream.

Therewith fantastic garlands did she make
Of crowflowers, nettles, daisies, and long purples,
That liberal shepherds give a grosser name,
But our cold maids do dead men's fingers call them.
There on the pendent boughs her crownet weeds
Clamb'ring to hang, an envious sliver broke,
When down her weedy trophies and herself
Fell in the weeping brook. Her clothes spread wide,
And mermaid-like awhile they bore her up,
Which time she chanted snatches of old lauds,
As one incapable of her own distress,
Or like a creature native and indued
Unto that element. But long it could not be
Till that her garments, heavy with their drink,
Pulled the poor wretch from her melodious lay
To muddy death. (4. 7. 165)

Through the sad pastoralism of Ophelia's madness and death, Shakespeare makes us look out in the surrounding natural world, much as Hamlet, also cast upon waters, is doing at the time. When, a few lines later, Hamlet returns, he, too, has become native and indued unto his element, displaying a new acceptance of fated death and discerning a "divinity that shapes our ends."

Without purporting to sum up the foregoing discussion with a single generalization, we can see that shifting the action from inside a court to outside tends, in Shakespeare's hands, to widen our perspective upon the central problem; to leave behind a false and constrictive environment; to bring into play freer, resolving forces of fresh action, acceptance, and sometimes laughter. Always we are invited on a more mysterious and magical foray than we could have anticipated. Perhaps it is the sense of introduction to remote and unsuspected powers governing life that accounts for a large part of our peculiar absorption.

VI

Hamlet and *King Lear* are not, in any conventional sense, "pastoral" plays (though *Lear* may profitably be approached as one[22]), and the significance in what I have termed the *pastoral design* of actions that circuit from court to country and return lies beyond the need for conventional rustics, pastoral topoi, or

22. See David Young, *The Heart's Forest*, pp. 73–103.

even any conviction that Shakespeare consciously worked in the genre.

Considered generically, to be sure, groups of Shakespeare's plays may usefully inform *The Winter's Tale*. The histories, for example, alert us, when confronted with a protagonist king, to the assumed vulnerability, if not essential guilt, of power, to the likelihood that the King's weaknesses (often suspiciousness and jealousy) will be anatomized, to a mixture of cyclical and linear time that is analogous to the ambiguous alliance between Fortune and divine guidance, and to the overweening problem of succession as related to a need for political and domestic stability. The supreme didactic thrust of the histories, moreover, helps account for defensive allusions to the lack of verity in "old tales" and for the kinds of questions about dramatic and imaginative truth encountered in *The Winter's Tale*.

Through the comedies toward the late plays may be traced Shakespeare's deepening investigation of problems of sexual identity, of false masculinity, of friendship's relation to love, of passionate self-deception, of entangling artifice in language, of confusions between material and spiritual values, of cross-qualifications between freedom and marriage and between rejuvenation and expense. Ultimately, however, generic differences between the plays matter less that similarities that cut across generic lines. Oftentimes in action and affective experience, the plays, whether divided into the three categories of the Folio, the four categories of modern editions, the many categories of Poloniusn or even finer subdivisions of tragicomedy, problem comedy, festive comedy, satire, anti-pastoral, and the like, the plays present a single, if multiform, content. Shakespeare continually asks: How can men and women come together and stay together in societies that do little to sustain them, that is, how can they establish and maintain proper bonds in a competitive and metamorphic world?

Usually, as might be expected, the plays begin with an eruption of envy or jealousy that breaks the ritual order of a marriage or monarchy, festival or peace, and forces a rearrangement of the social pattern, generally after many episodes of error and wandering. In this context, the so-called pastoral journey represents but one of several ways in which central characters find themselves exiled or otherwise extruded, often unfairly, from the court or other locus of law and power. (Among those banished: Titus's son Lucius, the Duchess and Suffolk in *2H6*,

Valentine, Romeo, Bolingbroke, Falstaff, Duke Senior, Rosalind, and others in *AYL*, Kent, Alcibiades, Coriolanus, Posthumus Leonatus, Belarius, Perdita, Prospero, and Arcite.[23] In addition to banishment and extrusion or ostracism, also common to Shakespearean history, comedy, tragedy, and romance is the instructive journey or labor through which a protagonist matures and attains a valuable perspective upon his former self and native society. One thinks of such figures as Hal/Henry V, Hamlet, Bertram, Antony, Pericles, and Posthumus Leonatus. Indeed such plays as *1 Henry IV*, *All's Well*, *Othello*, *Antony and Cleopatra*, and *Cymbeline*, if not others, show Shakespeare exploiting with incredible skill contrasts revealed by the journeys from Westminster to Eastcheap, France to Florence, Venice to Cyprus, Rome to Egypt, England to Rome, journeys east and south (like that from Stratford to London?) from a culture of relative order and stability to one of disorder and instability, intrigue and sensuality.

Potentially, then, any play by Shakespeare may help to inform the action of *The Winter's Tale* as it presents the familiar dissolution of established relations and raises the perennial Shakespearean questions: What are the "bonds" of society? How can friendship and love coexist? How should men and women respond to the power of mutability? How can our journeys through time and space be made redemptive? And if the instructive journey appears to take a specially conventional form, so that, for example, it may properly be labeled "pastoral," still the convention is always at the service of larger dramatic purposes. Thus *A Midsummer Night's Dream* and *Timon of Athens* both present flight to a wood near Athens, but the organizing aims of *Timon* are such that the search for solitude and simplicity yields a perversely literal mockery of the Golden Age. Digging for a root, Timon finds gold that, in pastoral tradition, is the root of artificial values. (See Drayton's *Idea, the Shepherd's Garland*.) And so the pastoral journey merely brings him closer to "damned earth," the "common whore of mankind" (4. 3. 42). Connections between gold, greed, and lechery are not absent from the pastoral of *The Winter's Tale*, but there the connections are lightly assimilated into the harmless tomfoolery of the rustics. Neither pastoral, nor any other genre, then, determines

23. Decrees of banishment in the plays are noted by Paul V. Kreider, *Repetition in Shakespeare's Plays* (Princeton: Princeton University Press, 1941), p. 286.

dramatic meaning, but rather the classifications provide con-
venient ways of grouping elements and patterns that serve
related functions and interrelate the plays.[24]

VII

Just as a few of Shakespeare's earlier plays may help us to
understand the central journey of *The Winter's Tale*, so earlier
plays may help us to understand another major feature, the
puzzling character of Leontes. Leontes, we can agree, is never
consistently comic, tragicomic, or tragic. Hence again, we may
seek instructive analogies in whatever sorts of play they arise.

Leontes is presented initially as a lover. His first speech of any
extent gives his memory of courtship. He takes shape in our
consciousness from Polixenes' description of their innocent
boyhood turning to the guilt of "stronger blood" (1. 2. 73), from
his own memories of "dangerous" sexuality (1. 2. 157) together
with "crabbed" and "sour'd" courtship, and from his full-scale
attacks upon "affection" as leading to "infection" of his brains
(1. 2. 145) because it coacts with the unreal and is fellow to
"nothing." This latter view, particularly, has deep roots (com-

---

24. This is not to deny that an understanding of the conventions and
vision of pastoral and romance adds greatly to an understanding of *The
Winter's Tale*, the late plays, and indeed all of Shakespeare's drama. Shakespearean critics—Frank Kermode, Introduction to *The Tempest*, Arden ed.
(ed. of 1958; Reprinted, with corrections, London: Methuen, 1962); Stanley
Wells, "Shakespeare and Romance," in *Later Shakespeare*, Stratford-upon-
Avon Studies 8, ed., John Russell Brown and Berard Harris (London: Arnold,
1966), pp. 49–79; Thomas McFarland, *Shakespeare's Pastoral Comedy*
(Chapel Hill: University of North Carolina Press, 1972); Rosalie Colie, *Shakespeare's Living Art* (Princeton: Princeton University Press, 1974), pp. 243–316;
and others (see those listed above in note 8)—as well as interpreters of
pastoral and romance generally—Ernst Robert Curtius, *European Literature
and the Latin Middle Ages*, trans. Willard R. Trask (1953; Reprinted, New York:
Harper, 1963), pp. 182–202; Frank Kermode, *English Pastoral Poetry from the
Beginnings to Marvell* (London: Harrap, 1952), pp. 11–44; Renato Poggioli,
"The Oaten Flute," *HLB* 11 (1957): 147–84; Northrop Frye, *Anatomy of Criticism* (Princeton: Princeton University Press, 1957), pp. 186–206; Bruno Snell,
The Discovery of the Mind, trans. Thomas G. Rosenmeyer (New York: Harper,
1960); Northrop Frye, *A Natural Perspective: The Development of Shakespearean Comedy and Romance* (New York: Columbia University Press, 1965);
Thomas G. Rosenmeyer, *The Green Cabinet* (Berkeley: University of California
Press, 1969); Harold E. Toliver, *Pastoral Forms and Attitudes* (Berkeley University of California Press, 1971); Peter V. Marinelli, *Pastoral* (London: Methuen,
1971)—have performed a valuable service in elucidating the structure and
meaning of pastoral and romance and in establishing their immense importance in Shakespearean drama and elsewhere.

pare *MV* 2. 2. 115; *Ado* 2. 3. 118; *Tro*. 2. 2. 59). In *Love's Labor's Lost,* Boyet remarks:

> If my observation (which very seldom lies)
> By the heart's still rhetoric disclosed with eyes
> Deceive me not now, Navarre is infected.
> *Princess*. With what?
> *Boyet*. With that which we lovers entitle affected. (2. 1. 226)

Affection, in other words, feeds on seeming impossibility, unreality, and nothing, as noted again in *A Midsummer Night's Dream*:

> Lovers and madmen have such seething brains,
> Such shaping fantasies, that apprehend
> More than cool reason ever comprehends. (5. 1. 4)

"O brawling love, O loving hate," cries Romeo (1. 1. 174), harping on the same string, "O anything, of nothing first create!"

Scratch a lover, in other words, and find a philosopher, usually an idealist headed for trouble. Shakespeare's jealous lovers are disappointed idealists; the lover who can see "Helen's beauty in a brow of Egypt" (*MND* 5. 1. 11) can see a brow of Egypt in a Helen. We easily remember Othello's example:

> Her name, that was as fresh
> As Dian's visage, is now begrimed and black
> As mine own face. (*Oth*. 3. 3. 386)

And Claudio's:

> Out on thee seeming! I will write against it.
> You seem to me as Dian in her orb,
> As chaste as is the bud ere it be blown;
> But you are more intemperate in your blood
> Than Venus, or those pamp'red animals
> That rage in savage sensuality. (*Ado* 4. 1. 54)

Leontes expands the complaint further. Not only is Hermione false, but everyone and everything is false, "false / As o'er-dy'd blacks, as wind, as waters" (1. 2. 132).

The King's jealousy is founded upon an almost metaphysical mistrust of reality. As wind and waters epitomize what is false, so mutability is equated with deceptiveness; whatever changes also lies. The advent of sexual passion is man's chief introduction to deceit. Polixenes changes his mind and stays longer. "Ay, but why?" asks Leontes (1. 2. 231). "At my request he would not" (1. 2. 87). Is this the affection whose intention stabs the center? Is this the end of being "boy eternal" (1.2.65)? "All's true that is mistrusted," says the King (2. 1. 43). Nothing true or innocent can last. Like the speaker of Sonnet 15, Leontes considers that

> everthing that grows
> Holds in perfection but a little moment,
> That this huge stage presenteth naught but shows.

His jealousy is a way of expressing antipathy to change, therefore, to life itself. Appalled at man's capacity for indiscriminate sexuality and deceit, he reasons downward toward a sense of the general curse:

> Physic for't there's none;
> It is a bawdy planet, that will strike
> Where 'tis predominant; and 'tis powerful, think it,
> From east, west, north, and south; be it concluded,
> No barricado for a belly. (1. 2. 200)

Like Hamlet and Lear, Leontes is presented in a state of shocked reaction to a vision of spreading unfaithfulness. Like them, he overemphasizes the existing duplicity and nurtures a sense of offended trust as if to justify the extremism of his protective measures. His alleged bawdy planet resembles the world Hamlet terms (more excusably in view of the reality he encounters) "rank and gross in nature," or that adulterous one described by Lear (again more excusably) as one in which copulation thrives. The absolute physical extremity of his shock links Leontes to all Shakespeare's tragic protagonists. His *"tremor cordis"* recalls Hamlet's madness, Timon's lunacy, the distracted frenzy of Titus, Othello's epilepsy, Lear's "Hysterica passio," and Macbeth's "restless ecstasy" and "fits" of trance. It is an expression of obsession.

Shakespeare often images the tragically obsessed figure as a man caught in a play that forces upon him a disgraced part. Hamlet feels unequal to "the motive and the cue for passion" that is given him and calls himself a "John-a-dreams." Othello sees himself (like an effigy) a fixed figure for scorn to point its finger at. Lear cries upon a stage of fools. Macbeth soliloquizes upon life's walking shadow, the "poor player / That struts and frets his hour upon the stage." Leontes speaks of how "disgrac'd a part" he must play (1. 2. 187). He is victim of "a game play'd home" (1. 2. 248).

Leontes' jealousy, then, expresses a deeply rooted fear and hatred of the mutability and deceit that seem to inhere in life and make an ephemeral game of it. Within, he feels himself "a feather for each wind that blows" (2. 3. 153). Without, he tries to manufacture certainty out of a rigid absoluteness that brooks "no gainsaying" (1. 2. 19), denies Hermione the right to entertain with a "free face" (1. 1. 112), makes up "foundations" of evidence (2. 1. 101 [compare Brutus in *JC* 2. 1. 10−34]), and celebrates a sole claim to truth: "How blest am I / In my just censure! in my true opinion!" (2. 1. 36).

Once we see, with the help of Shakespeare's earlier protagonists, that Leontes' condition (however unfounded) extends far beyond jealousy into a universal mistrust, we are ready to consider what, if anything, the other plays tell us about Shakespeare's handling of this mistrust.

VIII

When his intense vision of duplicity and pell-mell passion casts him into a play world, Leontes responds as did his tragic precursors. His response, like theirs, is to clench the will and reach for the role of director. He accuses Hermione. She asks, "What is this? sport?" He then conducts the scene:

> You, my lords,
> Look on her, mark her well: be but about
> To say 'she is a goodly lady,' and
> The justice of your hearts will thereto add
> ' 'Tis pity she's not honest, honourable':
> Praise her but for this her without-door form
> (Which on my faith deserves high speech) and straight
> The shrug, the hum or ha, these petty brands
> That calumny doth use—O, I am out,
> That mercy does; for calumny will sear
> Virtue itself—these shrugs, these hum's and ha's,
> When you have said 'she's goodly', come between,
> Ere you can say 'she's honest': but be't known,
> From him that has most cause to grieve it should be,
> She's an adultress! (2. 1. 64)

Arrogating to himself all governing power over the action, he tells his lords:

> We need no more of your advice: the matter,

> The loss, the gain, the ord'ring on 't, is all
> Properly ours. (2. 1. 168)

In the same spirit, he conducts the trial of Hermione, who this time proclaims it cruel theater (3. 2. 35 – 42). Combating a sense of being mocked, he mocks in turn, as did Lear in his "arraignment" of Goneril and Regan, and Hamlet in his conscience-catching play. The jealous Othello, too, mocks Desdemona in much the same vein:

> Sir, she can turn, and turn, and yet go on
> And turn again; and she can weep, sir, weep;
> And she's obedient: as you say, obedient,
> Very obedient.—Proceed you in your tears.—
> Concerning this, sir—O, well-painted passion!— (4. 1. 246),

and so does Claudio mock Hero:

> Would you not swear,
> All you that see her, that she were a maid,
> By these exterior shows? But she is none. (4. 1. 36)

All of these moments in preceding plays help suggest the tremendous sarcasm—based on a monstrous illusion of certitude—that Leontes' words should convey. They also suggest something else. Most of the tragic heroes attempt like Leontes to penetrate appearance, to figure out the world. They say to us, "I'll get to the bottom of it all, even if I have to harrow hell to find it," and an increasing awareness of pervasive mutability and deception, a preternatural sensitivity to ambiguities in language, often accompanies their drive toward definition. Meanings of honesty, affection, nature, nothing, dream, saying, and swearing—in *The Winter's Tale*, but not only there—sway in opposing winds of doctrine in which the audience is inevitably caught up. "Who's there?" is the question that begins not only *Hamlet* (1. 1. 1), but all the tragedies. Lear, similarly, asks, "Who is it that can tell me who I am?" (1. 4. 220). And Othello and Macbeth enthrall their audience in the awful process of their self-examinations.

At the same time, in reaction to his sense of universal deception, the hero attempts to fix his mind, to fortify some inner citadel against the forces plaguing him. Hamlet thinks he has that within which passes show; Leontes seeks it. The inner tensions grow into a fist of will that clenches tight and finally strikes out. In the end, Macbeth, Lear, Othello, and Hamlet all turn and kill. So does Leontes. These protagonists, through action, finally come physically and mentally back into the world. The perspective of the play and of its audience then shifts from tense interrogation and introspection to a freer active view. Contemplation yields to participation, suspense to catharsis.

The participation fostered by *The Winter's Tale*, however, differs greatly from that of the tragedies. In the tragedies, the major interest centers upon investigation of a particular character and upon seeing why, given the conditions of his world, his fate leads toward destructive self-assertion. Leontes' self-assertion, by contrast, lacks this quality of fated appropriateness. The vision of corruption that Leontes dredges up, no Claudius, Iago, Goneril, or Lady Macbeth appears to represent or to affirm. Each tragedy portrays a tremendous struggle to hold onto the self in the face of attacking forces. The hero seeks to realize an ideal image in opposition to an invading environment. So great is the tension between inner will and outer world that the former seems able to maintain itself only by denying all other reality or by laying the world to waste:

> Was't Hamlet wronged Laertes? Never Hamlet.
> If Hamlet from himself be ta'en away,
> And when he's not himself does wrong Laertes,
> Then Hamlet does it not, Hamlet denies it.
> Who does it then? His madness. (5. 2. 222)

> This she? No, this is Diomed's Cressida.
> If beauty have a soul, this is not she;
> If souls guide vows, if vows by sanctimonies,
> If sanctimony be the gods' delight,
> If there be rule in unity itself,
> This was not she. (*Tro.* 5. 2. 133)

At the end of *Othello*, Gratiano observes: "All that's spoke is marred" (5. 2. 357). When Leontes says, "All's true that is mistrusted" (2. 1. 48), he shows us not tragic loss and waste but rather a largely self-willed irony. When he says, "I have too much believ'd mine own suspicion" (3. 2. 151), it is not the same as if he had loved not wisely but too well. The world's stage has not brought him, blow by blow, to this pass. The whole dramatic progress that encloses him in hints of great creating nature shows that he is only at a way station. He has neither stiffened in a world of comedy where his solipsistic jealousy seems ultimately frivolous in comparison to the social solidarity that surrounds it, nor has he unraveled a tragic skein to its end in a realm that will let him preserve his vision only at the cost of death. Instead of having to count the world well lost, he can replace antagonistic struggle with redemption and reconciliation.

IX

The vision of Shakespeare's comic lovers often grows toward an ideal that lasts even after the pageant is over, when "reason wonder may diminish (*AYL* 5. 4. 133). His tragic heroes, similarly, who often see "more devils than vast hell can hold" (*MND* 5. 1. 9) justify their seeing and make it timeless through the personal intensity with which they define themselves against an opposing world. Leontes and Hermione appear briefly as lovers (in part, retrospectively) and then as tragic figures. In the first three acts, however, there are hints that they participate in a design extending far beyond them, a design that attenuates their individual reality, making them both players and played upon in a literal sense. Hermione is not only the entertaining manipulator of the second scene, who beats Polixenes from his "best ward" (1. 2. 33), who acts as "gaoler" and "hostess," and who becomes, later, more unhappy than history can pattern, "though devis'd / And play'd to take spectators" (3. 2. 36) but is also that participant in a larger scheme who says, when accused of adultery: "This action I now go on / Is for my better grace" (2. 1. 121). She refers repeatedly to the gods who behold human actions (2. 1. 106; 3. 2. 28; 3. 2. 75) and says she values life little (3. 2. 42, 93, 110). When she enters a deathlike swoon and later when she appears in the dream of Antigonus (as well as much later in the statue scene), these etherealizing hints have prepared the way.

Leontes, too, is a creature not wholly defined by tragic realities; there is too strong an awareness in the first three acts of "powers divine" that may oversee the action and be capable of leading it beyond tragedy. He resembles the man in the winter's tale of his son (see 2. 1. 25), the folk figure who dwells near a churchyard, a scene of death but also of redemption. When, after Hermione's supposed death, Leontes betakes himself to the chapel for daily prayer, the analogy becomes complete.

The process of coming to know Hermione and Leontes in the full force of their individual expressions involves the dawning realization that they figure in an overarching pattern. When they disappear behind the sorrowing storm and the dream of Antigonus, they dissolve and melt in a manner faintly reminiscent of previous Shakespearean characters. Antony "cannot hold this visible shape" (*Ant*. 4. 14. 14). Cleopatra becomes fire and air. *The Winter's Tale* yields the same sense of tragic reality that is compromised or perhaps etherealized toward dream. Like Antony in that through jealousy and the supposed death of his Queen he, too, is beguiled to the heart of loss, Leontes closes the tragic movement by a deathlike withdrawal to sorrow. But the storm-darkened shore of Bohemia seems no more appropriately final than does the darkness of Antony's death. All along, as described above, the spectator has been gazing past loss toward a creative or redemptive harmony. *Antony and Cleopatra* prefigures the breakthrough from the tragic world into the redemptive one. Cleopatra's death takes on a tinge of unreality. Her dream of Antony, her sighting of him through immortal longings, her marble-constant resolve that brings her beyond the snake's love play into a toil of grace like sleep, all suggest the promise of waking into a new world. She dreams of an Antony whose bounty "grew the more by reaping," an Antony "past the size of dreaming."

> Nature wants stuff
> To vie strange forms with fancy, yet t' imagine
> An Antony were nature's piece 'gainst fancy,
> Condemning shadows quite. (5. 2. 97)

This Antony foreshadows an art that nature makes, not just a statue that lives but the exemplar of a life instinct with such beauty and worth that it can submit to the capture of neither art nor death. In the persons of Perdita and the later Hermione, indeed in the whole post-tragic world, loss becomes an inexplicable preface to gain. As the dreamed Antony grows more bountiful after reaping, so Hermione, imagined by Leontes and Paulina, yields to the King treasure from her lips and yet leaves them "more rich for what they yielded" (5. 1. 55).

It might seem too easy, if engaging, a simplification to observe that Leontes and his world progress successively through stages of love, madness, and poetry. Such an ontogeny might then assert that it recapitulates the phylogeny of Shakespearean protagonists who are first impressed, then oppressed, and finally expressed by their imaginations. The notion, however, helps get at one's sense of progression through the plays from stylistic and thematic exuberance, marked by ornateness, speechifying, and romantic action (the comic vein), into puzzlement and horror at faithlessness, mirrored in an infinitely manipulative language (the tragic vein), and so through to a placement of the word-action enterprise in a wider, more creative setting (the last plays). This is no doubt too simple. Yet a tertium quid of some sort, which is neither comic lover nor tragic confronter of devils, is needed to define Leontes, who wins through to a specially imaginative, dreamlike world. Here is no aura of reasserting logic in which error unravels to restore order, as in *Much Ado*. Nor is there the sense of a tragic ending in which the gains, if any, must be found at the center of destruction, as in *King Lear*. No, the world here becomes truly metamorphic and magical. Loss fades in time and turns into gain. After the appearance of Perdita as goddess, Florizel's catalogue of deities metamorphosed for love, and the singing and dancing at the feast, tragic constriction and individual focus begin to seem petty and unreal. The real world is one of spirited renewal.

The rest of the play echoes with elements from the other romances. Hermione's waking is prefigured in the waking to music of Thaisa and, perhaps, Imogen (and, prototypically, in Hero's restoration in *Much Ado*). We can gain some hint of the effect purposed if we consider the words of Cerimon, who, as a sort of physician-magician, performs the ceremony of restoring the "dead" Thaisa (compare *All's Well*, where Helena's magical "physic" cures the King). To explain his early rising, he says:

> I hold it ever
> Virtue and cunning were endowments greater
> Than nobleness and riches. Carless heirs
> May the two latter darken and expend;
> But immortality attends the former,
> Making a man a god. 'Tis known, I ever
> Have studied physic, through which secret art,
> By turning o'er authorities, I have,
> Together with my practice, made familiar
> To me and to my aid the blest infusions
> That dwell in vegetives, in metals, stones;
> And I can speak of the disturbances

> That nature works, and of her cures; which
>   doth give me
> A more content in course of true delight
> Than to be thirsty after tottering honor,
> Or tie my treasure up in silken bags,
> To please the fool and death. (*Per*. 3. 2. 25)

The "content" and "delight" of "cures" lie in the dramatic emergence of apparently spiritual wonder out of mortal, time-bound woe. Upon finding Thaisa in her "coffin" and reading the scroll left by Pericles, Cerimon, somewhat like Cordelia ministering to Lear (*Lr*. 4. 7. 25), is determined to kindle again the "fire of life":

> The still and woeful music that we have,
> Cause it to sound, beseech you.
> The viol once more. How thou stirr'st, thou block!
> The music there! I pray you, give her air.
> Gentlemen, this queen will live;
> Nature awakes a warm breath out of her.
> She hath not been entranced above five hours.
> See how she gins to blow into life's flower again!
> *I. Gentleman*.   The heavens,
> Through you, increase our wonder, and sets up
> Your fame for ever.
> *Cerimon*.   She is alive! (3. 2. 87)

The same elements of music, waking, stirring, warmth, wonder, and heavenly influence are repeated in *The Winter's Tale* (5. 3. 98−109). In all his romances, Shakespeare shows onstage brave women—Thaisa, Imogen, Hermione, Miranda—waking from sleep, as much as to suggest that he knew no better image of our human capacity to face separation, loss of identity, and the seeming still finality of death, and, somehow, to "blow into life's flower again."

The redemption of Leontes is also prefigured in *Pericles* and *Cymbeline*. Marina, whose embroidered art "sisters the natural roses" (*Per*. 5 Chor. 7), sings to wake Pericles from his distemperature of grief. And Posthumus Leonatus, caught in a similar despondency, imagines Jupiter in a dream peeping through a marble mansion and then descending to stir his hope.

Shakespeare's romances share interests and procedures that help us respond with confidence to each. In all, an initial familial disruption, associated with a court context, leads to estrangement and to wandering far in space and time, to intri-

cate contrasts between nature and art as well as between ar-
tificers (Dionyza-Cerimon, Cymbeline's Queen-Cornelius, Auto-
lycus-Paulina, Sycorax-Prospero), to crises of near-despair
(for Pericles, Posthumus, Leontes, Alonso), to purgative storms
and music, and to miraculous reconciliations. In all of these
late plays, individuals or groups (Thaisa and Pericles, Imogen
and Posthumus, Leontes and Hermione, Ferdinand and
Miranda) become submerged eventually in dream and wonder,
as if to stimulate their, and our, faith in a wider, more benevolent harmony than can be seen in the limiting context of
egocentric and anthropocentric society. Always the great re-
sidual problem becomes the lively maintenance of that faith
against forces both of solidification and decay.

In considering the romances as a group, we can, however,
advance further toward identifying specific patterns that they
share. All of them suggest the same daring and fascinating
connections between familial and sociopolitical destinies.
From one important perspective, for instance, the plays tell of
threats to patrilineal succession and dramatize how those
threats may be overcome. Thus in each play a ruler—Pericles,
Cymbeline, Leontes, Prospero—becomes embroiled in con-
troversy involving another male who is viewed as a sexual or
political rival or both. Pericles confronts Antiochus; Cymbeline
confronts Caius Lucius (Posthumus confronts Iachimo);
Leontes confronts Polixenes; Prospero confronts Antonio (and
Alonso). In each case, the ruler begets or has begotten a single
daughter, and this event, as if it betokened a guilty loss of
patrilineal procreative power,[25] becomes intimately associated
with the ruler's loss, in every case, of his wife and sons, if any.
Each daughter, moreover, is shown as lost to her father's court
and cast into an anti-court environment, while the father-ruler
becomes a scapegoat figure—alienated and sterile. Pericles'
wife, Thaisa, in giving birth to Marina, seems to die at sea;
Marina eventually comes to the brothel in Mytilene, and Pericles, all-unknowing, withdraws into silent grief. Cymbeline, too,
has lost his daughter's mother and has no prospect of a son
(other than those sons who were kidnapped); Imogen flees to
the Welsh wilds. Leontes, shortly after Perdita's birth and loss,
appears to lose Hermione and does lose Mamillius; Perdita, of

25. Compare Jürgen Schäfer, " 'When They Marry, They Get Wenches,' "
SQ 22 (1971): 203–11.

course, reaches Bohemia. Prospero has no sons and has lost Miranda's mother in the pre-play past; he is extruded, along with Miranda, to the island.

Often the ruler is involved in an incestuous or otherwise taboo relationship, and jealousy and illicit sex, real or imagined, provide the catalyst for much of the action. Pericles finds the incestuous Antiochus and daughter poisonous serpents that are tempting him with dangerous fruit. The incident prevents him from returning home to rule. Cymbeline, like other fathers in the romances, appears jealous of his daughter and suffers accordingly until his son-in-law rival proves his ally. At the same time, Posthumus suspects Imogen of adultery and must engage in the familiar Shakespearean journey from the male martial world of capture, possessiveness, and material measure of values to the less deadly world of free respect, revalued kinship bonds, and prime emphasis upon the will to trust. Leontes cannot support a close male friendship simultaneously with marriage and incapacitates himself with jealousy; "brother" and wife, he thinks, mingle dangerously. Prospero may have let his brother too close, like sucking ivy on the princely trunk, until Antonio could "believe / He was indeed the Duke" (1. 2. 102). As a consequence, Prospero loses his dukedom.

Behind the plays appears a master myth of the ruler who loses both the full power to govern and the patrilineal line. His sole daughter, far from home, chastely redeems the tainted world and wins a husband and a son-in-law for her father. Thus Marina tames the brothel and wins Lysimachus; Imogen thwarts Cloten's attempted rape and regains Posthumus; Perdita bypasses the licentious revelry of Autolycus, Mopsa, and Dorcas to win Florizel; Miranda fends off the would-be rapist Caliban and wins Ferdinand. Generally the son-in-law provides a bridge of reconciliation between once-antagonistic cultures or nations. Thus the plays yield a parable of how warring families and countries can come together peacefully and fruitfully.

If it be asked why the tragedies do not allow this solution of the welcomed son-in-law, part of the answer—beyond the obvious fact that the author aims at tragedy—lies in changed assumptions about parental relations. Whereas in the romances the potential sons-in-law escape clogging parental relationships, in the tragedies we often find that such sons have mothers and fathers who assert constrictive claims to loyalty and affection. One thinks of Romeo and Hamlet and of Othello, whose mother, even after death, could help to sow "prophetic fury" in his heart by means of her gift, the spotted handkerchief. Tragedy often stresses incomplete severings of the heterosexual parental bond. Prime examples, in addition to those just mentioned, are the relations of Lear and Cordelia, Volumnia and Coriolanus, Titus and Lavinia, Polonius and Ophelia. In the romances, the male suitors have less trouble in winning over their fathers-in-law. But in the tragedies the father-figures hover like a curse and blight over the daughters as Capulet and Juliet, Polonius and Ophelia, Calchas and Cressida, Brabantio and Desdemona. The tragedies, in other words, view clans as inherently inimical to each other, and yet they show that the consequence of trying to maintain self-enclosed families is a horrible channeling effect wherein the sins of the fathers are passed to the children. The romances break the absorption with patrilineal succession, eliminate or banish the ruler's sons, and bring forward his daughter as means to rejuvenate the clan or culture by introducing new male blood from a son-in-law. In the tragedies the claims of the fathers are so strong that they become chains of fate. History dominates. In the romances, parental dominance diminishes, and the future, more free and, hence, hopeful, moves into prominence.

The drama of the romances is generated from interrupted marriages and trothplights, the drama of the tragedies from interrupted political triumphs or settlements.[26] Thus the open-

---

26. It is interesting to note, in this connection, the surprising frequency with which a ritual choice and its aftermath, often expressed in the term *election*, plays a part in Shakespeare's plots. The Roman plays turn on election of leaders by the mob, and many of the history plays turn on election of the king's successor. But consider others as well. Hamlet, of course, says of Claudius: "He that hath killed my king, and whored my mother, / Popped in between th' election and my hopes" (5. 2. 63). Edmund and Macbeth think themselves similarly slighted. It is Othello's "election" of Cassio that Iago first attacks (1. 1. 27). *Measure for Measure* opens with the Duke's announcement that he has "elected" Angelo his deputy (1. 1. 18). Election, in Shakespeare's world, far from ensuring the orderly reception of a new dispensation, usually leads to unexpected and adverse consequences. Even matrimonial choice may be seen in the same way. Imogen's fated "election" of Posthumus is thrice mentioned. Troilus "elects" Cressida, and Helena, Bertram. Bassanio's choosing among the caskets is an "election," and Burgundy, at the opening of *King Lear*, refuses "election" of Cordelia. Emilia, in *The Two Noble Kinsmen*, declares that she is guiltless of electing either Palamon or Arcite. When a Shakespearean character faces an election, then ,the atmosphere is ominous,

ing triumph of Titus is soon spoiled; the edict of Prince Escalus in the Verona of Romeo and Juliet is soon broken; Caesar's triumph turns to disaster; Claudius's Danish peace quickly crumbles; in *Troilus and Cressida*, the Greek and Trojan truce sours; Othello's triumph over the Turks precedes his ruin; Lear's intended settlement explodes; Macbeth puts down rebellion only to rebel; every apparent political victory of Antony presages new defeats; and the successes of Timon and Coriolanus engender the reversals they soon face.[27]

The romances, like the comedies, concentrate instead upon journeys that end in lovers' meetings. But, whereas the comedies laugh at love's many varieties of blindness and show the traps and snares in the way of love that delay its consummation in a wedding, the romances examine later stages in the process when love seems to be won but finds itself invaded. Pericles wins and loses first Antiochus's daughter, then Thaisa; Posthumus no sooner marries Imogen than he must leave her and then doubt her; Leontes recalls his wooing and winning of Hermione in the moment before he suspects her of adultery; Florizel and Perdita plight their troth just as Polixenes interrupts; even in *The Tempest*, it is the unfortunate marriage of Alonso's daughter Claribel, in Tunis, that takes her from him (2.1.105) and precedes the shipwreck; Miranda and Ferdinand, of course, find their betrothal masque strangely interrupted by Prospero.

---

and ceremonies of election in the plays, far from facilitating the happy exercise of choice, usually prove unfortunate. Shakespeare seems to have taken a dim view of attempts to ritualize choice, including such acts as swearing promises and making contracts. Hermione's " 'I am yours for ever' " (1.2.105) is fraught with consequence, and *The Winter's Tale*, more than most plays by Shakespeare, increasingly attacks man's desire to fix and determine the course of his affairs through rigid laws and promises. In the Shakespearean universe, "ceremony," properly understood and welcomed, lies in imitating and reverencing the natural and divinely constituted rhythms of life.

27. Beneath his obvious ploy of creating drama out of unfortunate falls from high places lies Shakespeare's profounder psycho-play of forcing male protagonists, who excel in traditionally male occupations such as politics, battle, and the like, to solicit female approval. One thinks of Othello and Desdemona, Lear and Cordelia, Macbeth and Lady Macbeth, Antony and Cleopatra, Coriolanus and Volumnia. Prototypically, such warriors and governors move beyond the arcs of their hierarchical, military competence and beyond the ambit of their legislative egos to seek love, not war. The results are devastating. Reciprocal relations, it seems, are not easily entered by those accustomed to killing and command.

The romances in general present a world of broken rituals and miraculous restorations. All drama thrives on interruptions of ceremony, as at the trial in *The Merchant of Venice*, the play within the play in *Hamlet*, or the banquet in *Macbeth*. But the number and frequency of interrupted trothplights, feasts, trials, flower givings, masques, religious ceremonies, and other rituals in the romances so intensify that they become a way or the way of life, as if the playwright and the gods, in making the pattern of interruptions more and more formal and purposeful, were preaching a kind of serendipity, proving that grace is best won from apparent misfortune, that all crosses are redemptive.

In some ways the message of the romances that local loss often engenders greater gain, that breakdowns in human ceremonies may serve larger divine purposes, appears as a radically religious affirmation of a perfect teleology. But within the poetry and progress of the plays themselves, the affirmation assumes a beautiful and convincing variety of kaleidoscopic forms. Not only do we find everywhere the action of happy shipwreck and fortunate fall as well as direct assertions of benign providence such as that of Jupiter in *Cymbeline*, "Whom best I love I cross; to make my gift, / The more delayed, delighted" (5.4.101) but we also find embedded everywhere in the texture of the plays the vital principle of hurt leading to wholeness, death to life.

In *Pericles*, Gower describes Marina embroidering:

> When she would with sharp needle wound
> The cambric, which she made more sound
> By hurting it. (4. Chor. 23)

Upon finding Marina, Pericles says:

> O, come hither,
> Thou that begets't him that did thee beget;
> Thou that wast born at sea, buried at Tharsus,
> And found at sea again! (5. 1. 196)

Here the negative incest of the play's beginning is converted to the legitimate spiritual union of parent and child so stressed in the last plays. The younger generation, appearing as procreative progeny who guarantee succession, instead of constituting a disruptive threat or signaling the parents' decline, is welcomed by the older generation as making old hearts fresh, providing a participatory rebirth. Upon being restored to Imogen and his sons, Cymbeline cries:

> O, what am I?
> A mother to the birth of three? Ne'er mother
> Rejoiced deliverance more. (5. 5. 369)

Leontes does not at first recognize Perdita and Florizel:

> O, alas!
> I lost a couple, that 'twixt heaven and earth
> Might thus have stood, begetting wonder, as
> You, gracious couple, do. (5. 1. 130)

Prospero, too, thinks of Miranda as that for which he lives and rejoices at what will breed between Miranda and Ferdinand (3. 1. 76; 4. 1. 4).

How different from the tragic vision is the insistence of the romances that what was lost or dying may be found or reborn and that, in the aphoristic phrasing of Cymbeline, "Some falls are means the happier to arise" (4.2.403). Gonzalo, near the end of *The Tempest*, concludes:

> In one voyage
> Did Claribel her husband find at Tunis,
> And Ferdinand her brother found a wife
> Where he himself was lost; Prospero his dukedom
> In a poor isle; and all of us ourselves
> When no man was his own. (5. 1. 208)

In all the romances, the gods make, in Pericles' words, "past miseries sports" that give way to "present kindness" (5. 3. 40). Posthumus, like other protagonists, is "happier much by his affliction made" (5. 3. 40). The romances thus continually thwart and divert men from their accustomed ritual, ceremony, and art, only to suggest that the world may be rendered finally more alive, more awake, more new and valuable, as a result of encountered strangeness. In *The Winter's Tale* not only are Polixenes' visit of state, Mamillius's tale, the trial of Hermione, and the sheepshearing festival all rudely interrupted, but the final scene as well presents art literally giving way to life. In the same fashion, the ceremony at the temple of Diana in the last scene of *Pericles* is interrupted by the revelation of Thaisa's identity; Cymbeline's triumph becomes a cacophony of surprises; and Prospero, in the most mysterious advance of all, abandons his art forever. The romance world is animated, finally, by endless wakings from ritual assumptions, from attempts to pin down, order, and define character and role, and from the nightmare of death's finality. The last plays all say "yes, but" to tragedy, inviting us to look beyond one affliction, one death, one winter, to the totality of life's weather. If only, the plays seem to say, men would reconnect, reconnect themselves to themselves, each other, and all the ongoing forces of "great creating nature" that signal, even in the face of death's power, the triumph of life.

In attempting such wide-ranging journeys in his late plays toward interrelation and communion with "everything that lives," Shakespeare was not a sole pioneer. Before we turn to the inner working of *The Winter's Tale*, therefore, we should see how its concerns and development become informed, by contrast and agreement, through a fellowship of the time.

X

Sidney, in his *Apologie for Poetrie*, seems to set the poet above Nature, alluding to the free Zodiack of his wit and to his golden world, so superior to Nature's world of brass.[28] He praises the "*Idea* or fore-conceite" of the work, its ideality in conception as opposed to its particular, time-bound reality, once made. In *The Winter's Tale*, Shakespeare takes a less confident and more subtle view of the matter. Here, no clearly established hierarchy subordinates the natural to the heavenly. Imagination, through Leontes' jealousy and, to a lesser extent, through the beguiling songs and tricks of Autolycus, works permanent loss. If the loss seems local and the gain general, that gain takes place within and as part of the sheltering rhythms of seasonal and generational development—the rhythms of nature. Unlike Sidney, Shakespeare hesitates to idealize poetic imagination, seeming to fear, like Perdita, that imagination, so purified and abstracted from ordinary life, may woo us the false way (4. 4. 15). The fantastic ballads of Autolycus satirize the gullibility of those who assume truth in imaginative creations, as if they necessarily emanated from a realm of Platonic ideas (4. 4. 261−85). If Hermione's statue represents the art spirit outdoing or mocking life, her physical reality gives the power of mockery back to life. The play concedes art's persuasive power but denies its self-enclosed sufficiency. Perhaps life in its widest version is miraculously like an old tale, but we do

28. *Elizabethan Critical Essays*, ed. G. Gregory Smith (Oxford: Clarendon Press, 1904), 1: 156.

right, Paulina and others suggest (5. 2. 26−67; 5. 3. 115), to question such seeming unreality. Even Sidney, elsewhere than in the *Apologie*, must, on occasion, ruefully concede as much. His Astrophil, for example, celebrates the transforming grace of Stella's spirit. He scoffs at those who attribute his skill at arms to "Nature" when the true causes issue from Stella's heavenly look.[29] His sobs remain unheeded because, in Stella's celestial mind, they are "metamorphosd straight to tunes of joyes" (Sonnet 44). Yet when she ignores the woeful Astrophil to weep at an insubstantial fable, her fancy drawn by false imagined things, then Astrophil prays that she will read in him "some sad tragedy; / I am not I, pity the tale of me" (Sonnet 45). This humorous foray is, however, atypical of Sidney's method. Shakespeare, like Theseus in *A Midsummer Night's Dream*, is much more prone to question deeply all false imagined things that cannot be incorporated into a natural harmony.

XI

Indeed, the most peculiar and keenly perceived paradox of *The Winter's Tale* and the major works upon which it draws is, as we have seen, that intensification of the spiritual and imaginative leads simultaneously to fixed ideals of love, beauty, truth, and goodness and to awareness of insubstantiality, metamorphic energy, deceit, mutability, and decay. The paradox, if it be one, goes beyond mere polarization, that is, that knowledge of A comprehends knowledge of not A. Her wedding interrupted, Perdita questions her dignity. Florizel answers that his faith supports her, even as it supports the sides of nature's earth and the seeds within. He is, he says, heir to his "affection," advised by his "fancy," pleased with such "madness" even if reason rejects it. The whole of creation is seen to depend upon such steadfast purpose, a kind of fanciful fixity or ethereal order. Hermione's statuesque stillness contributes the same ordering patience stretched to its limit, a white, cold, chaste, wintry tension upon which the expressive energy of nature ultimately depends. Art brings us close to the baffling ambiguities of creation, of life issuing from no life, spring from winter. Hermione stands "coldly" (5. 3. 36), yet "the very life seems warm upon her lip" (5. 3. 66). All interest centers in the point of

29. *Astrophil and Stella*, Sonnet 41, in *The Poems of Sir Philip Sidney*, ed. William A. Ringler, Jr. (Oxford: Clarendon Press, 1962), p. 185.

crossing over, the strange margin between timeless being and timeful becoming. "The fixture of her eye has motion in't" (5. 3. 67). When the stillness breaks, references to time flood forth (5. 3. 99, 118, 128, 154).

Through the imaginative and spiritual, one approaches extremes of order and energy, nothingness and flux, combined in fascinating but dangerous ambiguity. The obverse of Florizel's creating faith or the faith that wakes with Hermione is the faith of the jealous Leontes. Camillo tells Polixenes:

> Swear his thought over
> By each particular star in heaven, and
> By all their influences; you may as well
> Forbid the sea for to obey the moon,
> As or by oath remove or counsel shake
> The fabric of his folly, whose foundation
> Is pil'd upon his faith, and will continue
> The standing of his body. (1. 2. 424)

Faith in this sense combines suspicious love and vile imagination.[30] It masks, moreover, a monstrous egoism. Leontes inevitably challenges the Oracle itself. When Polixenes disrupts the wedding of Florizel and Perdita, he chooses the same course. He professes to believe in cooperation between his courtly world, that of art, gentleness, and nobility, and Perdita's country world, that of nature, wildness, and baseness:

> You see, sweet maid, we marry
> A gentler scion to the wildest stock,
> And make conceive a bark of baser kind
> By bud of nobler race. (4. 4. 92)

But what he accepts in theory he rejects in practice. Although he purports to see nobility in Perdita (4. 4. 159), in the end, his concept of "honour," limited to his royal line, blinds him to her worth (4. 4. 437).

Leontes and Polixenes are unable to make pragmatic, ad hoc, flexible connections between their ideals and surrounding appearances. We see each err in applying stiff doctrine to malle-

---

30. The typically Shakespearean perception of jealousy proceeding from myopic, over-concentrated love is foreshadowed in works such as *The Rare Triumphs of Love and Fortune* (1589), ed. W. W. Greg, Malone Society Reprints (Oxford: Oxford University Press, 1930), second act, ll. 296−30, Sig. B2ʳ, wherein Hermione, a male character, is told: "Sure is it that jealousie, proceedes of fervent love."

able fact. Queens, thinks Leontes, should show deep friendship
only to their husbands; one who appears to give a friendship
that violates this rule must be adulterous. Princes, thinks
Polixenes, should love only princesses; one who appears to love
a non-princess must be stopped.

But if Leontes and Polixenes lose touch with reality because
of opinionated beliefs, why is not Florizel open to the same
charge? Is his not a lover's madness, believing that virtue is
betokened by a gracious appearance? Polixenes says:

> Reason my son
> Should choose himself a wife, but as good reason
> The father (all whose joy is nothing else
> But fair posterity) should hold some counsel
> In such a business. (4. 4. 407)

When Florizel says that his reason must obey his "fancy" (4. 4.
483), that he is heir to his "affection" (4. 4. 482), does he not
display either a naive faith in the emblematic clarity of Perdita's
gracious appearance or else a disregard of her apparent un-
suitability as shepherdess to be his wife? Certainly, the couple,
once denounced by Polixenes, are "slaves of chance" and are
headed, in Camillo's estimation, "most certain / To miseries
enough" (4. 4. 568).

Florizel, Polixenes, and Leontes all raise, in varying forms, the
problem raised by Spenser in his "Hymne in Honour of
Beautie." It is there made wonderfully apparent that any absolute vision or scheme must be either painfully qualified in
contact with reality or else followed to the point of rejecting the
less than visionary or schematic world:

> So euery spirit, as it is most pure,
> And hath in it the more of heauenly light,
> So it the fairer bodie doth procure
> To habit in, and it more fairely dight
> With chearefull grace and amiable sight.
> For of the soule the bodie forme doth take:
> For soule is forme, and doth the bodie make.
> Therefore where euer that thou doest behold
> A comely corpse, with beautie faire endewed,
> Know this for certaine, that the same doth hold
> A beauteous soule, with faire conditions thewed,
> Fit to receiue the seede of vertue strewed.
> For all that faire is, is by nature good;
> That is a signe to know the gentle blood.

Yet oft if falles. . . .[31]

And with this "Yet oft" the speaker is forced to consider manifest violations of his theory, concluding:

Nothing so good, but that through guilty shame
May be corrupt, and wrested vnto will. (pp. 157–58)

The inevitable direction of this thought is to question all physical reality when compared to the superior beauty of the spiritual ideal, ascending, like the later Spenser in his "Hymne of Heavenly Beautie," to "the loue of God, which loathing brings / Of this vile world" (298–99, *Minor Poems*, 1: 230).

In *The Winter's Tale*, Shakespeare refuses so to trade world for spirit. The play mocks theorists and absolutists, who retreat toward timeless, spiritual apprehension to hold onto the purity of their beliefs. Just as Polixenes' schematic correspondence between the aims of art and nature evaporates under pressure, so Leontes' contrary vision of absolute deceit proves unreal. Approached philosophically, or even lyrically, without benefit of dramatic development or the directional guide of time, all of the great shaping forces in life, Shakespeare seems to be saying, become problematic, ambiguous, insubstantial. Caught at such timeless points, Hermione's statue is both cold and warm, the voice of the Oracle like Jove's thunder "surprises" the sense to nothingness, Florizel and Leontes both have a faith that is in some way "madness."

XII

A basic problem, then, posed by the play as it comes to us, is the problem of triumphing over deceptive affection and seemingly random change in the world, without retreating to a dreamworld of static idealizations whose essence is perforce ambiguous and unreal. Perceived directly without temporal, worldy mediation, the sources of change and affection, the ideas of nature and love, must seem hopelessly paradoxical:

Great *Nature*, euer young yet full of eld,
Still moouing, yet vnmoued from her sted;
Vnseene of any, yet of all beheld.[32]

31. Ll. 127–41, in *The Works of Edmund Spenser: The Minor Poems*, ed. C. G. Osgood, H. G. Lotspeich (Baltimore: Johns Hopkins University Press, 1943), 1: 207-8.
32. 7. 7. 13. 2, in *The Faerie Queene: Books Six and Seven*, ed. Edwin Greenlaw, et al. (Baltimore: Johns Hopkins University Press, 1938), p. 169.

Tracked to their timeless extremity, all sources of change and order exhibit only a godlike inscrutability. For Spenser, Love, like Nature, is veiled. Sir Scudamore finds that Venus stands upon an altar of unnameable substance. She is double sexed (*F.Q.* 4. 10. 41. 7). Such ambiguity runs through the whole of *The Faerie Queene*. Its unceasing emphasis upon mutability, the endless succession of mixed, protean, magical figures, suggests an inexhaustible fecundity in life, but the endlessness leads as well to a deepening sense of insubstantiality. None of the quests ends in clear-cut and final victory, and the consuming power of mutability overtakes all things. Spenser concludes by longing for a steadfast eternity. He would trade change for rest.

At the end of *The Faerie Queene*, Nature attempts to refute the claim of Mutability to absolute power, saying:

> I well consider all that ye have sayd
>> And find that all things stedfastnes doe hate
>> And changed be: yet being rightly wayd
>> They are not changed from their first estate;
>> But by their change their being doe dilate:
>> And turning to themselues at length againe,
>> Doe worke their owne perfection so by fate:
>> That ouer them Change doth not rule and raigne;
> But they raigne ouer change, and doe their states maintaine. (7. 7. 58)

Though this answer does not sum up the development and tone of *The Faerie Queene* as a whole, it gives the clue for the conversion of mutability as decay into change as a perfecting process, the conversion that dominates *The Winter's Tale*. In its shift from things dying to things newborn (3. 3. 113), the play rejects Leontes' attempt to possess a selfish and unrealistically pure love and to protect an unchanging "centre" (1. 2. 138; 2. 1. 102), or "foundation" of faith (1. 2. 429; 2. 1. 101), from stabbing change and deception. The flight from time in its fall-and-winter aspect of death and entropy changes to an embrace of time in its spring-and-summer aspect of growth and re-creation.

The key to the re-creative world is the conviction that timeless and temporal are not antithetic but cooperative. The divine and the mundane, the ideal and the actual, works of art and works of nature join in one creation; the first element of each seeming polarity is welcomed by the second, so that it comes to signify not protection from the world but perfection in the world.

In constructing his version of a re-creative world, Shakespeare could draw upon a variety of minor motifs and major models. Peele, in *The Araygnement of Paris* (1581), shows the early use of one contributory motif. He makes Flora welcome Juno, Pallas, and Venus with perfect floral images of them. The colors and kinds of flowers suit, in each case, the goddess whose image they compose. Yellow flowers fit Juno's jealousy. Red "Julie-flowers," cunningly "graffed in the grounde," portray the bloody, warlike Pallas. Venus is decked partly in true-blue violets. In each image, "Arte and nature" meet.[33] Peele's use of this device, while pretty and harmonious, serves no special dramatic purpose. In *Philaster* (1609?), Beaumont and Fletcher introduce a similar inset of cooperation between art and nature and place it within the close confusion of court intrigue. Philaster's account of how he acquired his page opens a view out into a world of delicate, interanimating harmonies:

> Hunting the Bucke,
> I found him, sitting by a fountaines side,
> Of which he borrowed some to quench his thirst,
> And payd the Nymph againe as much in Tears;
> A Garland lay him by, made by himself,
> Of many severall flowers, bred in the bay,
> Stucke in that misticke order, that the rarenesse
> Delighted me: but ever when he turnd
> His tender eyes upon um, he would weepe,
> As if he meant to make um grow againe.
> Seeing such pretty helplesse innocence
> Dwell in his face, I ask'd him all his story;
> He told me, that his Parents gentle dyed,
> Leaving him to the mercy of the fields,
> Which gave him rootes; and of the Christall springs,
> Which did not stop their courses; and the Sun,
> Which still, he thank'd him, yeelded him his light.
> Then tooke he up his Garland, and did shew,
> What every flower, as Countrey people hold,
> Did signifie: and how all, ordered thus,
> Exprest his griefe: and to my thoughts did reade
> The prettiest lecture of his Countrey Art,
> That could be wisht.[34]

33. 1. 3. 129, in *The Life and Works of George Peele*, gen. ed., Charles Tyler Prouty (New Haven: Yale University Press, 1970), 3: 69. *The Araygnement of Paris* is edited by R. Mark Benbow.

34. 1. 2. 113-35, in *The Dramatic Works in the Beaumont and Fletcher Canon*, gen. ed., Fredson Bowers (Cambridge: Cambridge University Press, 1966), 1: 413–14. *Philaster* is edited by Robert K. Turner.

The use of this scene by Beaumont and Fletcher resembles the use by Shakespeare not only of Perdita's flower giving but also of interstitial scenes such as the briefly described visit of Cleomenes and Dion to Delphos (3. 1), in which pure climate and religious ritual gracefully blend.

Apprehension of a "misticke order," mysterious but humanly relevant, grows steadily through *The Winter's Tale*. It becomes ever clearer that the impression of nonhuman forces, divine and natural, upon human affairs contributes to an artful ordering that may properly be marveled at no matter how imperfectly understood. The heavens speak through Oracles, frown through storms; gods take animal shapes; flowers have human meaning; mistrusting winter yields welcoming spring; the seemingly dead awake; and men of faith find a gracious issue and sense that each creature may answer, as Leontes puts it, to its "part performed" (5. 3. 153).

In the pastoral scenes, particularly, Shakespeare seems to be reaching back toward that special sense of the interanimation of animal, human, and divine forces that everywhere underlay the great flowerings of Elizabethan creativity. In Lyly's *Endimion* (1586?), for example, the Earth, Tellus, boasts:

> Is not my beauty diuine, whose body is decked with faire flowers, and vaines are Vines, yeelding sweet liquor to the dullest spirits, whose eares are Corne, to bring strength, and whose heares are grasse, to bring abundance? Doth not Frankinsence & Myrrhe breath out of my nostrils, and all the sacrifice of the Gods breede in my bowels? Infinite are my creatures, without which neyther thou, nor *Endimion*, nor any could loue, or liue.[35]

Body, beauty, and divinity of man, earth, and gods are one. Says Florizel:

> These your unusual weeds, to each part of you
> Do give a life: no shepherdess, but Flora
> Peering in April's front. (4. 4. 1)

Participating in natural regeneration, the human form expresses divinity. Those who find and fix the beauty of nature personify the divine. In the midst of Peele's satiric play, *The Old*

---

35. 1. 2. 9−26, in *The Complete Works of John Lyly*, ed. R. Warwick Bond (Oxford: Clarendon Press, 1902), 3: 24.

Wives Tale (1591?), the "Fowle Wench" Celanta dips her pitcher in the Well of Life; a head comes up full of gold. The voice says:

> Faire maiden, white, and redde,
> Combe me smooth, and stroke my head;
> And every haire, a sheave shall be,
> And every sheave a goulden tree.
> *Celanta*. Oh see Corebus, I have combd a great
>   deale of golde into my lap, and a great deale of corne.[36]

The head and the girl produce an unwittingly innocent bounty, both human and supernatural.

In such scenes the human actor becomes wonderfully transparent and furthers natural and divine purposes without the cloudiness of individualizing will. Because there is no attempt to segregate a personal, willful, selfish being away from the flow of natural processes, the surrounding environment, in all of these scenes, manages to avoid appearing as something "other," which attacks an atemporal and remote being with destructive mutability. Instead, the view is extensive, cooperative. All things live the life of all as parts of Tellus, earth's body. There are deaths but no final death, because life is so clearly ongoing. In the midst of the summer festival, Perdita speaks, mysteriously, of "the birth / Of trembling winter" (4. 4. 80) and "blasts of January" (4. 4. 111); she blushes warmly, yet her hand is as white as "the fann'd snow that's bolted / By th' northern blasts twice o'er" (4. 4. 365). In the smallest details of the play as well as in its largest movement, we are made to sense how completely seeming polarities really meet and interanimate each other.

XIII

"To look for a positive structural principle in English Renaissance literature is to miss its essential point. Mutability, though certain, is after all unpredictable."[37] Whatever the merits of this view when applied to the widest range of Renaissance writing, when applied to *The Winter's Tale* and to those moments or

---

36. Ll. 783-88, in *Works*, 3: 415. *The Old Wives Tale* is edited by Frank S. Hook.

37. F. W. Bateson, *A Guide to English Literature*, 2d ed. (Garden City, N. Y.: Doubleday, 1968), p. 55.

larger patterns of literature that lead toward its re-creative center, the view fails to distinguish disintegration from metamorphosis. *The Faerie Queene* ends in a swirl of mutability, and *The Winter's Tale* shares, to a degree, its nostalgia and hope for a creatively triumphant world. The play allies itself more positively, however, to the recurring confidence of each Spenserian quester that virtue and spirit are energized through metamorphic forces. Such forces do not simply confound life, they support it. This support rises above such reassuring examples of beneficent nature as are contained in the rescue of Una by satyrs or in the rescue of Calepine by the salvage man, or in the Garden of Adonis, or on the Acidalian Mount. A progressive, problem-solving struggle between man's constant spirit and magical or protean forces leaves a conviction of balance, of artfully significant nature, of ritual fullness.

In Fletcher's *Faithful Shepherdess*, Amarillis has the Sullen Shepherd dip her in a Holy Well to change her to the likeness of her rival Amoret. The Shepherd intones:

> Truth that hath but one face,
> Thus I charm thee from this place.
> Snakes that cast your coats for new,
> Camelions that alter hue,
> Hares that yearly sexes change,
> *Proteus* alt'ring oft and strange,
> *Hecate* with shapes three,
> Let this maiden changed be,
> With this holy water wet
> To the shape of *Amoret*. [38]

The Well works the wished-for change. Later, when the true Amoret, wounded, is cast into the Well, the God of the River rises to save her, heal her, and invite her to come live in his waters. The metamorphic powers invoked by the Shepherd give way to a view of the River as a calm source of ultimate order, "Sometimes winding round about, / To find the evenest channel out" (426–27). The River protects and nourishes all that live in its water or touch its banks. Amoret, before leaving to pursue her love for a swain, returns a protective blessing to the River, praying that it remain free from all noisome invasion. The final stress on a redeeming oath of nonpromiscuous love, a kind of

38. John Fletcher, *The Faithful Shepherdess* (1610?), 3. 1. 27–36, in *The Works of Francis Beaumont and John Fletcher*, ed. Arnold Glover and A. R. Waller (Cambridge: Cambridge University Press, 1906) 2: 400.

"faith," serves to emphasize the possibility of control over the surging, protean energies to which the lovers are supersensitized. Chastity, in the sense not of pale celibacy but of the "truth that hath but one face," symbolizes man's capacity to order his nature and to know all nature so ordered.[39]

In *The Winter's Tale*, Shakespeare captures this same sense of metamorphic energy channeled to one purpose. Florizel says to Perdita:

> The gods themselves,
> Humbling their deities to love, have taken
> The shapes of beasts upon them: Jupiter
> Became a bull, and bellow'd; the green Neptune
> A ram, and bleated; and the fire-rob'd god,
> Golden Apollo, a poor humble swain,
> As I seem now. Their transformations
> Were never for a piece of beauty rarer,
> Nor in a way so chaste, since my desires
> Run not before mine honour, nor my lusts
> Burn hotter than my faith. (4. 4. 24)

Both isolated passages and the dramatic progress itself gather incidents of metamorphosis toward a faithful love or reconciliation: Florizel turns from prince to shepherd to disguised traveler to prince again; Perdita turns from shepherdess to queen of the feast to beggar-maid denounced to true princess; in Polixenes an appreciative and philosophical wedding guest becomes a wrathful king but later is seen as a consenting father and as a "brother" to Leontes (5. 3. 147); Leontes, whom we last saw just rousing from his jealousy, we next encounter as a proven penitent (5. 1); Hermione's change of state is, of course, the most remarkable and stands as a symbol for the coming to renewal of the others.[40] All the changes converge collectively into a late and hopeful version of Shakespeare's basic view, once

39. Even such diverse plays as Greene's *Friar Bacon*, Dekker's *Shoemakers' Holiday*, and Beaumont's *Knight of the Burning Pestle*, none of which aims at a serious exploration of pastoral meanings, all manage to place maids in a pastoral setting to be wooed by lovers seeking ideals of faithful constancy. Forest or garden, the *locus amoenus* generates and fosters true love.

40. Shakespeare's post-tragic optimism concerning man's capacity for self-renewal harks back to pre-Reformation humanists such as Pico della Mirandola, who celebrates, in his *Oration on the Dignity of Man*, man's mutability and self-transforming nature (*"versipellis huius et se ipsam transformantis naturae"*). And see Thomas Greene, "The Flexibility of the Self in Renaissance Literature," in *The Disciplines of Criticism*, ed. Peter Demetz et al. (New Haven: Yale University Press, 1968), pp. 241–64.

described by Eric Auerbach as "the conception, so difficult to formulate in clear terms although everywhere to be observed in its effects, of a basic fabric of the world, perpetually weaving itself, renewing itself, and connected in all its parts."[41]

XIV

The "conception" of an ever-renewing world, of which Auerbach speaks, is in my view not so much an idea to be gleaned from the works mentioned as the immediate temporal process of encountering them affectively. *Endimion* and *The Faithful Shepherdess*, *Arcadia* and *The Faerie Queene* all require hours to absorb. The repeated encounters of their protagonists with transforming forces and figures are not presented as a gallery of pictures to be glanced at. The encounters take time, are themselves triumphs of time in which the process of growth equals in importance the final result. Endimion, the symbol of constancy, is cast into a magic sleep through the jealous machinations of Tellus who is, as Lyly puts it, affected with the spice and infected with the poison of love. Somewhat like Hermione, he sleeps many years and finally wakes, as an old man, to his love's kiss. But he seems to be restored to his youth. By his persistent and poetic expression of love, he has come finally to a position in which his life is filled with life, with values of beauty and faith, so that he seems "vowed to a service, from which death cannot remove him." Lyly's delicate and haunting play itself embodies the same service.

In *The Faithful Shepherdess*, again there is an emblematic figure of faithfulness, Clorin, about whom swirl various triangles of jealousy and through whose influence all are finally instructed in the ways of chaste constancy. Jealousy is the "great foe to faith," and it is stressed that general ruin may follow from a breach in affection, for true love between two persons is thought to provide a "center" of "fixed being." A tremendous feeling for the life of the river that saves Amoret and for the "great working powers" of the four elements leads toward a conviction that man and nature join in and express a single creation.

These plays do not seem to have as their purpose a raising of problems, such as the tragic one of man's fate. They do not

---

41. *Mimesis: The Representation of Reality in Western Literature*, trans. Willard Trask (1953; Reprinted, Garden City, N.Y.: Doubleday, 1957), p. 287.

suggest a larger subject matter than that contained in their immediate experience. The amount of time it takes to read or see them permits a nearly complete assimilation of the thoughts and feelings pointed to or engendered. Like the characters within the plays, the reader ends up not out of phase with his object of perception, not wishing his time longer or his understanding greater or his aesthetic sense more satisfied, but rather in phase with it. Instead of trying to imagine through the surface to a strange time and place for the restorative experiences of Endimion and Clorin, we find a perfect equivalent in the present re-creation of the plays themselves, in the dissonance of jealousy and strife turning to the music of trust and concord. We grow in confidence that an apparently mysterious and remote nature, Cynthia the moon and the nocturnal forest, when viewed aright with innocence and love, will become a benevolent, artistic harmony.

Another way of expressing the effect of these works is to say that, when they win through to a portrayal of the natural world as consonant with the shape of man's thought and desire, their subject matter or content becomes more easily absorbed into our direct experience or apprehension. To illustrate: in Sidney's *Arcadia* (Book 2, Chapter 11), Pyrocles, who is disguised as the girl "Zelmane," spies upon Philoclea as she bathes. Zelmane watches Philoclea tenderly move her feet "till the touch of the cold water made a prettie kind of shrugging come over her bodie, like the twinckling of the fairest among the fixed stars."[42] Zelmane "had the coales of her affection so kindled with wonder" that, taking up "her" lute:

> Her wit began to be with a divine furie inspired; her voice would in so beloved an occasion second her wit; her hands accorded the Lutes musicke to the voice; her panting hart daunced to the musicke; while I thinke her feete did beate the time; while her bodie was the roome where it should be celebrated; her soul the Queene which shoulde be delighted. And so togither went the utterance and the invention, that one might judge, it was *Philocleas* beautie which did speedily write it in her eyes; or the sense thereof, which did word by word endite it in her minde, whereto she (but as an organ) did onely lend utterance. (218)

As the beautiful motion of Philoclea's body expresses the twinkling of stars, so Zelmane's song expresses Philoclea's beauty. In

42. Sir Philip Sidney, *The Countesse of Pembrokes Arcadia*, ed. Albert Feuillerat (Cambridge: Cambridge University Press, 1912), 1: 217.

fact the beauty becomes the song. Zelmane is only an instrument converting beauty of body to beauty of song.

In experiences like these, normal distinctions between invention and utterance, between the subject of the song and the song itself, collapse. The bounty or grace of the pastoral world expresses itself equally through the bather, dancer, reaper, or flower giver, and through the poet or maker who expresses the same bounty or grace. Florizel says to Perdita:

> When you speak, sweet,
> I'd have you do it ever: when you sing,
> I'd have you buy and sell so, so give alms,
> Pray so, and, for the ord'ring your affairs,
> To sing them too. (4. 4. 136)

Both singers, Perdita within the lyric and Florizel with it, order affairs. Seer and seen express equally the art of a poetic, shaping world. Later, Perdita says of Florizel:

> I cannot speak
> So well, nothing so well; no, nor mean better:
> By th' pattern of mine own thoughts I cut out
> The purity of his. (4. 4. 381)

Object and subject correspond and merge.

A correspondence between objective purity and subjective pattern, between natural grace and human art, comes to be taken quite literally. When Sidney describes, for example, "the faire field, appointed for the shepherdish pastimes," the reader is not encouraged to give the field any external being independent of its aesthetic function in the tale:

It was indeed a place of delight; for thorow the middest of it, there ran a sweete brooke, which did both hold the eye open with her azure streams, & yet seeke to close the eie with the purling noise it made upon the pibble stones it ran over: the field it self being set in some places with roses, & in al the rest constantly preserving a florishing greene; the Roses added such ruddy shew unto it, as though the field were bashfull at his owne beautie: about it (as if it had bene to enclose a *Theater*) grew such a sort of trees, as eyther excellency of fruit, state-lines of grouth, continuall greenes, or poeticall fancies have made at any time famous. (118−19)

The trees are equally famous through attributes or through poetic description because there is really no distinction between the two.

The entire action of the *Arcadia* works upon the reader in a similar fashion. Pyrocles and Musidorus are thinly, conventionally characterized and made to represent questing states of mind rather than three-dimensional, original persons. The accumulation of similar incidents in which they fall in love with Philoclea and Pamela, disguise themselves as Zelmane and Dorus, fight lion and bear, perform rescues, escapes, and the like, is, when compared to the progress of a naturalistic novel, relatively artificial and self-conscious, coincidental and manipulative. Such reduplication of characters and incidents, the large number of conventionalized figures, the descriptions of poetical nature, the patterned prose and frequent ascents to lyric expressions of feeling all lead, in my view, to the gradually intensifying impression in the reader's mind of a ceremonial world. It is a world in which the many temporary impediments to the realization of love and virtue—kidnap, enforced disguise, jealousy, enchantment—only prove, minute by minute, the unshakable course of that realization. The reader is not called upon to penetrate behind the characters and action to ask what they stand for. Instead the reader follows for several hours a sustained expression of courtesy and fidelity in the face of all obstacles. The reader does not, perhaps, believe in Pyrocles or Musidorus as an individual but absorbs the confidence of the whole. The book is, then, less a representation of reality calling for suspended disbelief than an admitted artifice whose content lies close to or within the form of the reader's temporal encounter with it, much as music assumes its shape and meaning only in the listening.

In the Sixth Book of *The Faerie Queene*, similarly, after Calidore's long entanglement with Crudor, Briana, Priscilla, Aladine, Serena, Pastorella, and the Blatant Beast, the reader is left with a hard-won sense of equilibrium between all the forces that would confound the quest and all those that would support it. His knowledge that the forwarding and thwarting forces interanimate each other and provide meaning for the quest resembles the quester's acceptance of meaningful detour. Perceiver and perceived share a psychic journey of similar dimensions. Spenser asserts as much when, in the opening to the twelfth canto, he compares himself as poet, whose course is often stayed yet never astray, to Calidore, whose quest has been interrupted for courtesy's sake but not forgotten:

Like as a ship, that through the Ocean wyde
　　Directs her course vnto one certaine cost,
　　Is met of many a counter winde and tyde,
　　With which her winged speed is let and crost,
　　And she her self in stormie surges tost;
　　Yet making many a borde, and many a bay,
　　Still winneth way, ne hath her compasse lost:
　　Right so it fares with me in this long way,
Whose course is often stayd, yet neuer is astray.

For all that hetherto hath long delayd
　　This gentle knight, from sewing his first quest,
　　Though out of course, yet hath not bene mis-sayd,
　　To shew the courtesie by him profest,
　　Euen vnto the lowest and the least.
　　But now I come into my course againe,
　　To his atchieuement of the *Blatant beast*;
　　Who all this while at will did range and raine,
Whilst none was him to stop, nor none him to restraine.[43]

Elsewhere in *The Faerie Queene*, Spenser pictures himself as
the captain of a ship, the readers are his mariners, and the
characters in the poem are passengers (see, for example, 1. 12. 1;
1. 12. 42). At the end of the Sixth Book, Calidore is made to
capture the Blatant Beast, but the Beast soon breaks his chain
and the book ends with him at liberty. "Ne may this homely
verse," says Spenser, "of many meanest, / Hope to escape his
venemous despite" (6. 12. 41. 1).

What justifies Spenser in writing as if he had gathered the
figures in his poem, himself as poet, and his readers all together
in the same dimensions of time and space is the fact that he has
done just that. He makes no attempt to give an inner time
scheme or to map the topography of Faerie Land. Nor are we
encouraged to plumb the psychological depths, for the most
part, of the protagonists or of other characters (though the
accumulation of incidents and reflections yields great
psychological insight). On the other hand, it is not simply a
crude allegory in which we match up characters and moral
qualities and let it go at that, as if working a puzzle. For two or
three hours, in each book, we follow the central Knight and his
(or her) friends as they pursue their dreamlike series of adventures. They are dreamlike because on nearly every page there
arises a new embodiment of evil, intemperance, injustice, dis-

43. *Faerie Queene: Books Six and Seven*, p. 139.

courtesy, and the like, or else a new ally in the struggle, and the scene shifts as often. Our imagination is not asked to be structurally intensive, miniscule in its detail, but rather temporally extensive, sweeping in its survey. The effect is one of creative energy moving forward, meeting reverses, finding reinforcements, struggling ahead once more, facing harassment, finding rest, setting out again. Calidore reforms Crudor and Briana from their hair-raising ways. Tristram slays the discourteous knight who wounded Aladine, Calidore chases the Beast away from Serena, Turpine harasses Serena's knight Calepine, the Salvage man saves Calepine from Turpine, Calepine rescues a baby from a bear, the Hermit helps Serena and Timias cure themselves of the Blatant Beast's wounds, Arthur strips Turpine, Timias is captured by Disdain whom Arthur subdues, Calepine rescues Serena from cannibals, Calidore comes upon Pastorella, he plays the part of a shepherd, he sees the graces dance on Mount Acidale, he rescues Pastorella from a tiger and later from the Brigants, at last Calidore completes his quest, but the Blatant Beast escapes. I mention these relatively few incidents from a single book simply to suggest the surging, ever-renewing energy that pulses throughout.

Despite Spenser's complaint against the Blatant Beast of detraction biting at his work and his more serious and final complaint against a Mutability that makes him wearily seek the final Sabbath rest, his poem as a whole, far from overwhelming the reader with negative forces of decay, yields the experience that he claims for himself in opening the Sixth Book:

> The waies, through which my weary steps I guyde,
>> In this delightfull land of Faery,
>> Are so exceeding spacious and wyde,
>> And sprinckled with such sweet variety,
>> Of all that pleasant is to eare or eye
>> That I nigh rauisht with rare thoughts delight,
>> My tedious trauell doe forget thereby;
>> And when I gin to feele decay of might,
> It strength to me supplies, and chears my dulled spright.

Endimion, *The Faithful Shepherdess*, *Arcadia*, and *The Faerie Queene* all help us, I believe, to see why in *The Winter's Tale* the re-creative vision relies little upon proofs of content and much upon persuasions of form. The attempt to see life whole takes us beyond the confines of a single place, Sicilia, or a single time, the period of jealousy, or a single personality, Leontes. The tragic focus of the first three acts is the one we normally consider realistic for it gives back our own sense of life as lived by the individual in a local perspective of place and time with youth and vigor behind and old age and death before. But in the last two acts, in the journey to Bohemia, the changed time, the introduction of many new characters, the emphasis upon a new season and generation of growth, the rapid alternation of disguises, the journey back to Sicilia, and the waking of Hermione, we as the audience are asked to abandon our single perspective in favor of pluralistic perspectives that take us beyond the normal confines of one time, one place, one action. As in the works mentioned, a speedup and extension of our perception here elevates into great prominence the formal qualities of the world presented and the work presenting it. Because of the closely spaced appearances of new persons— Shepherd, Clown, Autolycus, rustics, Florizel, Perdita—characterization becomes thin, the emphasis shifts from introspection—the soliloquies of Leontes and the other speeches analyzing him—to interaction (Antigonus meets bear but Shepherd finds baby, Autolycus steals from Clown but the shearing festival still goes forward, Florizel and Perdita are momentarily thwarted by Polixenes but press ahead, deceive Leontes for a moment until Polixenes arrives but then prevail, while, finally, Leontes' lonely sorrow turns to companioned joy). In close succession we are confronted with differing persons, differing defeats and victories. The dispersal or scattering of the central probing consciousness into a variety of actors who enact a rhythmic succession of blocking and forwarding movements produces a musical, ceremonial effect much like that produced by Spenser in following the various reverses and triumphs of knight, salvage man, hermit, and fair lady or by Sidney in tracing the alternate woes and wonders of Pyrocles, Musidorus, Cynecia, and Basilius.

Such works intensify not only a morphogenetic sense of life in speeded up, perpetual renewal but also a concomitant awareness of rhythm and formal organization that make the worlds so described seem particularly artlike. After the recognition of Perdita, a Sicilian Gentleman exclaims: "such a deal of wonder is broken out within this hour, that ballad-makers cannot be able to express it" (5. 2. 23). There is more here than the notion that the world seems like a play, the notion expressed by Perdita, for instance, when she says:

> Methinks I play as I have seen them do
> In Whitsun pastorals. (4. 4. 133)

> I see the play so lies
> That I must bear a part. (4. 4. 655)

As we have seen, many of Shakespeare's characters, including Leontes, remind the audience that life may seem like a play. The references of the Gentleman, however, point toward a particular kind of art that the re-creative world resembles, the art of the ballad or tale in which events are condensed, characterization is thin, and stress falls upon the improbable and miraculous. "This news," the Gentleman continues, "which is called true, is so like an old tale, that the verity of it is in strong suspicion" (5. 2. 27), and his associate characterizes the events as being "like an old tale still, which will have matter to rehearse, though credit be asleep and not an ear open" (5. 2. 62). Paulina, too, upon the waking of Hermione, notes:

> That she is living,
> Were it but told you, should be hooted at
> Like an old tale. (5. 3. 115)

Time, himself, or the playwright "in the name of Time" (4. 1. 3), refers to the play as "my tale" (4. 1. 14). His intervention is reminiscent of Lyly's prologue to *Endimion*:

> Most high and happy Princesse, we must tell you a tale of the Man in the Moone, which if it seeme ridiculous for the method, or superfluous for the matter, or for the means incredible, for three faultes wee can make but one excuse. It is a tale of the Man in the Moone.
> ... Wee present neither Comedie, nor Tragedie, nor storie, nor anie thing, but that whosoeuer heareth may say this, Why heere is a tale of the Man in the Moone.[44]

The Man in the Moon is the subtitle to *Endimion*. Time, through his reference to "my tale," points to the title of his play, too, and through talk of ancient order and overwhelmed custom reminds us that such tales seem as old as time, harking back to myths and their miracles. Mamillius's winter's tale was to be of "sprites and goblins" (2. 1. 26), and the last two acts are replete with curious myth dreams: Florizel's vignettes of gods in metamorphosis, Perdita's anthology of buds that "take / The winds of March with beauty" (4. 4. 119) or else "die unmarried,"

---

44. *Works*, Bond, 3: 20.

Autolycus's ballads of the usurer's wife who breeds money and of the cold woman who turns into a cold fish. Hermione wakes a la Galatea. The characters stand half in myth, half out. Florizel loves Flora. We see Autolycus, we hear of Mercury. Perdita calls to Proserpina. In all this, we become aware of the play as a tale that openly, ritually, views life itself as a tale, a synoptic and holistic account of patterned regeneration.

The world in which gods and men freely intermingle in a natural environment, the one evoked by Endimion and Cynthia, Basilius and the Oracle, Amoret and the river god, Scudamore and Venus, celebrates an integrative force, call it love, which brings all creatures together rhythmically and enlivens them. In perceiving each work, the essential act of understanding is not a piercing of character or situation to say what it stands for, nor adoption of a comic or tragic perspective, but rather a gathering of interrelated events, a listening to the pulse that quickens the actors: we need not decide whether Hermione comes alive as a woman surmounting death or a god descending from immortality so long as we realize, as we must, that her awakening recapitulates and sums up the awakening of the season from winter to spring, the awakening of Florizel and Perdita to the latter's true identity, the awakening of all on the stage and perhaps before it to renewed community and hope.

XV

Through such study of the background as has been attempted here, we become responsive, I believe, to our community of interest in the play. In a sense, Shakespeare worked through his own career and in association with his contemporaries[45] to

45. In concentrating upon what I take to be the central impulse of *The Winter's Tale* and upon works that inform that impulse, I have tended to slight works outside the general ambit of pastoral romance. Other forms, of course, illumine the play. One typed domestic tragedy is, for example, Thomas Heywood's fine play, *A Woman Killed with Kindness* (1603), which shrewdly delineates many connections between marital fidelity and broader ranges of faith and hope and which dramatizes movingly the perfecting powers of forgiveness and reconciliation. Another form is the type of popular, if crude, dramatic romance exemplified by *Mucedorus*, with its wild man Bremo dramatically tamed by Amadine's chastity, the onstage Bear, and the familiar motif of pastoral disguise. See also, Patricia Russell, "Romantic Narrative Plays: 1570–1590," in *Elizabethan Theatre*, ed. John Russell Brown and Berard Harris, Stratford-Upon-Avon Studies 9 (London: Arnold, 1966), pp. 107–29. *The Winter's Tale* is, indeed, so multifarious in its concerns and

reauthorize man's conviction that, despite lesser losses, all parts of life may gather and grow in concert. When we inform ourselves of what the play seems designed to achieve, we enrich our potential encounter with it. And we enhance the possibility that we may work with others toward the kind of shared journey from isolating doubt to reuniting faith that is so openly encouraged by the play.

It remains for me to sketch in a final chapter an outline of that journey as I envisage it being undertaken by readers and spectators seeking the high rewards of direct performance, the living play.

---

design that it sets up telling reverberations with most Elizabethan plays brought within its force field. It would be instructive, for example, to connect *The Winter's Tale* and the intensifying debates between male chauvinism and feminism that crop up in such plays as John Heywood's *The Four PP*, Stevenson's *Gammer Gurton's Needle*, Greene's *Friar Bacon and Friar Bungay*, Jonson's comedies, and Jacobean satires such as Middleton and Rowley's *The Changling*. Or one might profitably work out the parallels and distinctions between the semitragic Leontes of the first three acts and Marlovian freethinkers who vacillate between pride and despair, or between Leontes as revenger manqué and similarly ambivalent figures in plays of Tourneur, Webster, and Ford. Specially rewarding work remains to be done, I suggest, on connections between the *The Winter's Tale* and Lyly's comedies such as *Gallathea* where, again, old mythologies, religions, and rituals are portrayed as withering and renewing themselves in triumphant expression of love's or faith's great purgative force.

Chapter IV.

The Play in Time

A good way to join ruminative understanding and direct experience of *The Winter's Tale* would be to attend a performance after, or before, reading (or writing) criticism concerning the play. This attempt to respect both the thematic insights of our schematizing intellect and the moment-to-moment revelations of our theatrical consciousness is emulated here in the chapters on history and backgrounds that have sought natural perspectives on the play as structure of ideas and as sequence of events. I seek next to emulate the movement from rumination to attended performance as I consider the play somewhat more intrinsically. I make no attempt, however, apart from an initial comparison of the first two scenes, to give a reading of the play in its minute-by-minute unfolding. I shall attend, primarily, to larger clusters of scenic rhythms, features of style, patterns of actions, and the like that mark out the distinctive orchestration, metabolism, or drive of *The Winter's Tale*. I begin at every reader's or playgoer's starting point, with a meditation upon the first words met, the title. Then I take up major organic features of successive parts of the drama.

I

Romance tales, like dreams, often invite both casual and intense regard. "The Winter's Tale" presents, similarly, a lingering, even ever-deepening, ambiguity. Dismissing Macbeth's apprehension of Banquo's ghost, Lady Macbeth says it "would well become / A woman's story at a winter's fire" (3. 4. 63). (Compare Prince Edward's derisive reference to an "Aesop fable in a winter's night" [3H6 5. 4. 25].) Yet Macbeth and his Lady find that phantasms may produce the spasmed terrors of nightmares. Mamillius, too, who notes that "a sad tale's best for winter" (2. 1. 25), confronts an audience both credulous and incredulous in Hermione and her attendants. They mock this "good sir" and his attempted best to fright them with "sprites" (2. 1. 26–28), but they concede that he is "pow'rful at it," and

they must find prophetic force in the way that Mamillius's sad
winter's tale of a man who dwelt by a churchyard becomes
interrupted, or more accurately invaded, by a man stalking
death and redemption, by Leontes, "That winter lion, who in
rage" (2H6 5. 3. 2) enters to manufacture his own ultimate sad-
ness. "The Winter's Tale" may differ, moreover, from "a sad tale"
best for winter or from "a woman's story" at a winter's fire in that
"The Winter's Tale," may mean not only "your typical tale told in
winter" but also "the tale told *by* winter," the tale that *every*
winter tells, and, if we think from the outset of winter as the
teller of the tale, then we obtain for the whole play a high
perspective upon its winter lion and its seasons of loss and gain
that can substantially enrich its life.

Appealing no doubt to our deepest and most universal readings of the season, Shakespeare in his works consistently
connects "rough," "furious," "sap-consuming," and "barren"
winter with personified qualities, qualities that pervade *The
Winter's Tale*. The first portion of the play concentrates on
equivalents in the human world of winter's cold, hostile bluster
or, as Paulina puts it, "winter in storm perpetual" (3. 2. 212). Not
only is Leontes mired in Richard's famous winter of "discon-
tent," behaving like the Hal described by his father "as humorous as winter" (2H4 4. 3. 34), caught in an "angry winter" (MND
2. 1. 112), emulating "churlish winter's tyranny" (2H4 1. 3. 62) but
also Leontes must find his way through the stages of storm,
sickness, death, and rebirth that Shakespeare associates with
winter. In human terms, the wages of wintry anger are sickness
and death. After Harfleur, Henry V notes "the winter coming on,
and sickness growing" (3. 3. 55); Shakespeare's materializing
imagination often finds a seasonal reading for war, alienation,
and banishment. "How like a winter hath my absence been"
(*Son.* 97). To Bullingbrook, King Richard says:

> Six frozen winters spent,
> Return with welcome home from banishment.
> *Bull.* How long a time lies in one little word!
> Four lagging winters and four wanton springs
> End in a word. (1. 3. 211)

Leontes, moving through Paulina's image of repentant fasting in
winter (3. 2. 211), "shuts up himself" (Time, 4. 1. 19) and fades
behind the "loud weather" of the journey to Bohemia, the
Shepherd's rescue of the cold baby Perdita ("they were warmer

that got this than the poor thing is here" [3. 3. 75]), and the drowned sailors "cold under water" (3. 3. 104).

In Bullingbrook's and Shakespeare's minds, furthermore, the image of "lagging winter" implies dependence on the image of "wanton spring," when "April on the heel / Of limping winter treads" (*Rom.* 1. 2. 27). The winter's tale is of itself but also, perforce, of spring. In Perdita's phrase —"the birth / Of trembling winter" (4. 4. 80)—much of the play's mystery lies enfolded. Born in winter yet "grown in grace" (4. 1. 24), Perdita speaks this phrase with special authority; she is destined to be welcomed by Leontes "as is the spring to th' earth" (5. 1. 151). Ultimately the winter's tale, the winter's tail, the winter stale yields birth.

II

To renew one's engagement with *The Winter's Tale* through musings on its title is to enter, swiftly, its pastoral perspective. The title introduces the first scene, just as that scene introduces what follows. The "Winter" is Nature; the "Tale" is Art. But the "Winter" is also the grave of Fall: dead, timeless, abstract, artlike. And the "Tale" is Time's own narrative: moving and regenerative. This essential cross-qualification is taken up in the first scene where the Bohemian Archidamus and the Sicilian Camillo represent not only two countries but two climates and two sets of attitudes that similarly intersect.

> *Arch.* If you shall chance, Camillo, to visit Bohemia, on the like occasion whereon my services are now on foot, you shall see, as I have said, great difference betwixt our Bohemia and your Sicilia.
> *Cam.* I think, this coming summer, the King of Sicilia means to pay Bohemia the visitation which he justly owes him. (1. 1. 1)

The Sicilian court, the art context, stands now in winter and, as we soon see, a kind of dream ("my life stands in the level of your dreams" [3. 2. 81]). Winter and dream equal nature and art or nature as art. Bohemia, too, may mix nature and art. Archidamus continues:

> Wherein our entertainment shall shame us: we will be justified in our loves: for indeed—
> *Cam.* Beseech you—
> *Arch.* Verily I speak it in the freedom of my knowledge: we cannot

with such magnificence—in so rare— I know not what to say—
We will give you sleepy drinks, that your senses (unintelligent
of our insufficience) may, though they cannot praise us, as
little accuse us. (1.1.8)

The accusation of the "magnificent" winter court lodges
against a vaguely defined Bohemian "insufficience"; artful "entertainment" may think to shame the natural innocence of
justifying "love." Camillo, resisting this division, tries to go back
to the twinned origin of the two Kings in one "rooted" affection:
"Sicilia cannot show himself over-kind to Bohemia. They were
trained together in their childhoods, and there rooted betwixt
them then such an affection which cannot choose but branch
now" (1.1.21). The first sentence no doubt means: "Sicilia
could not possibly give Bohemia too much love." "Kind" also
refers to genetic relatedness and to natural bonds of various
sorts. The ironic, undercutting meanings here are that Sicilia
may be only showing, not feeling, his affection for Bohemia or
that, harking back to the Sicilia/Art and Bohemia/Nature connection, Sicilia cannot establish a total identity with Bohemia
or cannot show himself too closely related.

The play's title and the little opening scene work together,
bringing season and story, nature and art, Bohemia and Sicilia,
into teasing juxtapositions. In their prologue-like exchange,
Archidamus and Camillo image a society poised as well between nostalgia and anticipation, memory of youthful kings
and hopes for a young prince. Shakespeare makes this
emblematic preview cover the whole range of the play's degen-
eration in aging friendships and regeneration in the "promise"
of youth (1.1.36). But the hopes of regeneration remain, in this
scene, somewhat incomplete and weak. The hints of menace,
such as Sicilians needing an "excuse to live," await the scene to
follow. We are led directly from foreboding of "mature dignities" to welcoming promise in the hopes of gallant youth that
"physics the subject, makes old hearts fresh," and the scene
closes on an insistent refrain, three references in four sentences to men's "desire to live." It is the root desire we hope to
see survive drought and winter to flourish anew. But for the
present, the imminent prospect, we face the tension created by
this brief, subtle opening. In a theater, the hints of menace fall
perhaps faintly on the ear. But to verbal nuance live attention

adds visual presence—costumes, makeup, gesture, movement, setting, lighting—an amalgamation of cues as they gather toward a generalization of atmosphere, a developing world. One who knows the play may expect to follow easily the courtly canter of these elder statesmen through background essential for the uninformed and expect to relish the dramatic ironies they so unwittingly provide. But, as Archidamus, referring to "such magnificence," makes an abashed gesture toward sumptuous ornaments and hangings about him, as he casts down his eyes a moment and fumbles with his cloak at "I know not what to say," he appears part of a more sincere, self-conscious struggle than merely competitive exchange of compliments. Through Archidamus's earnest glances as he enlarges upon the great difference between the countries, through Camillo's attempt to render bluff assurance that boyhood friends naturally grow to kingly embrace, even "from the ends of opposed winds," one observes that the courtiers face threats and rewards of growth and change. If persons at first together grow older apart, what could make them feel young and one again? What keeps men from becoming, in Archidamus's phrase, "content to die"? The two counsellors, musing across the stage, at last seek plain agreement in plain language: the "promise" and the "hopes" of progeny lead men to plant the end of their own lives in the beginning of other lives. As Camillo and Archidamus now draw aside, having completed their introduction, they have expressed in their tentative, somewhat stiff handclasp of agreement all the combined wishfulness and anxiousness of the scene.

The stage has been cast in the optative mood. Even those spectators who "know" the play are caught in it, surpassing their knowledge and experiencing the numinous envelopment of the mind by dramatic circumstance. In one sense, nothing at all happened during the first scene: there occurred no tempest, no quarrel, nor even any mid-scene entrance or exit to rouse attention. There was only modest talk. Yet the watchers are drawn into a distinctive medium of Sicilian magnificence, of confrontation and half-resolution, of conversational mode turning from starched and elegant to more nearly blunt, of evaluations in word, tone, and gesture already beginning to assess the projected action and the core of characters. Sicilia will pay what is "justly" owed; Bohemia will be "justified" in love. "Our loves," which Archidamus professes to own, soon contrast with "their loves," which Camillo prays to continue. Here, in short, is man hoping, man seeking to find a balance and belief in generational continuity and finding himself uncomfortably faced with time and change. The Sicilian winter's tale combines things passing and to come, "old hearts" and new, a transition hinted at, yet hardly defined, from a closing to a beginning. An audience can scarcely resist being beckoned into this drama of rooted affection; it is led irresistibly by the first scene's quiet, kind, yet uneasy and even ominous welcome.

III

As Camillo and Archidamus draw upstage, a moment remains to ponder the "comfort," attributed to Mamillius, a comfort made the more precious by a threatening if-clause (which closes the scene as conditionally as it opened): "If the king had no son. . . ." That very king and son enter now, hand in hand, together with the other principals and a sweeping entourage — in marked contrast to the introductory pair of counsellors. Though we may recognize that the first scene begins to reduplicate its form when the Bohemian speaks first (again of time as chance and change) and the Sicilian replies (again measuring what's to "pay"), thus reinstituting a debate, we must reckon more fully with the swelling grandeur of both scene and speech. The stage fills with royalty and all its accoutrements of power and service. The courtiers' prose changes now to a more musical cadence as magnificence of metaphor proclaims the presence of regal imagination.

At the forefront of attention stand Leontes and Polixenes, flanking the visibly pregnant Hermione. Mamillius plays beside Leontes. Upstage, a few attendants group themselves not far from Archidamus and Camillo. Polixenes became discernible when he entered behind the Sicilians (King and Queen) and offered a passing nod to Archidamus. If we missed such identification, we soon know upon whom we fix our attention when Polixenes, raising his hands in a sweeping gesture, extending all fingers but one, begins:

> Nine changes of the watery star hath been
> The shepherd's note since we have left our throne
> Without a burden. (1. 2. 1)

As he continues, with measured, orotund phrase, to deliver his elaborate thanks, a minute is created in which to assess his

character. That "watery star," the moon, points toward sea
changes and points us, however dimly, overseas to Bohemia, a
"shepherd's" country. The shepherd notes the changes of a
Cynthia or Diana who seems here less chaste than generative.
Time, the general subject of the two courtiers' preceding conversation takes on, in Polixenes' reference to nine months and
perhaps to "burden," a pregnant reality.

His juxtaposed images of tending shepherd versus abandoned throne may initiate one's questioning of Polixenes as he
focuses more singly upon his royal friend:

>   Time as long again
> Would be fill'd up, my brother, with our thanks;
> And yet we should, for perpetuity,
> Go hence in debt: and therefore, like a cipher
> (Yet standing in rich place) I multiply
> With one 'We thank you' many thousands moe
> That go before it.
>
> *Leon.*   Stay your thanks a while,
>   And pay them when you part.
>
> *Pol.*   Sir, that's to-morrow.
> I am question'd by my fears, of what may chance
> Or breed upon our absence; that may blow
> No sneaping winds at home, to make us say
> 'This is put forth too truly'. Besides, I have stay'd
> To tire your royalty.
>
> *Leon.*   We are tougher, brother,
>   Than you can put us to 't. (1. 2. 3)

Given the predictive tensions of the first scene and the present
pregnancy of Hermione, these ascending references to filling
up, standing in rich place, multiplying, and fearing what may
breed or put forth are references that *could* cause wonder.
There may be yet no hint of adultery to any save Leontes, if
indeed to him, but the mind of the audience, intent upon hints
of the trouble endemic to a play's beginning, should be in a way
sensualized by this language of impregnation. And even though
the entering edge of doubt appears tentative, at first only a
cautious and probing uncertainty, still the momentum gathers
quickly, and directional signals point to the oncoming storm.

In his brief responses to the hyperbolic excuses of Polixenes,
Leontes may appear curt, even perhaps menacing. The midline
beginnings and halts of his speeches may suggest a sense of
interruption and abruptness. The similar patterns of the two

sentences, each divided into two clauses of three beats, may
suggest a kind of ritualizing refrainlike, capstone quality to
Leontes' replies. The tension takes a quantum leap forward,
however, when Polixenes next proclaims that "no tongue" save
Leontes' could "win" him and a moment later Hermione's does.
Hermione, moreover, gives Leontes the dangerous assurance
that she loves him at least as much as other ladies love their
lords. Then we see into the possessiveness of Leontes' mind as
he describes his courtship when "three crabbed months had
sour'd themselves to death" before he won his queen. The
direction in which play and audience proceed signals itself. But
there are further intimations of why they proceed in that particular direction.

As Leontes and Hermione work on Polixenes to persuade him
to stay, they expose more fully the world described earlier by
Camillo, the world made up of "mature dignities and royal
necessities." Gracious thanks of Polixenes give way, under
countering pressure from Leontes, not only to "fears" of "what
may chance," "sneaping winds," and dragging affairs of state
but also to immediate unease: Polixenes presents himself as in
pain. "Press me not, beseech you" (1. 2. 19). Leontes' hindering
is a "whip" to him. To offend, he tells Hermione, "is for me less
easy to commit / Than you to punish" (1. 2. 58). As the conversation unfolds, present and future time seem less than carefree,
seem tinged with worrisome concern. The only happy glimpses
are of younger generations. Hermione says of Polixenes, "To
tell, he longs to see his son, were strong" (1. 2. 34). Here again is
the note of youth that heals the subject. Polixenes, however,
describes youth as a time of brief-lived innocence (1. 2. 67−75),
and it is into that context beneath the royal banter, into that
view of inevitably burdensome, sinful maturity, that Leontes'
description of his courtship fits. Marriage itself involves, in the
words of Hemione, fault and slipping. No one can answer "not
guilty"; hereditary imposition is the lot of all. At the very least,
we in the audience are made to wonder that the visual setting of
"such magnificence," as Archidamus put it, encloses speakers
"question'd" by their fears and musing on "temptations."

In the talk of Hermione and Polixenes we hear, certainly,
balance and grace. But we note as well entering edges of alienation. After Hermione tells Leontes that he charges his brother
king "too coldly," Leontes draws aside with Mamillius. We see
Hermione jibe at Polixenes: "a lady's Verily's / As potent as a

lord's. Will you go yet?" (1. 2. 50). She catches his sleeve, walks
with him to the other side of the stage. On the opposing side
stands Leontes, silent and contemplative next to his son, figures for comparison as Hermione questions Polixenes concerning the kings' boyhood: "You were pretty lordings then?" (1. 2.
60). And as guest and queen continue to discuss that lost time
prior to knowledge of "ill-doing," they stroll back toward
Leontes and gain his attention just after Polixenes tells Hermione that temptations were born only when she "cross'd the
eyes" of Leontes. She replies:

> Of this make no conclusion, lest you say
> Your queen and I are devils. Yet go on;
> Th' offences we have made you do, we'll answer,
> If you first sinn'd with us, . . . (1. 2. 81)

Hermione's persuading Polixenes thus juxtaposes itself to her
marrying Leontes. It makes an unusually tense moment in
Shakespearean drama when the hinted, germinal questionings
of "stronger blood," persuasive "tongues," "limber vows," and
Sicilian "entertainment" come together in a point of visual
focus: clasped hands. Hermione, pregnant and charged with
sensual energy, draws Polixenes into a discussion of sex, tells
Leontes to praise her, speaks of being ridden with soft kisses,
and asks for news of her first good deed with "Nay, let me have't:
I long!" Leontes tells her that was when he "made" her open her
"white hand" and vow to be his forever. So saying, he takes one
of her hands in his. Hermione responds, " 'Tis Grace indeed."
Turning then from Leontes, she extends her hand to Polixenes,
saying:

> Why lo you now; I have spoke to th' purpose twice:
> The one, for ever earn'd a royal husband;
> Th' other, for some while a friend. (1. 2. 106)

And queen and "friend" (which could be taken by those so
inclined to include the sense of "paramour" [*Cym*. 1. 4. 62; *MM*
1. 4. 29]) draw off together, leaving Leontes to hiss his blistering
aside: "Too hot, too hot!" (1. 2. 108).

In that single instant of handclasps transferred through
Hermione, Camillo's image of the kings who "shook hands, as
over a vast" explodes into suspicion. The gesture that to Hermione and Polixenes means love and confidence to Leontes
means a lascivious breach of trust: "paddling palms, and pinching fingers" (1. 2. 115).

IV

In the simplest terms, an audience watching the first two scenes of *The Winter's Tale* hopes, then founders. It hears of amity but finds discord. Told of rooted affection between visiting kings, it sees one king seeking to leave the other. It sees two friendly counsellors replaced by a tense triangle wherein the host-husband takes a strangely peripheral position. The lingering description of affectionate childhood twists into one of lost innocence, of the doctrine of ill-doing, and prolonged discussion of sexual slipping. The son who should physic the subject takes no active part and is but a boy made to "go play."

An audience gathers in order and quiet expecting art to give that order a life, a meaning, a value. It first hears of friendship and generational continuity (albeit with vaguely discordant undertones), but it soon witnesses a questioning of such civilized forms. The forms are oddly devitalized. In the mind and speech of the central character doting is doubting, affection infection, time fearful, speech artificial, love suspicious, nature unstable, faith asleep.

Leontes, like many prominent figures in Shakespeare's later plays, turns inward, in possessiveness, away from a leader's role to that of brooder, speculator, self-questioner, domestic inquirer, inspector. Like Othello, Lear, Antony, he turns from ruling to railing, seeking to feed without confidence on a love at first too shallowly conceived. Far from representing, as potent king, man in his generative aspect, he turns in a de-creative circuit, finds himself stabbed by unhealthy affection, and turns suspicion into accusation. As suggested in the preceding chapter and worth reiterating, kings and leaders generally in Shakespeare tend to align their affections vertically up and down the procreative or martial chain whose continuance it is their prime function to assure. Lateral relationships—as here, between Leontes and Hermione—at first mean less to them, or at least to their function. Relations between Hamlet and his parents interfere with his affection for Ophelia; Lear seeks too strong an involvement with his daughters; even Macbeth's love for his wife might be tainted by a need for issue; the vertical relation between Coriolanus and his mother Volumnia nearly exlcudes his wife Virgilia; Pericles is excluded by the incest of Antiochus and daughter; Cymbeline's queen advances her son Cloten in enmity to her husband. Martial heroes like Othello and Antony can never quite abandon command and its implicit vertical relations for lateral relations of friendship and love.

Through many devices of speech and stagecraft, Shakespeare presents a Leontes of isolation and constriction. It is singularly appropriate that his first extended speech should be an aside. He who was curt when Hermione and Polixenes were loquacious, who charged "coldly" when they spoke warmly and laughed together, who commanded and judged where they conversed as equals, who stayed still with his son while they moved freely, he is allowed to relieve his feelings only in a cramped aside. And in that aside he shows himself bound to insidious limitations of interiority and obsession with self:

> To mingle friendship far, is mingling bloods.
> I have *tremor cordis* on me: my heart dances,
> But not for joy—not joy. (1. 2. 109)

For a moment he can imagine liberal "entertainment," the "free face," "heartiness," "fertile bosom." But such imaginings are bracketed by the more material reality of his unhearty bosom, his finger pointing at smiles upstage, his imitative sigh of sexual dying, and his hand at his brows feeling for cuckold's horns that (does he half remember at "bawcock"?) derive from spurs implanted on combs of cockerels to mark that they have been castrated.

As he looks at Mamillius, he reflects that, if the smiles of Hermione are practiced "as in a looking glass," then as a result other "copies," even his son as the copy of himself, may be false (1. 2. 121−35). The truth of vertical reproduction, king to son, depends upon truths of lateral sincerity, queen to king. If the steer, the heifer, and the calf—husband, wife, and child—are all "neat," that is, horned, then the world is indeed "wanton." He tries to believe in the truth of Mamillius's seeming to be a slice of his flesh, his "collop," but even the germinal analogy of eggs comes under question, because, at least in Leontes' mind, something in affection itself cuts to the quick, and, as it turns out, like the cuckoo, foists in life (161) from outside:

> Come, sir page,
> Look on me with your welkin eye: sweet villain!
> Most dear'st, my collop! Can thy dam?—may't be?—
> Affection! thy intention stabs the centre. (1. 2. 135)

Staring into the sky of his son's welkin gaze, Leontes imagines innocence lost in sexuality that stabs through to man's earthy center. Shakespeare, I think, has done much to help an audience hear and see the innocence of youth—from the first scene's glance at the happy childhoods of the kings and the promise of Mamillius through this scene's stress upon the same theme: "he longs to see his son," "when you were boys," "to be boy eternal," "we were as twinn'd lambs." But it is an innocence of youth under instant siege.

Not only has Polixenes proposed a theory of adolescent sexuality in which stronger blood gives birth to "temptations," and not only does Leontes exhibit, in reference to stabbing affection and, later, to his "dagger muzzl'd / Lest it should bite its master," an outspoken fear of sexuality, but also the visual structure of the play concentrates upon the dangerous fragility of youth's promise. When Archidamus and Camillo invited a bilateral perspective upon the stage where Bohemia and Sicilia were balanced against each other, Mamillius was summoned up between them in imagination. Now, when Polixenes and Leontes present the same bilateral perspective, Hermione and Mamillius stand between—Hermione at one side next to Polixenes during their conversation and Mamillius in the center and then before Leontes as he watches the other pair. As Leontes speaks to the question of "affection," he can enact, by looking vertically at his son and horizontally across to his wife and "brother" King, a dramatic visual emblem of the cross-tensions in his mind. Before him stands his youthful self, recoiled "twenty-three years," "unbreech'd," a squash, a kernel, offered "eggs for money." Across from him stands his wife opening her white hand, as in the archetypal act he has just described, and, to his eyes, enticing Polixenes. In a single instant, there is offered for sight the image of man (as child) growing vertically toward sexually mature selfhood and then (as husband) laterally into sexual experience.

It is important to see that Leontes' outburst against affection appears within a matrix of primal relationships. Posited first was the "affection" (1. 1. 23) rooted between the kings as boys. They continually call each other "brother." Polixenes insists upon a background in which the youthful "brothers" exchanged only innocence for innocence. Now, onstage, one brother, Leontes, stands speculating upon his growth and change away from youthful innocence. Mature affection, capable of infectious dreams, takes a different cast. The other

brother, Polixenes, not only takes Hermione's hand, in imitation
of Leontes' courtship, but also speculates, as did Leontes, upon
his relationship to his own son:

> He's all my exercise, my mirth, my matter:
> Now my sworn friend, and then mine enemy;
> My parasite, my soldier, statesman, all.
> He makes a July's day short as December;
> And with his varying childness cures in me
> Thoughts that would thick my blood. (1. 2. 166)

The tangle of identities is complete. Polixenes seems to mimic
Leontes and the thought that "friends" may dangerously
mingle "blood." He speaks, again, as does Leontes, of a curative
"childness," but his final emphasis, like that of his "brother,"
falls on blood-thickening thoughts. This speech hardly reas-
sures the seething Leontes, who, instead of seeking cure from
Mamillius, dismisses him, after first bidding Hermione and
Polixenes an ironic adieu to the "garden" (1. 2. 178) of, so he
thinks, their temptations.

The pace of the play has been swift; less than fifteen minutes
have elapsed. In that time, the almost material density of relationships, common in Shakespeare's openings, has been fully
adduced. Bonds of loyalty between friend and friend, brother
and brother, husband and wife, wife and friend, father and son,
have been defined and counter-defined into what is, at least for
Leontes, a cheerless and all-suspicious knot. As the company
clears the stage, the audience must hope that the king's clear
sanity may return to him once free from the disturbing presence of Polixenes and the others. On the contrary, however, the
perception of his anguish intensifies as he establishes an open
though mocking rapport with the audience. First he forces the
spectators to become aware of him as an actor imagining a
derisive audience:

> Go, play, boy, play: the mother plays, and I
> Play too; but so disgrac'd a part, whose issue
> Will hiss me to my grave: contempt and clamour
> Will be my knell. Go, play, boy, play. (1. 2. 187)

Then, shunting Mamillius aside, he turns directly to the
spectators, even points into the observing throng:

> There have been,
> (Or I am much deceiv'd) cuckolds ere now,

And many a man there is (even at this present,
Now, while I speak this) holds his wife by th' arm,
That little thinks she has been sluic'd in 's absence
And his pond fish'd by his next neighbour, by
Sir Smile, his neighbour. (1. 2. 190)

No more immediate challenge to an audience can be made. I
have seen several productions of the play and noted varying
degrees of incredulity toward Leontes' first ravings, but I have
never seen his reference to "many a man . . . that little thinks"
fail to find its mark. That Leontes seems deceived in his jealousy
only makes more bitter his pointing to true adulterers and
cuckolds in his audience. If we try, furthermore, to protect
ourselves with the reflection that Leontes feels the disease but
has it not, we are nonetheless assaulted by the actor's ad-
monishments—"think it . . . be it concluded . . . Know't "—to
admit that "many thousands on's / Have the disease, and feel 't
not" (1. 2. 202). The speech, in other words, is genuinely, per-
sonally, unsettling.

Shakespeare thus persuades the spectator to remember that
play—child's play and the play of affection—can point to reality. Far from distancing the theatrical event by such open address as that of Leontes to an audience, Shakespeare enlivens
the theater by encouraging each spectator not to suspend
disbelief but to enter a conscious complicity with the play.
Most of them will have entered the theater from the relatively
humdrum order of daily domestic and business affairs.
Leontes, deluded or not, forces each one of them to re-examine
the foundations of complacency toward trusted friendships.

V

For the next hour, the playhouse is charged and tyrannized
upon by the monarch's accents and actions. Any attempt, however, to chronicle the moment-to-moment exchanges of actors
and the audience's responses risks myopia. I propose instead to
trace features of idiomatic and scenic contrast that charac-
terize the tragic portion of *The Winter's Tale* and that, in my
judgment, account for the unified verbal and visual impact of
stage presentation.

Perhaps the most remarkable aspect of the tragic portion is
that so little changes. Leontes appears four times and each time
does the same thing: he denounces Hermione or her surrogate,

Paulina, and is rebuked by representatives of his court. To be more precise, in a theme with little variation, Leontes four times expresses his misogyny, separates mother from child, and confronts indignant bystanders. Even if the play were dumb show, this re-enacted emblem of alienated affection would work deep into the consciousness of spectators.

In the second scene, Leontes watches Hermione as she holds Polixenes' hand; they withdraw from him, and soon he dismisses Mamillius. His violent argument with Camillo follows. In the third scene, he comes upon Hermione and Mamillius, pulls the boy from her, forces them to separate exits, and faces the rebukes of Antigonus and the Lords. The fifth scene shows the king attacking and dismissing Paulina and banishing Perdita in the arms of her defender, Antigonus. In the seventh scene, the trial scene, Leontes attacks Hermione, loses Mamillius and her, and suffers the stinging rebuke of Paulina.

The purpose of this reduplicating structure is not primarily to advance the plot, nor is it to explore the King's motivations. It serves instead to amplify the dimensions of his nightmare and to demonstrate in wider ambit the consequences of his condition. An audience will persist in finding Leontes mad but will find it harder and harder to ignore the implications of that madness. His idiom spawns violence, and the audience sees an increasingly violent series of expulsions:

> Bear the boy hence. (2. 1. 59)
>
> Away with her, to prison! (2. 1. 103)
>
> Go, do our bidding: hence! (2. 1. 125)
>
> Leave me solely: go, . . . (2. 3. 17)
>
> Away with that audacious lady! (2. 3. 42)
>
> Hence with her, out o' door: . . . (2. 3. 68)
>
> Will you not push her out? (2. 3. 73)

As the audience *hears* Leontes conceive his jealousy, accuse Hermione, debate Paulina, and conduct the trial, it also *sees* him rejecting advice and comfort, dismissing women, losing company, being left alone, so that, while he orally projects an image of alienated man, he iconographically enacts the part as well.

Many of the exits away from Leontes, moreover, are lingering

and pointed. Twenty-five lines elapse between his first command to Mamillius—"Go, play" (1. 2. 187)—and the completed
exit. Nearly as many form the interval between his dismissal of
Hermione and her exit, and then the queen delivers a pointed
withdrawal speech:

> Who is't that goes with me? Beseech your highness,
> My women may be with me, for you see
> My plight requires it. Do not weep, good fools,
> There is no cause: when you shall know your mistress
> Has deserv'd prison, then abound in tears
> As I come out: this action I now go on
> Is for my better grace. Adieu, my Lord:
> I never wish'd to see you sorry; now
> I trust I shall. My women, come; you have leave. (2. 1. 116)

When Paulina brings the infant Perdita to Leontes at night, the
entire scene becomes a drawn-out portrayal of the king's physical repulsion. Paulina's final speech points graphically to what
must be happening onstage:

> I pray you, do not push me; I'll be gone.
> Look to your babe, my lord: 'tis yours: Jove send her
> A better guiding spirit! What needs these hands?
> You, that are thus so tender o'er his follies,
> Will never do him good, not one of you.
> So, so: farewell; we are gone. (2. 3. 124)

Even the announcement of Mamillius's death is put in terms of
withdrawal, departure:

> O sir, I shall be hated to report it!
> The prince your son, with mere conceit and fear
> Of the queen's speed, is gone.
>
> *Leon.* How! gone?
> *Serv.* Is dead.

(3. 2. 143)

In the tragic part of the play, all the Leontean scenes are
presented in specific terms of "going." Not only does Leontes
physically repel Hermione, Mamillius, Polixenes, Camillo,
Paulina, Perdita, and Antigonus, he also seeks to disengage
himself from the very ongoing nature of life. His is a cold spirit of
negativism. Brooding like the winter on a procreative past that
brought with life a knowledge of death ("when / Three crabbed
months had sour'd themselves to death" [1. 2. 102]), Leontes

expresses his fear of time through hatred of sex, an hysterical misogyny, and obsessive threats of death.

The attitude toward sex is plain enough:

> Go to, go to!
> How she holds up the neb, the bill to him! (1. 2. 182)

One thinks of Lear's saying:

> The wren goes to't, and the small gilded fly
> Does lecher in my sight. (4. 6. 111)

For Leontes as well, the going-to of sex has become horribly repulsive; affection "stabs" and "infects," "revolted" wives are "sluiced" by paramours, the flax wench "puts to," his sheets are "spotted." But, unlike Lear, Leontes keeps his vision of sexual corruption within a relatively narrow focus; all the blame is heaped on women. Misogyny is his distinctive accent:

> Women say so,
> (That will say any thing): . . . (1. 2. 130)
>   O thou thing— (2. 1. 82)
> She's an adultress! (2. 1. 78)
>   She's
> A bed-swerver, . . . (2. 1. 92)
> He dreads his wife . . . A callat/Of boundless tongue, . . . (2. 3. 79)
>   I ne'er heard yet
> That any of these bolder vices wanted
> Less impudence to gainsay what they did
> Than to perform it first. (3. 2. 54)

Suiting the action to the word, he four time stands across from a woman whom he attacks for "going" and whom he then causes to "go" from the stage.

I think it crucially important to realize that such sex-combat or rejecton of women organizes the visual structure of the play's first half. Once we grasp the pattern, much that remains falls into place. Leontes' rejection of women accompanies his attempt to be self-sufficient, to protect his oft-mentioned "heart," to be the "center," and to found his "faith" only upon himself. He will not share the creative process with anyone else. He seeks to be the sole dispenser of life and death, to run the show:

> Is this nothing?
> Why then the world, and all that's in't, is nothing, . . . (1. 2. 292)

> You may as well
> Forbid the sea for to obey the moon,
> As or by oath remove or counsel shake
> The fabric of his folly, whose foundation
> Is pil'd upon his faith, and will continue
> The standing of his body. [Camillo describing Leontes.] (1. 2. 426)

> If I mistake
> In those foundations which I build upon,
> The centre is not big enough to bear
> A school-boy's top. (2. 1. 100)

> There is no truth at all i' th' Oracle. (3. 2. 140)

Leontes' faith is founded where it should not be, in himself alone. When he denies the Oracle, he openly presumes against the godhead, denies his created status. As king he has perhaps some reason to become trapped in divine analogy, but as man, dependent upon woman in order to play his part in creation, he cannot be self-sufficient. He cannot promise life by himself. He can only threaten death. And when he banishes woman, his becomes equally an idiom of death:

> Give mine enemy a lasting wink. (1. 2. 317)

> Make that thy question, and go rot! (1. 2. 324)

> You smell this business with a sense as cold
> As is a dead man's nose:... (2. 1. 151)

> Commit them to the fire! (2. 3. 95)

> The bastard brains with these my proper hands
> Shall I dash out. (2. 3. 139)

> For the fail
> Of any point in 't shall not only be
> Death to thyself, but to thy lewd-tongu'd wife (2. 3. 171)

> Look for no less than death. (3. 2. 91)

Shakespeare's reduplicating structure thus forces the audience to hear and see, remember and anticipate, the one strikingly obsessive act on Leontes' part, that is, rejection and expulsion of women, kin, and company, together with threats of death. In many ways, Leontes shows himself caught in the quintessential winter's tale, enacting the title of the play, unable to see ahead to "this coming summer," looking back in anguish to a time when lambs frisked in the sun. He has become the lion in winter, old man winter, the character in Mamillius's story ("a sad tale's best for winter") who "dwelt by a churchyard" of graves. Our penultimate image of him in the tragic portion of the play is as a man caught in the deepest winter of despair. After announcing Hemione's death, Paulina, at least momentarily, denies Leontes the power of effective repentance:

> A thousand knees
> Ten thousand years together, naked, fasting,
> Upon a barren mountain, and still winter
> In storm perpetual, could not move the gods
> To look that way thou wert. (3. 2. 210)

Shakespeare's materializing imagination will immediately produce a wintry storm and present onstage the violent death of Antigonus.

VI

An audience watching and weighing the four great pulsations of madness outlined here should find, during a well-directed and well-acted performance, that Leontes' storm perpetual is regularly if briefly interrupted by a still small voice. All four of the king's scenes are crowded, loud, violent, rhetorically flamboyant. Each is self-fragmenting as exits are made away from Leontes. Hatred and death are the topics; fear and alienation the results. This deepening human winter is in essence the plot. But there is a counterplot.

The counterplot consists of the four relatively brief moments when Leontes is offstage. They are: (1) the conversation of Camillo and Archidamus (1. 1. 1−45), (2) the meeting of Camillo and Polixenes at the end of the second scene and the byplay with Mamillius beginning the third scene; (3) Paulina at the prison (2. 2. 1−66); and (4) the Messengers returning from Delphos (3. 1. 1−22). What the audience sees when Leontes is onstage is opposition leading to static isolation. What it sees when he is offstage is cooperation leading to the forward movement of a pair. Archidamus turns from fending off imagined accusations to agreeing with Camillo in hopes of the young Mamillius; the two counsellors pass across the stage in final amity. After Leontes reveals his jealousy, Camillo meets Polixenes and they decide to escape together. We see them pass across the stage as friends. Paulina, in the prison, gathers Emilia to her purpose and exits with her. Cleomenes and Dion marvel at their Delphic journey and hasten forward to court.

Leontes, like the last season of the year, appears to look back and view all the generative goings-on of life as repugnant and ineffectual delays against death: "go to," "go, play," "go rot," "go," he says continually. The actors in the small, interstitial scenes are cast in a wholly different perspective. They look forward to *going* forward, and they grasp hopefully at generative continuity and renewal. Archidamus and Camillo forecast the great "going" of the play itself, the summer visit to Bohemia, and they see that the "promise" of youth freshens old hearts. Polixenes and Camillo find faith in each other by concentrating upon hereditary gentleness and honor, the regenerating opposites of the hereditary imposition noted earlier in the play. Polixenes speaks of "our parents' noble names, / In whose success we are gentle" (1. 2. 393). Camillo says: "by the honour of my parents, I / Have utter'd truth" (1. 2. 442), and Polixenes concludes: "Come, Camillo, / I will respect thee as a father if / Thou bear'st my life off" (1. 2. 460). In the four brief scenes, the audience can hear brave and hopeful redefinitions of the human family. Not only do the counsellors take physic from the Prince and not only do the fleeing men find a certain family identity or bond between themselves but also Paulina manages to absolve Perdita of inherited taint by stressing that she shares the higher and more universal parentage of us all:

> You need not fear it, sir:
> This child was prisoner to the womb, and is
> By law and process of great nature, thence
> Free'd and enfranchis'd. (2. 2. 58)

And, finally, as the minor scenes take us further and further from Leontes' court and closer to the journey of the play itself, we experience a wider perspective upon the generative continuum that binds us together. The Messengers sense that they have journeyed to the quick of nature:

> The climate's delicate, the air most sweet,
> Fertile the isle. (3. 1. 1)

Privileged to glance upward toward higher powers and to hear the "voice o' th' Oracle, / Kin to Jove's thunder" (3. 1. 9), they gain intimations of a new birth in the "event o' th' journey":

> When the Oracle
> (Thus by Apollo's great divine seal'd up)

> Shall the contents discover, something rare
> Even then will rush to knowledge. Go: fresh horses!
> And gracious be the issue. (3. 1. 18)

This "going," unlike the goings that leave Leontes self-enclosed, rushes toward hope of issue. The whole image is one of birth as the seal gives way, the contents are discovered, and what is rare bursts forth. All four of the non-Leontean scenes thus have to do with accepting and indeed welcoming the progress of generation that makes life ongoing. Carefully opposed and interposed, as they are against the blustering wrath of the king's scenes, these four moments invite the spectators to recall and anticipate a more sane idiom of praise, prayer, and hope. In them it is hinted that red blood may someday reign in the winter's pale.

VII

In the light of these scenic contrasts and their implications, we can better understand the theatrical force of *The Winter's Tale* in its tragic portion. The four scenes in which Leontes misdefines Hermione or Paulina are all statue scenes. In each, he points an accusatory finger at a woman, centrally observed, and charges her with artifice and deceit. Hermione "plays"; she hangs "like her medal" about Bohemia's neck. Leontes sees his wife in terms of an art object, like a statue, to be examined by bystanders:

> You, my lords,
> Look on her, mark her well. (2. 1. 64)

He takes all for show: "Praise her but for this her without-door form" (2. 1. 69). He lives in a world of deceitful appearances. Earlier he confessed: "I am angling," "I / Play too." His scenes with Hermione and Paulina have a staged quality. He forgets his lines and responds as would an actor: "O, I am out" (2. 1. 72). He thinks that Paulina was "set on" by Antigonus. He refuses, in other words, to accord to either of these women any sincerity, or stable inward faith. Believing that all is artifice and play, he seizes the role of artificer and playmaker. The trial scene is intended to be his masterpiece; there too Hermione stands like a statue in central isolation. "My life stands in the level of your dreams" (3. 2. 81), she tells Leontes. It is a terrible truth. Leontes has become caught up in the nightmare of unfaith. To him, others lack reality; he thinks of them as being cold as are dead men (2. 1. 151), past all shame (3. 2. 84). In the play's final scene, he will help wake a statue, but now he treats the living woman as if she were sleeping marble. When Hermione swoons and appears to die, Paulina aptly challenges Leontes to see if he

> can bring
> Tincture, or lustre in her lip, her eye,
> Heat outwardly or breath within. (3. 2. 204)

We say that a picture is worth a thousand words. Yet we think of Shakespeare primarily as a verbal artist. Forgotten is his amazing power to enthrall us with sheer pictographic debate. Leontes at first out-Herods Herod, rising through a crescendo of furious gestures, secretly then openly denouncing Hermione, striding forward to taunt among the spectators "many a man" with cuckoldry, pointing Hermione offstage, forcing Paulina's exit, stalking around the infant Perdita, plucking Antigonus's beard, striking the Oracle from the hand of his astonished officer. Against his jealous rantings, Hermione, Paulina, and the rest can and do unite in an opposing voice, but against the physical force of his mad agony they can present little counterforce. And so they continually withdraw.

Shakespeare, I believe, swiftly rouses the audience to resentment against this actor of sneers and scorn who, when he speaks to the crowd, seems to imagine a kind of theatrical contract in which he plays the part of jealous tyrant for those who make him, as he thinks, their sport:

> How blest am I
> In my just censure! in my true opinion!
> ... and I
> Remain a pinch'd thing; yea, a very trick
> For them to play at will. (2. 1. 36)

> Camillo and Polixenes
> Laugh at me; make their pastime at my sorrow:
> They should not laugh if I could reach them, nor
> Shall she, within my power. (2. 3. 23)

To an audience Leontes is peculiarly unsettling because of his direct, aggressive gestures and speeches, his self-consciousness, and his hypocritical designs:

> This sessions (to out great grief we pronounce)
> Even pushes 'gainst our heart: the party tried
> The daughter of a king, our wife, and one

> Of us too much belov'd. Let us be clear'd
> Of being tyrannous, since we so openly
> Proceed in justice, which shall have due course,
> Even to the guilt or the purgation. (3. 2. 1)

Having just expressed privately a determination to commit Hermione "to the fire," he strikes us as stupidly devious, specially tyrannical. By this point in the play, the trial scene, the audience in the theater, as well as the audience onstage, needs an alternative to the prolonged scenes of disagreement and defeat. It longs to escape this winter of death-centered discomfort. The four non-Leontean scenes have pointed a way toward a regenerating journey, reminding men of summer, Bohemia, "great nature," and fertile climes. But, at least in terms of their visual weight and energy, they have been wholly insufficient to counterbalance the oppressive burden of Leontes' violence. Only through counterviolence will the balance be restored. When the panic-striken Messenger rushes in to shout that Mamillius is dead, when Hermione falls senseless, only then does Leontes halt, in the act of blaspheming Apollo. He stands still at last, reduced now to silence, sculpted into the image of mortified man.

Now the tables are reversed as Leontes becomes subjected to the scalding stream of Paulina's conscience:

> Thy tyranny,
> Together working with thy jealousies
> (Fancies too weak for boys, too green and idle
> For girls of nine), O think what they have done,
> And then run mad indeed: stark mad! (3. 2. 179)

The spectators now gaze, not yet with much sympathy, upon a figure of iniquity exposed and humbled. As Polixenes, on hearing of Leontes' suspicion, thought of Judas who "did betray the Best," so Paulina tells Leontes: "thou betray'dst Polixenes" (3. 2. 185). It was a "damnable" act. That and the attempted corruption of Camillo were "trespasses." Even a "devil" would have repented before casting out Perdita. Following hard upon Leontes' contrast between Camillo's glistering "piety" and his own "black" deeds, Paulina's tirade (3. 2. 174–214) smacks of exorcism. Here is an energetic and sustained recognition of the king's madness and a convincing rejection of it, a theatrically impressive and satisfying purgation.

In the theater, in the presence of the play, Leontes faces an audience that has heavily borne his tyrannical ranting and murderous actions. That he should lightly bear, or get away with, the action of proclaiming the Oracle mere falsehood and relegating Apollo to *deus otiosus* is unthinkable. Divinity makes its immanent power known; the stage shakes with the impact. The stricken monarch cries:

> Apollo, pardon
> My great profaneness 'gainst thine Oracle! (3. 2. 153)

"Profaneness" has been the overriding horror of the play. Shakespeare's conception of profaneness, here as in many plays, centers upon a king's denial of the bonds of nature, of a created order, and of the need for trust, sympathy, and faith among all orders of friends, family, and state. Leontes' staged trial was to have been the obverse of the reverential sacrifice— "ceremonious, solemn and unearthly"—described by Dion and Cleomenes, but it turned into a trial of Leontes himself. And whereas the Messengers merely described, secondhand, the ritual that so surprised their senses, making them "nothing," at the trial scene we actually see the Oracle scroll and are read its contents, experience the sacrifice of Mamillius, watch Hermione die (apparently, though Paulina may hint otherwise), listen to Leontes address the great god Apollo directly, and respond to the sacral perspective of Paulina's exorcism. When, therefore, Leontes, rising at last in slow pain, reinforces our ritual view—

> Once a day I'll visit
> The chapel where they lie, and tears shed there
> Shall be my recreation— (3. 2. 238)

we find the counterplot nearly triumphant. Like the Messengers, he too has been reduced to "nothing" and can hope to renew or re-create himself only in a place of devotion, the "chapel" where they lie.

To witness Leontes reaching for Paulina's hand—"Come, and lead me/To these sorrows" (3. 2. 242)— is to measure the distance he has traveled. The first image we had of him was (in Camillo's description) shaking hands with Polixenes "as over a vast," but then we saw Hermione take her hand from Leontes and give it to Polixenes, and we heard Leontes' ranting disgust at "pinching fingers," to him the emblem of unfaith. Shakespeare, indeed, carefully establishes a kind of gestural dialogue between hands either clasped in trust or used in opposing ways: "Give me thy hand," says Polixenes to Camillo as they grope toward mutual support; "What needs these hands?" says Paulina as she is shoved from Leontes' presence. The focus upon hurting and helping hands will become more and more prominent in the play. For now, as Leontes takes Paulina's hand to walk offstage with her and thus close the trial scene, he demonstrates graphically the degree to which his misogyny and his mistrust of human contact have been replaced by a search for sympathy and trust. But the transition toward the smiles and tears that are a better way can hardly be begun as yet. Like Leontes, the audience, to be re-created as the play seems to intend, must be led on its own instructive journey toward faith.

VIII

What was alluded to in the Messengers' scene and evidenced at the trial was the felt presence of unseen powers founding and guiding the actions and destinies of men. Now, as the audience gradually frees itself from the dominance of Leontes' anarchic will, the operation of those unseen powers becomes more and more apparent.

Seen in terms of Shakespeare's constructive technique, the emotive curve of the main plot toward an exorcising ritual and the curve of the counterplot toward Bohemian revelations of "great nature" (2. 2. 60) now intersect in the pivotal scene of the play. In some respects the storm represents Leontes' mental state (as well as the gods' frowning thunder), and indeed the entire mid-portion of the play could be his re-creating dream. But, more importantly, the scene provides an audience with just the rite of passage it requires at this particular moment in the play.

The passage is not so much from death to life—though the Shepherd's famous reference to things dying and things new-born is central enough—the passage is from the old theatrical relation or contract to a changed one. The old relation between stage and spectators was suspicious, even hostile: Leontes worked to divide the audience against itself. Even as he announced that he "played" a disgraced "part," he insisted, as we saw, that many a man in the theater audience deserved the title of cuckold. His reiterated sense of himself as part of a "game play'd home," as a "pastime," "sport," a "pinch'd thing," a "trick," suggested an almost sado-masochistic relation with the spectators who came, as it were, to see him tormented like themselves. The frustration of the audience, moreover, steadily increased, because it had no way of coming together to reject the posture into which it was cast by Leontes, nor could it take part in the drama, convince Leontes of his error, or hasten the peripeteia.

If Leontes, who dominated the tragic part of the play, did much, through his harsh, unilaterally imposed decree, to define the audience as divided, suspicious, and ungentle, the transition to pastoral comedy works effectively in the other direction to unite the audience and to express confidence in it and its goodwill, as if the play sought to decompose a false social structure in order to build a true one. There is, first of all, the fact that Antigonus, the Shepherd, Time, and Autolycus, in fairly rapid succession address the audience through soliloquies, confide in it to an increasing degree, and encourage it to adopt a participatory attitude. Antigonus explains his presence in Bohemia and tries to justify his abandoning Perdita there:

> I do believe
> Hermione hath suffer'd death; and that
> Apollo would, this being indeed the issue
> Of King Polixenes, it should here be laid,
> Either for life or death, upon the earth
> Of its right father. (3. 3. 41)

The Shepherd plainly speaks out to the audience: "Hark you now!" (3. 3. 63). Time explicitly asks the "gentle spectators" to exercise their imaginations, and Autolycus gives himself an elaborate introduction to and for the audience alone. The whole drama thus admits its artifice and begins to open itself in frank welcome. Gone is the tragic constriction of the first part, the intense, repetitive focus upon Leontes, the incessant argument and questioning of appearances, the careful pairings and balanced oppositions onstage, the slow movements, the limited range of colors, the gritty naturalism of subject matter. With the storm scene, death of Antigonus, and entry of Shepherds, there is a marked shifting of dramatic gears. Immediately upon the entrance of Antigonus and the Mariner, we are not only told that we are in Bohemia but are made to feel out of doors where "the skies look grimly, / And threaten present blusters" (3. 3. 3). We are far from the weatherless stale winter of Leontes' court; feeling tone floods in with the "loud weather" and descriptions of the raging sea. This interest in natural phenomena will intensify. It is, moreover, a world where all that happens may be explained in terms of unseen powers, divine forces:

> The heavens with that we have in hand are angry,
> And frown upon 's.
> Their sacred wills be done! . . . (3. 3. 5)

>   Dreams are toys:
> Yet for this once, yea, superstitiously,
> I will be squar'd by this. . . . (3. 3. 39)

> It was told me I should be rich by the fairies. (3. 3. 116)

Finally we encounter Time himself and are openly assured that we are in good hands.

The new world is also a dreamworld. Antigonus is guided by a dream vision that points toward his death. The Shepherd wishes that youth would "sleep out" its time of promiscuity and fighting. Time asks his audience to imagine such growing of his scene "as you had slept" between the arrival in Bohemia and Perdita's emergence into a maiden's grace. Autolycus says: "for the life to come, I sleep out the thought of it" (14. 3. 30). We should pass, the play seems to suggest, across the great margins of growth and death as in a dream. Yet this dream may take us not away from but toward reality. Of his vision Antigonus says: "ne'er was dream / So like a waking" (3. 3. 18). He thought: "This was so, and no slumber" (3. 3. 39). Before the play is out, we too will see a version of Hermione's ghost as in a dream. Time suggests that the play itself may be thought of as our dream of the winter's tale. In the transition scene, Perdita, abandoned on the stage and seemingly destined to have a "lullaby too rough," sleeps out the death of Antigonus and her discovery by the Shepherds. As we watch, the whole scene may appear to be as well her dream of life miraculously preserved and fostered.

To all of the elements in the transition—the repetitions of

direct address, the perceived workings of higher powers, the
sense of dream vision, the explosive mixture of horror and
humor in the bear's appearance and in the Clown's descriptions
of sailors drowning and bear dining, the winking charity of
Perdita's rescue, and the magnificient artificiality of Time's
appearance—the audience is encouraged to respond with a
new wakefulness, self-consciousness, laughter, and delight.
The play has, obviously, broken wide open, and, seeing that
more shocking departures from tragic realities and unities are
in store, the figure of Time enters as apologist to welcome and
woo spectators to a new perception of the play and its
significance.

Time's speech, ostensibly and truly a plea for indulgence
toward artistic license, proves its point by subjecting its hearers
to a teasing, cajoling threat of too much order:

> I that please some, try all: both joy and terror
> Of good and bad, that makes and unfolds error,
> Now take upon me, in the name of Time,
> To use my wings. Impute it not a crime
> To me, or my swift passage, that I slide
> O'er sixteen years, and leave the growth untried
> Of that wide gap, since it is in my power
> To o'erthrow law, and in one self-born hour
> To plant and o'erwhelm custom. Let me pass
> The same I am, ere ancient'st order was,
> Or what is now receiv'd. I witness to
> The times that brought them in; so shall I do
> To th' freshest things now reigning, and make stale
> The glistering of this present, as my tale
> Now seems to it. (4. 1. 1)

On the one hand, Time slyly presents himself as the emblem
of order, even stasis. He speaks through the stale sameness of
ancient rhymes. He subjects our human population to a single
test: some are pleased but all are tried. In the first two lines the
four balanced pairs apparently imply a comprehensive and pat
ordering of affairs: please-try, joy-terror, good-bad, makes-
unfolds. But the last pair, as it alludes to "error," actually reverses the sequence of positive-to-negative. And yet to be un-
folded, error must be made. The terms are complementary, and
Time encompasses both phases. A similar dialectical interchange appears between the figure itself—white-haired, ancient, slow—as old as Time, we would say, and the figure's

declared intent to use its wings. Nothing is as old as Time, yet Time flies. The two facts are interdependent; it is because Time sees and moves his own "swift passage" and "speed so pace" that he also participates in divine stability: "The same I am." The audience is thus encouraged to broaden its horizons, to accept a multi-generational perspective as most true and stable.

Onstage, Time turns his hourglass (or perhaps his mirror?) and signals a shift from emphasis upon the past, Time's age, his being and power, toward emphasis upon the future, Time's growing scene and his wishes. The turn of the glass signals as well the whole shift in focus of the play from the egocentric, authority-ridden, past-examining, closed world of Sicilia to the open world of Bohemia where we envisage growth and what remains to be "brought forth." The audience is cast into the future of what Time may "prophesy," of what "follows after." In the course of Time's address, the "gentle spectators" have become thoroughly implicated in the action of the drama, and, in closing with lightly cynical well-wishes, Time even invites his hearers to set the value of the play within the larger context of their own lives:

> Of this allow,
> If ever you have spent time worse ere now;
> If never, yet that Time himself doth say,
> He wishes earnestly you never may. (4. 1. 29)

In these last lines the word "Time" is intoned more insistently than ever, yet Time now refers to himself in the third person as if he were fading backward while the focal center shifts to "you" the spectators. Time, while he daringly adverts to and yields to the extra-dramatic life of his audience, still links the play to that life. "Of *this* allow" contains a rich ambiguity tracking backward to the "argument of Time" and forward to Time's wishes for time well spent. Time, like the playwright working through "one self-born hour," would have his argument bear fruit.

The entire speech works to leave the spectators amused, bemused, faintly flattered, partly activated into an earnest search for didactic rewards and partly skeptical of the process in which they participate. No more than any other activity in life can art give something for nothing. In seeking the fresh meaning of this "tale," in forfeiting the unities, in trading tragedy for what comes after, the spectators must be at least half-consciously aware of sacrificing accepted conventions for strange ones, of putting up with a special artifice for the sake of a special reward that, as yet, in Time's speech, remains tantalizingly indefinite. The audience knows that the glass has turned, but it has yet to perceive just what that may signify.

IX

An account, such as the one attempted above, of certain ways in which speech and spectacle join to steer the theater audience through tragic and transitional portions of *The Winter's Tale* may fear to falter as it approaches the great central scene, the shearing festival. The festival—functioning as it does largely through music, dance, laughter, song, and color all of which have meaning primarily in immediate temporal experience—might seem little susceptible to the sort of analysis we have been pursuing. Yet it may be possible, nonetheless, to point out a few principal devices by which Shakespeare leads playgoers toward a special participation in the drama and toward a species of awakening faith.

First, is the matter of disguise and play. To Leontes, play was deadly serious. In the midst of his self-deception, he tried to become the artificer of his world, creating false roles not only for himself but also for all those around him. He seemed for a protracted time all too easily to deny the superior, truth-divining art of higher powers such as the poet-maker Apollo or "great creating nature" (4. 4. 88). Now, with the entrance of the Chorus, an author surrogate, "me, in the name of Time," the audience is reminded that, at least in some ways, all that has happened onstage has served wider artistic purposes and is the argument of Time. The focus shifts, accordingly, to a host of characters who deliberately use disguise and play in order to sound out the true nature of others and themselves, just as the audience seeks through the purpose of play to see as in a mirror its own nature.

Florizel and Perdita, of course, are not presented in their natural garb but in special costumes: Florizel a "poor humble swain" and Perdita "no sherpherdess, but Flora," the "queen" of the feast, "most goddess-like prank'd up" (4. 4. 10). Florizel shrewdly takes their costumes as emblems of a superior reality; even Apollo, he says, humbled his deity to love and took a shepherd's form. Later, in response to Perdita's remark, "sure this robe of mine / Does change my disposition" (4. 4. 134), he will prove in poetry the sense in which all her acts are, as he says, queens (4. 4. 146). Then, too, their costumes are not only emblems of their most ideally real state but also mirrors wherein each reflects the other, so that their play, like the play itself, yields both a glassy reflection of the quotidian world and a window through which may be glimpsed realities that are normally unseen.

But though Florizel and Perdita, the testing of whose "play" is at the heart of the festival scene, occupy the center of our vision, other figures in costume contribute to their meaning. "We must disguise ourselves" (4. 2. 55), says Polixenes to Camillo as they head for the feast. Once there, Polixenes, too, will play the role of his true self, a stranger to his son, and he will look into the mirror of his past as Florizel says:

> O hear me breathe my life
> Before this ancient sir, who, it should seem,
> Hath sometime lov'd. (4. 4. 361)

The third major party in disguise at the feast is Autolycus, the most deliberate and ingenious player of them all. As in Florizel the audience is invited to see a renewed version of Leontes (the connection is made even more clear when they meet [5. 1. 218]) and of Polixenes in youth, and as in Polixenes it sees a reduplication of the suspicious, jealous, and condemnatory Leontes, so in Autolycus it sees a reminder of the Leontes who slyly delivered confidences in soliloquy and aside, who angled and gave line, and who was an outsider, preying upon society. But the pranks of Autolycus prove relatively harmless; we have journeyed from the haunt of the "lion" to the home of the "very wolf" who intends to make the "shearers prove sheep," (4. 3. 117), but now we know that the scenes he stages are overseen by a master plotter and are part of "Time's news." In other words, when the audience sees Florizel, Perdita, Polixenes, and Camillo in disguise, when it hears Autolycus change his voice to fool the Clown and Shepherd (who themselves are more than dabbling in pretense—to earned wealth and kinship with Perdita), it accepts the artifice as potentially assimilable into benign reality, as ultimately life enhancing.

Implications of this induction to a vision of providential disguise and play are far-reaching. Not only are the spectators encouraged to feel that they share in a common venture with the players, that the play is "spent time" equally for actors and audience, with the result that the music and dance of the feast,

its laughter and overflowing harmony, cease to be entertainment and become the thing itself, perfectly natural art, but
also—and this is perhaps more startling—the spectators are
brought to see that the interruption of the festival and reminder
of painful artifice merely prove an occasion for reasserted faith
in an overarching harmony that can adapt the unmasking of
disguise to supremely artistic purposes.

The dramatic shape of the festival scene resembles that of the
trial (and the statue scene to come). Each builds to a climax in
its center that takes the form of a radical unmasking, and each
unmasking occasions a renewed search for order, trust, and
hope, a re-creation. But whereas the trial scene showed the
blighting limitations of Leontes' winter dream of unfaith, the
pastoral scene, even after Polixenes throws back his hood and
denounces the lovers, shows the unquenchable vitality of their
affection and trust. Much more is involved than a descent from
a play-within-a-play to the play itself that asks the audience to
see that its own reality, too, is art. For the events of the pastoral
celebration—the truth in costume of Florizel and Perdita,
Polixenes' identification of an art that nature makes, Perdita's
simultaneous incorporation into herself of the Prosperpina
myth (the art realm) and the dance of a wave (the natural realm),
and Autolycus's songs that point to true pains of unlove even as
they mock the rustics for seeking historical fact in them—all the
events that precede the interrupted betrothal bring the audience to a heightened belief in the truth of this particular expression of affection and trust. So that when Florizel takes
Perdita's hand, saying, "Mark our contract" (4. 4. 418), only to
have Polixenes reply, "Mark your divorce," as he forcibly breaks
the clasp, the spectators respond to this Leontean gesture with
a new resiliency. For the beauty and value, the warmth and
grace, of goodwill and faith have just been proved upon their
pulse. What they have seen and heard and felt cannot success-
fully be denounced as unmeaning play, and, even as they watch
Perdita remove her garland—

> this dream of mine—
> Being now awake, I'll queen it no inch farther— (4. 4. 449)

they do not see her reduced thereby but merely cast forward
into the task of becoming what she played. "What I was, I am,"
announces Florizel:

> It cannot fail, but by

> The violation of my faith; and then
> Let nature crush the sides o' th' earth together,
> And mar the seeds within! (4. 4. 477)

"Faith" in this sense denotes what remains when men and women set aside the artificial trappings of their love and seek the seed within which binds them to all forms of ongoing life. Perdita, another queen like the early Hermione jarred awake from a statuesque pose where she was observed and judged by a circle of bystanders, responds magnificently to Florizel's declaration: she, too, will accept and face the trial and testing of awakened faith:

> I think affliction may subdue the cheek,
> But not take in the mind. (4. 4. 577)

It is true that Autolycus, who also doffs his disguise after the climax of the pastoral scene, seems to add an abrasive comment upon the "faith" of Florizel and Perdita:

> Ha, Ha! what a fool Honesty is! and Trust, his sworn brother, a very simple gentleman! I have sold all my trumpery. . . . My clown (who wants but something to be a reasonable man) grew so in love with the wenches' song, that he would not stir his pettitoes till he had both tune and words; which so drew the rest of the herd to me, that all their other senses stuck in ears: you might have pinched a placket, it was senseless; 'twas nothing to geld a codpiece of a purse; I would have filed keys off that hung in chains: no hearing, no feeling, but my sir's song, and admiring the nothing of it. (4. 4. 596)

Speaking out to the audience, he reminds it, a la Leontes, that sworn trust may prove deceitful, that the festival was in part his balladeer's con-game, and that the ideals of love depicted by art may encourage a useless lethargy that cannot admit or cope with the protean realities of sensual time. The audience hears the critique, yes, but what it sees is an Autolycus made to change costumes with Florizel and stimulated to help assist, in various ways, the elopement and the new artifice to be practiced upon Leontes, one which itself will, in the pattern of the play, break down and yield again to a superior reality. Shakespeare in this way continually suggests that to abjure one's potent art or drown one's magic book may simply mean to enter the rhythm of the sea. "I see the play so lies / That I must bear a part" (4. 4. 655), says Perdita as the couple hasten in new costumes toward the shore and toward their journey to Leontes and the greatest "play" of all. Immediately after their exit, the Shepherd and Clown will enter, preparing to explain Perdita's background to Polixenes and so to unmask themselves in their turn, and it is marvelous to watch Autolycus swerve them (and himself) aboard ship and back into the play. But Perdita's remark best knits up for an audience its complex experience of the long pastoral episode where remembering the shocking hatred of Leontes, watching the general dance of goodwilled men and women, and anticipating what may come all can produce a fresh resolve to bear one's part, even beyond the theater.

I turn now to a second feature of the pastoral scenes that, like the handling of disguise, overthrows the constrictions of the tragic debate and encourages the audience to participate in a more inclusive and hopeful view of the action. I refer to the remarkably altered rhythm of characterological and scenic contrasts.

It is a commonplace in criticism of the play to observe that, when Perdita is found by the Shepherd and when Time turns his glass, we are invited to see that the action, in a profound manner, begins again. The "lambs that did frisk i' th' sun" mentioned by Polixenes (1. 2. 67) are of this new time and place in the Shepherds' Bohemia, and, after Time's speech, the first Bohemian scene is, again, of the king persuading his reluctant visitor to stay. What needs to be freshly noted is the way in which debate between the Leontean and non-Leontean scenes, previously explored, becomes reduplicated but in a much altered context and with vastly different implications.

Time's speech that tells of Perdita "grown in grace / Equal with wond'ring" (4. 1. 24) echoes the play's opening scene in which Archidamus and Camillo praised the grace of Mamillius. The scene following Time's speech (4. 2) echoes the play's second scene not only in Polixenes' persuading Camillo to stay but also because Polixenes explicitly compares Leontes to himself, suspects royal promiscuity (in the person of Prince Florizel), projects an atmosphere of spying—"eyes under my service" (4.2. 36)—and persuades Camillo to undertake a dubious business (compare 1. 2. 228–29 with 4. 2. 52). Polixenes, moreover, will appear, in extended analogy to Leontes, debating first Camillo, then Perdita (about grafting), then Florizel (about the betrothal). The alternations in focus, furthermore, between Perdita and

Florizel on the one hand and Polixenes on the other are extremely regular and highly reminiscent of the alternations in the first three acts between hopeful non-Leontean scenes and argumentative Leontean ones.

The vast difference between the former, tragic alternation of the audience's focus and the latter, comic one, in addition to the fact that the earlier weakly opposing voice now dominates the royal one, is the insertion into the latter pattern of a third, new, and highly significant center of focus—Autolycus and the Shepherds. (1) After (a) Time speaks hopefully of Florizel and Perdita and (b) Polixenes and Camillo question the "angle" that attracts Florizel to Perdita, then (c) Autolycus comes forward mixing daffodils and doxies, the red and the pale, his country moonshine thievery and his former "three-pile" service of Florizel at court, mixing, in short, nature and art, country and court, "here and there" (4. 3. 17). (2) After (a) Florizel and Perdita enter as lovers to initiate the celebration and (b) Polixenes debates Perdita who decides that he is a man of the middle summer marigold "that goes to bed wi' th' sun / And with him rises, weeping" (4. 4. 105) then (c) Autolycus enters to fleece the shearers by selling them love laces and false ballads of love's true longings, that is, again showing the natural and artificial inseparably mixed. (3) After (a) Florizel and Perdita attempt to complete their betrothal ceremony and (b) Polixenes interrupts, and Camillo steers them toward Sicilia, then (c) Autolycus engages Shepherd and Clown in bumpkin byplay of the sort that again mocks court and country (including in this case elaborate threats set off against naive fears). (4) And finally, in the fifth act, after (a) Florizel and Perdita have their audience with Leontes, and (b) the arrival of Polixenes and Camillo seems to threaten the lovers once again, then (c) Autolycus is shown eliciting the "issue" of the recognition scene from the Gentlemen and, lastly, joining Shepherd and Clown as a "true fellow" among "gentlemen born."

To adopt a musical analogy, instead of the 2/4 meter of the tragic half of the play, we find in the comic half a 3/4 meter. The audience consistently encounters Autolycus (at roughly 250 line intervals) as a figure who mediates humorously between the claims of Polixenes and those of Perdita and Florizel. He excites a laughter whose result is always to lessen the tension between opposing forces: age and youth, pretension and reality, greed and charity, wrath and forgiveness, lion and lamb.

Like all mediators, he is potentially caught in a cross fire, and in his case it is a comic one. In psychosexual terms he mediates as "dildo" (4. 4. 197), "poking-stick" (4. 4. 228), and bared "part" (4. 4. 293) between the masculine, warlike, courtly world, and the feminine, more peaceful, pastoral one. He dwells in realms of swift inflation —his boastings, songs, tricks, and disguise— and just as sudden deflation:

> Not a more cowardly rogue in all Bohemia: if you had but looked big and spit at him, he'd have run. (4. 3. 102)

> If they have overheard me now,—why, hanging. (4. 4. 628)

> I humbly beseech you, sir, to pardon me all the faults I have committed to your worship, and to give me your good report to the prince my master. (5. 2. 149)

The scene-stealing presence of Autolycus has been notoriously difficult for critics to explain. But if we keep in mind the great third beat of attention represented by the Autolycan scenes, the beat that breaks polarizing tensions, mediates between opposites, speeds up the pace, generates the energy of laughter, and consistently carries the action forward to new places and new drama, then we can begin to accept and feel more comfortable with the four, ever-surprising outbursts of parodic liberation. We can see how Shepherd and Clown, the third father-son pair, re-enact parental tensions in a way that eases burdens of their seriousness yet points, ultimately, toward instinctive forgiveness and support of kinship's bonds. And we can appreciate how, through the repeating three-focus pattern, Shakespeare continually injects a kind of refreshing, primitive vigor in the play, avoids late-act fatigue, and drives the action on in happy suspense:

> Jog on, jog on . . . . (4. 3. 119)

> Then whither goest? say whither? (4. 4. 309)

> Let's before as he bids us: he was provided to do us good. (4. 4. 830)

> Every wink of an eye, some new grace will be born: our absence makes us unthrifty to our knowledge. Let's along. (5. 2. 110)

> Hark! the kings and the princes, our kindred, are going to see the queen's picture. Come, follow us: we'll be thy good masters (5. 2. 172)

My third and last grouping of dramaturgic devices that promote the pastoral audience's awakening participation and confidence, I collect under the heading "persuasive harmony."
Under this heading I mean to gather and examine a few interac-
tions between visual and verbal presentations—such as between dance and dialogue—that stimulate the response of
spectators but that tend to elude textual analysis.

One reason that the harmony of the Bohemian scenes proves
persuasive lies in the continual imposition of order upon
enormous energy of motion. The first half of the play was
marked by generally slow, balanced movements onstage (such
as those detailed before Leontes' jealous outburst), scenes of
static opposition, and prevailingly lateral, cross-stage tensions
and contrasts. Or else Hermione and Paulina were surrounded
by a still circle of inquisitive onlookers. This was a stiffly fixed
winter order, a lifeless patterning that helped suggest the steril-
ity and iron obsessiveness of Leontes' anger. Consider now the
change in the latter half of the play. The first inhabitant of
Bohemia that we see is a *Bear*. And what happens? The text
shows that Antigonus, having placed Perdita on the stage, begins a slow exit (before the Bear's arrival), probably in the direction taken by the Mariner. Then:

> Farewell!
> The day frowns more and more: thou'rt like to have
> A lullaby too rough: I never saw
> The heavens so dim by day. A savage clamour!
> Well may I get aboard! This is the chase:
> I am gone for ever!
> [*Exit, pursued by a bear.*] (3. 3. 53)

"This is the chase" suggests at least some modicum of onstage
pursuit. "I am gone for ever!" cannot help but be funny, drawing
attention, as it does, to the actor's last exit in the part. Imagine a
circuit or two around the stage circumference—Antigonus
rushing, arms outstretched in horror, the bear lumbering after,
Perdita in the center oblivious—and one can make real, if also
macabre and grotesque, the distance traveled from Leontes'
court in Sicilia. The stage has expanded, a new world is freshly
circumscribed, the representative of the old world is consumed, and the baby waits at the center of the new. Over her
arch (from one side offstage) groans of the dying man and (from
the other side offstage) greetings of Shepherd and Clown:

"Whoa-ho-hoa!... Hilloa, loa!" (3. 3. 76). Good-bye and hello, death and birth, final things and first, emblematically succeed each other. Into the reconstituted world step primitive men, shepherds of the pastoral age and men to whom, especially in Christian tradition, the miracle of innocent birth is vouchsafed. "Blossom, speed thee well!" (3. 3. 46), prayed Antigonus as he placed Perdita upon the ground. She is like the seed buried in darkness and freshly springing to light and life. Antigonus's hint becomes one of many encouragements for an audience to sense the introduction of a new and invigorating perspective.

That perspective opens upon an inclusive harmony, one that, everyone agrees, assimilates winter to spring, death to life, and mistrust to renewed faith. Still insufficiently appreciated, I think, are some of the means through which Shakespeare, despite the wide-ranging and often apparently disparate concerns of his pastoral scenes, achieves a visual continuity and formal intensity that render the harmony persuasive. If we take as a starting point the audience's response to the bear, Perdita, and Shepherds in the scene just mentioned, we can see that its ingredients are repeated later. The circling of the bear, furious yet funny in its grimace, becomes transmuted in the circlings of Autolycus as he sings his metamorphic songs, sells to the innocent rustics, and, at the end of the Bohemian sojourn, stalks round about the quaking Clown:

> He has a son, who shall be flayed alive, then 'nointed over with honey, set on the head of a wasps' nest, then stand till he be three quarters and a dram dead; then recovered again with aqua-vitæ or some other hot infusion; then, raw, as he is, and in the hottest day prognostication proclaims, shall he be set against a brick wall, the sun looking with a southward eye upon him, where he is to behold him, with flies blown to death. (4. 4. 785)

The pastoral harmony persuades, ultimately, because it defines a full circle in which innocence, menaced by savagery, becomes that much more precious. As Polixenes twice wheels a threatening circuit from Florizel to the Shepherd to Perdita ("thou a sceptre's heir... Thou, old traitor... And thou, fresh piece / Of excellent witchcraft... For thee, fond boy... Thou churl... And you, enchantment..." [4. 4. 421–35]), he resembles, perhaps, the bear and Autolycus, but he most closely follows and may indeed be stimulated by the dance of Satyrs who weave their own circle of lustful leaps and orgiastic gestures about him until he responds with a profane and degraded interpretation of the lovers' desires. "Is it not too far gone?" (4. 4. 345), he asks, echoing the accents of Leontes ("too hot! / To mingle friendship far, is mingling bloods. . . . Gone already!" [1. 2. 108—85]) and then painting the relation of Perdita and Florizel solely in commercial and promiscuous terms (Perdita should be bought with "knacks" [4. 4. 350] for she herself is a "knack" [4. 4. 429]). Raging insanely at Perdita and (like Leontes) at the very circle of love, which must in time leave him out of its center, Polixenes stamps offstage:

> If ever henceforth thou
> These rural latches to his entrance open,
> Or hoop his body more with thy embraces,
> I will devise a death as cruel for thee
> As thou art tender to 't.   [*Exit.*] (4. 4. 438)

The spectators see death and the threat of death not only at the three nodal points of the Bohemian journey—beginning (Bear versus Antigonus), middle (Polixenes versus Florizel, Perdita, and Shepherd), and end (Autolycus versus Clown and Shepherd)—but also throughout:

> Gallows and knock are too powerful on the highway: beating and hanging are terrors to me. (4. 3. 28)

>   Sir, the year growing ancient,
> Nor yet on summer's death nor on the birth
> Of trembling winter, . . . (4. 4. 79)

>   O, these I lack,
> To make you garlands of; and my sweet friend,
> To strew him o'er and o'er!

Flo.   What, like a corpse?
Per.   No, like a bank, for love to lie and play on:
> Not like a corpse; or if—not to be buried,
> But quick, and in mine arms. (4. 4. 127)

What emerges for the audience out of the total presentation is, I believe, a new and convincing experience of ways in which death and life mock each other, bury each other, and rouse each other to responsive energies. As Perdita's great catalogue of flowers takes poignance from her vision of Proserpina "frighted" by the rapine of dark Dis, so her general fear in the scene, like the "fright" engendered by Mamillius's winter tale of churchyard goblins (2. 1. 28), lends luster to her innocence and, even as it acknowledges the threats to her new life and love, measures the strength of her desire. As Florizel pledges undying affection and praises the eternal pattern of Perdita's "dance" even in the teeth of the Mutability evidenced everywhere in the play, so the central "dance of Shepherds and Shepherdesses" (4. 4. 167)—a prime emblem of circular order and delight—must be matched in the eyes of spectators against the furious Satyrs' dance: an evocation of chaotic sexual energy equally at the heart of things. No formulaic, catch-all solution is offered to problems encountered at the court of Leontes. The harmony of the pastoral is not an answer but a kind of confession and avoidance that admits negative realities as it balances them off against positive ones. In the minds of playgoers, the shift to pastoral widens the view to include not only winter but all seasons. Jealousy and death remain part of the scene, but through the laughter, love making, poetry, and dance, the music and song, the new intermingling of men and women onstage when before they were divided, the new predominance of youth as against the earlier predominance of elders, the vastly expanded range of colors, costume types, kinds of characters, postures, gestures, movements, expressions of emotion, and the hints of a collective spring, summer, and harvest, Shakespeare makes the play enact in growth and time the relation of all seasons to winter. The audience experiences, basically, a waking from a closed world to an open one, a flowing over from static concentration upon mistrust, trial, and death to the full cycle of human loss and gain.

X

When, at the opening of the final act, Leontes, his hair powdered silver, face lined, and posture a trifle stooped, slowly walks in dignity toward the spectators and greets them with a long knowing look and smile, they answer with instant recognition of his meaning: he, too, has journeyed. For a moment in silence mutual voyagers welcome each other. The finale is structured about such points of silent recognition that lead through Leontes' shock upon beholding Florizel and Perdita—

> Most dearly welcome!
> And your fair, princess,—goddess!—O, alas!
> I lost a couple, that 'twixt heaven and earth
> Might thus have stood, begetting wonder, as
> You, gracious couple, do— (5. 1. 129)

Paulina's unveiling of Hermione as statue—

> I like your silence, it the more shows off
> Your wonder— (5. 3. 21)

and the moment before Hermione's waking—

> Proceed:
> No foot shall stir. (5. 3. 97)

Such dramatic stress upon purely visual meaning suggests a need for the sort of account attempted here that deals with immediate theatrical experience. The final part of the play, moreover, self-consciously advances the issue of seeing and believing versus hearing and doubting. In the next to last scene, when the Gentlemen of Court describe the recognition and reunion of Leontes, Perdita, Polixenes, Camillo, and Florizel, they tell much of what was done, little of what was said, and they disparage report itself in favor of direct witness:

> I make a broken delivery of the business; but the changes I perceived in the king and Camillo were very notes of admiration: they seemed almost, with staring on one another, to tear the cases of their eyes: there was speech in their dumbness, language in their very gesture; . . . (5. 2. 12)

> That which you hear you'll swear you see, there is such unity in the proofs. (5. 2. 32)

> Then have you lost a sight which was to be seen, cannot be spoken of. (5. 2. 43)

All this stimulates an eagerness in the audience actually to see such a reunion, an eagerness gratified by the statue scene. Even there Paulina reminds us:

> That she is living,
> Were it but told you, should be hooted at
> Like an old tale: but it appears she lives. (5. 3. 115)

The play, in other words, is not merely told to us; we see it. And this makes all the difference.

The final act sounds, in relative terms, verbally "thin," for the entire play moves away from ratiocinations and pyrotechnics of Leontes—his tortured philosophy ("Affection! thy intention stabs . . .") and introspection ("I have drunk, and seen the spider")—through the simpler lyricism of Florizel and Perdita and colloquial style of the rustics to the hushed vision of the statue scene. For an audience, the essential dramatic progress, which fits its proportions to the three hours of playhouse time, traces a violent domestic quarrel (or accusation) and reconciliation. Quarrels are often wordy, reconciliations are not.

The verbal tyranny of Leontes who debated, chopped logic, punned aggressively, shouted down, used high-flying Latinate rhetoric, and insisted upon his modes of thought, took prominence in the play's early battle of styles. The more the early Leontes spoke, the less he communicated, or learned; his language was legislative, never contractual or reciprocative:

> Why, what need we
> Commune with you of this, but rather follow
> Our forceful instigation? (2. 1. 161)

Leontes tried to make his world over in the image of his mind, of his words, and the flight to Bohemia was really a flight from that mind, that solipsistic language, and from the static verbal intensities of the alienated Court. In the final scenes, Leontes exemplifies a man who freshly sees and who longs to make contact with the waking reality of others, their light and life:

> Then, even now,
> I might have look'd upon my queen's full eyes. (5. 1. 52)

The playgoers hear Leontes wishing to embrace not only Hermione but also his new visitors (5. 1. 113), and they see him more than once with arms outstretched in wonder and welcome, as Camillo had predicted:

> Methinks I see
> Leontes opening his free arms and weeping
> His welcomes forth; asks thee there 'Son, forgiveness!'
> As 'twere i' th' father's person, kisses the hands
> Of your fresh princess. (4. 4. 548)

It is true that great stress is placed upon the power of Florizel and Perdita to beget wonder (5. 1. 130), to infuse spring into Sicilia's winter (5. 1. 151), and to foster an infection-purging climate (5. 1. 168). But the dominant image is of Leontes in greeting, Leontes deciding to help even after he discovers the deception practiced upon him—"I will to your father" (5. 2. 228)—Leontes as described by Paulina's "it should take joy / To see her in your arms" (5. 1. 80) and by the Gentleman:

Our king, being ready to leap out of himself for joy of his found

daughter, as if that joy were now become a loss, cries 'O, thy
mother, thy mother!' then asks Bohemia forgiveness; then em-
braces his son-in-law; then again worries he his daughter with
clipping her; now he thanks the old shepherd, ... (5. 2. 50)

What tends, therefore, to be slighted in reading but overwhelm-
ingly evident onstage is the central activity, the enlivening presence, of the king who continually proves his newfound power
to bless:

> O grave and good Paulina, the great comfort
> That I have had of thee! (5. 3. 1)

>   Let no man mock me,
> For I will kiss her. (5. 3. 79)

The marked change in Leontes that has been noted here
shapes in part the impact of the statue scene, but it leads first to
the recognition described in the little intervening scene (5. 2)
played by the Gentlemen, Autolycus, and then Shepherd, and
Clown. It was observed in the second chapter how often this
scene has been cut from productions and yet how often, when
played, it has been singled out by reviewers for surprised and
appreciative comment. Beyond its obvious humor, the scene
serves several functions crucial to this juncture in the play. By a
species of sleight of hand, Shakespeare makes the meeting of
Leontes and Polixenes and the recognition of Perdita (necessarily anticipated by the audience at the close of the preceding
scene) seem a thing almost of the present, then of the immediate past, then of a receding time, more finally elapsed and
distant. The First Gentleman tells of being present at the "opening of the fardel" (5. 2. 1). The Second Gentleman says that the
"king's daughter is found ... within this hour" (5. 2. 23). The
Third Gentleman disengages us further from the immediacy of
the event as he speaks in an affected, hyperbolical style that
makes the event seem filtered through a storyteller's personality and set apart in a shape given by imagination. When
Shepherd and Clown enter, we are told they have been "gentlemen born" for "any time these four hours" (5. 2. 136).

As the recognition of Perdita arrives and recedes in imagined
time, solidifying to an accepted event with both wonderful and
comical consequences (the Third Gentleman's witticisms, the
Shepherds in the "blossoms of their fortune"), it seems to
pervade as well a wider space and wider spectrum of social

strata. From the inner circle of participants the news spreads to the Gentlemen, who imagine both an "audience of kings and princes" for the event and also the inevitable "ballad-makers," and then on to the Shepherd and Clown who inflict their interpretation of the event's significance—its making them gentlemen and "gentle"—upon the now lowly Autolycus who promises in like fashion to amend his life. The spectators become invited in this way to perceive a radiating influence of the reported reconciliations, and the sense of radiating influence, when carried over to the statue scene, will serve to enhance its reconciliations.

The Gentlemen's scene further prepares us for the final scene by its predictive focus upon artifice that, paradoxically, reveals life and fosters natural and humane values. In their successive appearances, the Gentlemen become increasingly affected and art conscious as the first speaks of his "broken delivery," the second of "ballad-makers," and the third of the Shepherd standing like a conduit statue, of statuelike bystanders ("Who was most marble, there changed colour" [5. 2. 89]), and then of the Hermione statue: "They say one would speak to her and stand in hope of answer" (5. 2. 100). All this pre-conditions the theater audience, quite clearly, for the last marble metaphor of the play in which art shares itself with "great creating nature." After the Third Gentleman, moreover, ascends from stony shepherd to marble spectators to almost living statue, the curve of intensifying wonder in the scene spills over, surmounts the apex, and begins to descend into the excited bustle and gathering up of the three Gentlemen as they prepare to go to "piece" the rejoicing with their company. The concentration of "art," here as elsewhere in the play, tends to release its tension in concerted action, waking beholders to their fresh life and to renewed community of interest. We get a parodic variant of the same curve when the Old Shepherd and Clown come on next, dressed in outlandish finery. The Clown insists more and more upon unmeaning artifices of the court—his "robes," his being a "gentleman born," his daring Autolycus to give him "the lie," his right to "swear" what's false—yet the net effect is to reaffirm shared lives, interests, and wonder. The Clown promises to help Autolycus, heeding the Old Shepherd's reminder that "we must be gentle, now we are gentlemen" (5. 2. 152), and they troupe off in search of "the kings and the princes, our kindred" (5. 2. 172).

As the Gentlemen serve to parody the wonder of the nobles, so the Old Shepherd and Clown parody the "gentlemen," and so Autolycus parodies the parvenues. The ecstasies of royalty and nobility trickle down through the social strata with, it seems, ever more diluted content. But the scene (5. 2), while it distances the recognition, manages also to preserve the wonder of it and hence makes the audience eager for firsthand experience. This is not scornful parody, but delighted and embracing parody. Its tone, finally, can be best gauged by the much-changed role accorded to Autolycus. Speaking but twice to the Gentlemen and thrice to Shepherd and Clown, and each time briefly, he stands for the most part in observing posture and secondary status. When he gives his one extended speech, a soliloquy, he presents himself as a subdued, even a bit abashed, chap forced to admit the disadvantages of his "former life" and its "discredits." Like Caliban at the end of *The Tempest* and Parolles at the end of *All's Well*, Autolycus appears chastened: not, to be sure, apologetic and not really converted, but tamed and assimilable into the happiness and social solidarity surrounding him (unlike, say, Shylock or Malvolio). Stage tradition has him pick pockets in this scene, but stage tradition often prefers easy laughs to wonder.

XI

Despite the varied and well-modulated joys of the first two scenes of the fifth act, the scenes have borne throughout a sense of pre-climax. In each, the technique has been to have those onstage greeted by persons who enter only to impel a rush offstage in search of promised wonders. As the statue scene begins, there are present onstage all the principals of the play. The pattern of the preceding scenes appears necessarily foreclosed, and the audience must infer from this as well as other cues that it now will see, in terms used earlier by Leontes, the game played home.

The statue scene, once played, stands as recapitulation of earlier climactic scenes in which queen or princess, centrally observed, was "unmasked" by a king and made to face a new reality, though instead of the kings' earlier mistrust, their horror at handclasps of supposedly illicit lovers, and their imposition of disguise and deception upon the objects of their wrath, now there is substituted a new confidence and hope, hands extended in personal affection, and the redemption of art to life. Our first clue to the recapitulative thrust of the scene, however, lies in Paulina's welcome of Leontes to her "removed house":

> All my services
> You have paid home: but that you have vouchsaf'd
> With your crown'd brother and these your contracted
> Heirs of your kingdoms, my poor house to visit,
> It is a surplus of your grace, which never
> My life may last to answer. (5. 3. 3)

Here lingers a reminiscence of the instructive pastoral journey in which Florizel's (and Perdita's) royalty humbled itself to the poorer rustic scene and found there a revitalization out of surprisingly art-filled ceremonies. Disarmingly, Paulina creates an impression of welcoming "sovereign" "crown'd" "kingdoms" into her "poor house": behind the comparison lurks the idea invoked by Florizel at the shearing feast when he spoke of Apollo descending into a swain's form for the sake of rare beauty. When Leontes bestows the "surplus" of his "grace" upon the gallery and Paulina's "life," the realms of grace and of natural life once more approach each other as at the pastoral scene through the medium of art.

Now, instead of a theatrical shearing festival, a lively "Whitsun pastoral," the scene is a "gallery," a theater of silent figures wherein we "see the life as lively mock'd as ever / Still sleep mock'd death" (5. 3. 19). Again, as at the trial and pastoral scenes, there arises the suggestion that we are in the realm of "sleep." Shakespeare is at some pains to give Hermione's statue a reality superior to that of the onlookers. Leontes exclaims:

> I am asham'd: does not the stone rebuke me
> For being more stone than it? O royal piece!
> There's magic in thy majesty, which has
> My evils conjur'd to remembrance, and
> From thy admiring daughter took the spirits,
> Standing like stone with thee. (5. 3. 37)

The bystanders become like the playgoers as the art experience catches up their spirits and makes them participate in play:

> *Paul.*   O patience!
> The statue is but newly fix'd, the colour's
> Not dry.

> *Cam.* My lord, your sorrow was too sore laid on,
>   Which sixteen winters cannot blow away,
>   So many summers dry: scarce any joy
>   Did ever so long live; no sorrow
>   But kill'd itself much sooner.
> *Pol.*   Dear my brother,
>   Let him that was the cause of this have power
>   To take off so much grief from you as he
>   Will piece up in himself.
> *Paul.*   Indeed, my lord,
>   If I had thought the sight of my poor image
>   Would thus have wrought you—for the stone is mine—
>   I'd not have show'd it. (5. 3. 46)

Does not Camillo adopt the art metaphor and imitate Paulina when he describes Leontes' sorrow as "laid on" and not yet "dry"? Leontes becomes an equivalent statue, facing, as Hermione faced, sixteen years of purgative winter storms and summers insufficient to allay the grief. Even Polixenes finds himself drawn to substantiating analogies of art: to lessen Leontes' grief is to "piece up" that grief within his own person. As we yield and receive mutual griefs and hopes, we become, like Leontes, "wrought"—anguished with fellow feeling but also wrought into works of art sharing the universal substance of our humanity.

As the spectators in Paulina's gallery chapel become transfigured into motionless, stonelike wonder, they mimic the audience that accepts stillness for a time in order to witness the moving revelations of art. Shakespeare must have felt deeply the paradox of theater that reduces audiences to "nothing," "sleep," "stone," in comparison to and for the sake of the "life" upon the stage. The figure of Hermione chides, rebukes, and mocks them into but then out of stonelike postures. In this sense, it takes us beyond Lear's cry:

> O, you are men of stones.
> Had I your tongues and eyes, I'ld use them so
> That heaven's vault should crack. (5. 3. 258)

Here, in contrast, the lookers-on so devotedly seek blessing from Hermione that she becomes divinely authorized to bless, to become the benign image of the promised end, and to live through that slenderest "chance which does redeem all sorrows" (*Lr.* 5. 3. 267).

Paulina challenges the "transported" Leontes:

> If you can behold it,
> I'll make the statue move indeed; descend,
> And take you by the hand. (5. 3. 87)

Not "if you *will* behold it" but "if you *can*." Again, there is the suggestion that the beholder must somehow be equivalent to the deed. Compare the Gentleman's assertion in the preceding scene: "The dignity of this act was worth the audience of kings and princes; for by such was it acted" (5. 2. 79). Now, Leontes, instead of challenging the entire ceremony to seek the "truth," enters trustfully the ritual proposed:

> What you can make her do,
> I am content to look on. (5. 3. 91)

This sentence, especially the word *content*, may suggest an inappropriate passivity. Paulina responds:

> It is requir'd
> You do awake your faith. (5. 3. 94)

Faith is one of those multipurpose words used by Shakespeare in a variety of situations. The present context invites a rich coalescence of meanings: trust in Paulina, belief in providence, fidelity to vows of love, sincerity, uncritical confidence. Leontes, in particular, must reawaken his need for Hermione, his fidelity toward her, and his deepest acceptance of her abiding loyalty. All of the onlookers must have faith in the possibility and the meaning of the statue's life: that full community may be restored and hope renewed, that time brings not only withering loss but also rare triumphant regeneration. And Paulina speaks to the audience as well. For the scene to achieve its meaning, the audience must have faith that this supreme fiction is not only worth beholding, but is in some respects magnificently true. Art does awake life.

The notion that faith may exist yet be asleep is challenging. But the play has repeatedly pointed to dangers that married love may stiffen into hollow ritual, that faith in friendship may all too easily fall asleep and enter a nightmare, that faith in justice may mistake form for substance, that faith in divine powers may lose its force, that even the faith of lovers must awaken from the tendency to dream rather than constantly to renew itself. Faith, in terms of the play, must not become order without energy, hope without striving; it must be more than a stolid noun; it must be informed by an active, verbal, awakening.

I believe that a central rhythm of *The Winter's Tale*, an action that it repeatedly imitates, beats upon the reoccurence of waking out of dream only to sleep again and wake once more. The "dream" of innocence first described by Polixenes cannot last, and indeed the too-painful presence of lost innocence amid mature "entertainment" is foreshadowed in Archidamus's call for "sleepy drinks." The first shock of the play is to observe Leontes in that state wherein sleepers wake and yet still dream. He alone is alert and supersensitized to the bleak netherside of faith, those possibilities of betrayal, duplicity, and mockery that recur to negate the very enterprise. For him, to wake from the dream of innocence is but to enter the dream of affection. Sensual love, in Leontes' terms, communicates with "dreams," with the "unreal," with "nothing." Leontes, in his skepticism, seeks to put aside the dream of love. He challenges all, including the audience, to awaken from dogmatic slumbers. But the price of his negative insight is a restless sleeplessness, and expression of nightmare. Paulina comes "to bring him sleep," but he cannot sleep because he is already sleepwalking. As Hermione says, their lives stand in the level of his dreams. The tragedy of the trial scene awakens him. Or does it? Leontes enters the "recreation" of the great Bohemian inter-dream, itself filled with wakings. Yet every waking is to a new dream of reasserted faith, an art that nature makes. The central dream of mankind is "faith," faith in the powers of friendship, in the ordering harmony of love, in the redemptive continuity of generations, in the meaning and value of life itself. When Paulina says it is required that we awaken faith, she asks a realization of that dream.

Appropriately, if tensionally, the sign of awakening faith is quiet concentration. Paulina commands: "Then all stand still." The audience is implicated in this imperative, for it not only sees and hears but, like the characters onstage, remembers and anticipates. It has traveled the entire journey, seeking, beyond even the experience of any one character onstage, to find what lies behind Paulina's curtain, Hermione's expression, behind the inmost veil. The spectators would wake into a last true dream, a reality beyond the reach of ordinary dreaming. Now, if the actors and audience can achieve a perfect attention, a rapt stillness of longing, they may with courage enter the very condition of the statue. If, in the theater, for one moment, the silence can convey the unimpeachable transcendence of art, then the return to life can be, like Hermione's , unique and incorruptible.

All those who await Paulina's command to the statue must share certain feelings. If the statue is alive, as under the circumstances must be suspected, then a joke is played upon Leontes, the Leontes who said: "Thy mother plays, and I / Play too." Yet this punishment that exactly fits his crime gives Leontes the chance to change play into reality through his awakening faith. He can come out the way he went in. Then again the spectators may reflect that Hermione has been in truth a kind of statue for sixteen years, that the figure before them represents her long winter of marble stillness and constancy in waiting, and that waiting for the procreative adolescence of one's child may end properly, as here, in ritualized recognition of his or her growth to adulthood and decision to found a family, a recognition, therefore, of one's own extended power of regeneration. The spectators, furthermore, have come to the theater to be enlivened by art; the choice by Hermione and Paulina (and Shakespeare behind them) of the statue scene is a quintessential representation of that enlivening. In this sense, Hermione and the spectators are one. "Who was most marble, there changed colour" (5. 2. 89), said the Gentleman of the spectators at the recognition scene. We are invited to think in terms of equivalence between those acting and those acted upon.

The psychology of the moment before Paulina's address to the statue deserves mention, too, for every audience recognizes and indeed shares the peculiar strain of holding still. The law of life is motion, but the spectators respond to the onstage demands for silence and stillnesss with a silence and stillness of their own. For an interval, breaths are suspended and time halts. Paulina then calls: "Music. . . ." There is a teasing delay: " . . . awake her. . . ." Paulina waits a moment, raises her arm, and then lets it fall: " . . . strike!" (5. 3. 98). Music sounds. It is, of course, the perfect emblem of pure temporality and also the symbol of divine and earthly concord. Yet still the statue hesitates with its audience, awaiting the climax of kinesthetic tension. As if understanding the need to name the meaning of the instant, Paulina says: " 'Tis time." (5.3.99). The words have great resonance. Hermione has waited long on the moment; Time, we saw, has been the play's overseer; Leontes, who first feared time and its attendant mutabilities, now longs for time to enter the statue.

As Paulina continues to speak, the statue—responding to her creative labor, to the moving music, to the will of the single audience on and before the stage—visibly takes in breath, wakes toward animate facial expression, and attempts the beginnings of gestural motion. Expressing in simple terms the feelings of all present, Paulina says to Hermione:

> Descend; be stone no more; approach;
> Strike all that look upon with marvel. Come!
> I'll fill your grave up: stir, nay, come away:
> Bequeath to death your numbness; for from him
> Dear life redeems you. (5. 2. 99)

The statue's frozen "numbness" gives way to life. Winter's grave is filled. Here all our concentration is upon the redemptive process, the sheer value of "dear life." Soon, however, Paulina turns from Hermione to Leontes:

> You perceive she stirs:
> Start not; her actions shall be as holy as
> You hear my spell is lawful. [*To Leontes*] Do not shun her
> Until you see her die again; for then
> You kill her double. Nay, present your hand:
> When she was young you woo'd her; now, in age,
> Is she become the suitor? (5. 3. 103)

The audience is thus gently encouraged to let its focus widen from Hermione to Leontes and to place the process of rebirth in context. Leontes momentarily aghast, as the text clearly shows, overcomes his awe and slowly reaffirms his role of life-enhancing wooer by performing the central symbolic act of the play. He touches Hermione's hand: "O, she's warm!" (5. 3. 109). Everything is in this line: the red blood in winter's pale, returning spring, restored sanity after "Too hot, too hot!" It is the crowning proof of his own rebirth, for he, too, is touched alive like the new-waking Adam.

As the hands mingle, the spectators find metamorphosed into a single image of reconciliation all of those earlier troubled, mistrusted, hopeful, and charitable images:

> They ... shook hands, as over a vast.... (1. 1. 28)
>
> Ere I could make thee open thy white hand.... (1. 2. 102)
>
> But to be paddling palms.... (1. 2. 115)

> Give me thy hand,
> Be pilot to me.... (1. 2. 447)

What needs these hands? (2. 3. 126)

Lend me thy hand, I'll help thee: come, lend me thy hand. (4. 3. 68)

Take hands, a bargain! (4. 4. 384)

> The king's son took me by the hand, and called me brother....
> (5. 2. 140)

> Give me thy hand: I will swear to the prince thou art as honest
> a true fellow as any is in Bohemia. (5. 2. 156)

Give me that hand of yours to kiss. (5. 3. 146)

In the lastingly joined hands of Leontes and Hermione, as in the instant of the statue's waking, there is a power of gestural recapitulation that can hardly be overstated. Through its gradually accumulated wakings and greetings the whole drama flows into the two climactic moments, and the spectators can see feelingly the deepest impulse of alienated beings to wake and reconnect.

Leontes and Hermione embrace, they are joined by Perdita, and soon the reunion becomes general. With the actors the audience stirs, anticipates an ending, recovers consciousness of the theater, and readies to rouse itself toward the clapping and an exit of its own. Shakespeare gives Leontes appropriately concluding lines:

> Good Paulina,
> Lead us from hence, where we may leisurely
> Each one demand, and answer to his part
> Perform'd in this wide gap of time, since first
> We were dissever'd: hastily lead away. (5. 3. 151)

The spectators answer each actor's "part perform'd" with the self-joining hands of applause. The play stands played.

XII

It remains forever questionable whether words about art really do enhance it. If they do, they do so by changing our minds. This would seem to be an elusive, protean process of changing, but, just as stage traditions emerge, elaborate themselves, seem for a time secure, then wither or metamorphose, so cultural assumptions, expectations and evaluations prevailing among readers and audiences of a Shakespearean play likewise branch, put forth, and exfoliate with a marvelous consecutiveness, a cumulativeness that helps give meaning to "history." When we examine the stage and critical histories of *The Winter's Tale*, we see, no doubt, some of the same or similar errors, misconceptions, and stock responses propagating themselves afresh in each age. We also see, however, an advancing interest in the wholeness of the play. We may now be coming closer to a respect for the entire artifact. After two centuries of redactions, the full text flourishes upon our stage. And, whereas plays such as *A Midsummer Night's Dream* and *Hamlet* have become so overloaded with conflicting "straight" interpretations that directors and critics almost of necessity stylize them now toward some one or two prominent features of their personalities, *The Winter's Tale* remains relatively unburdened by overtheatricalization and over-interpretation, so that, as reviews of worldwide production and criticism suggest (see, for example, recent spring and autumn issues of *Shakespeare Quarterly*), producers and critics, probably for the first time, are trying to let the whole play speak for itself.

It even deserves arguing that our age finds itself specially attuned to the later plays of Shakespeare as essays in holistic, broadly ecological inquiry and faith. Not only are we resuscitating the fortunes of romance and celebrating it as a specially incorporative mode of vision that takes us in some ways beyond comedy and tragedy but also we are finding in *The Winter's Tale*, particularly, as outlined above, a vital combination of tensions between wrath and love, mistrust and faith, tensions between culture and nature, between vengeance and forgiveness, art and time. These terms, however, do not remain equivalent; the drama yields a resolution.

In his *Tales of the Mermaid Tavern*, Alfred Noyes has Robert Greene say to Shakespeare:

> My music made for mortal ears
> You flung to all the listening spheres.
> You took my dreams and made them true.[1]

Greene subtitled *Pandosto* "The Triumph of Time." But he could only conceive of the triumph in local, limited, all too "mortal" terms, for he slipped back at the end to his habits of

---

1. (New York: Frederick A. Stokes, 1913), p. 34.

shallow paradox and decided to "close up the comedy with a tragical stratagem," the death of Pandosto. Shakespeare took the risk of changing this mortal tune to immortal music. Through Perdita's restoration and Hermione's resurrection, he made the dream of time come true.

It has been fashionable for some years to see Shakespeare as the poet of paradox, of multivalence, complementarity, and plurisignation, as if he were relativist par excellence. But the truth is more nearly that Shakespeare works steadily in his plays toward justifications of service, forgiveness, and familial love. He consistently critiques our inauthentic responses to time. Define time as mortality and death and seek antidotes in power (ultimately to dispense death), fame, progeny, art. Define time as growth and life and seek to enter it in love, marriage, family, service to society. In the earlier part of his career, Shakespeare answers history with comedy; later, he answers tragedy with romance. Shakespeare's history and tragedy show men seeking power, fame, revenge against time's dark mortality. His comedy and romance show men yielding to the force of love, giving up their reliance upon power and place, wrath and vengeance, the themes of history and tragedy, and triumphing with time by entering it fully in reciprocal creative relations with women, family, and friends.

In the histories and tragedies, when aims of ambition and revenge dominate, then culture (or art) is dominated by conceptions of hierarchy, claims of older generations to direct destinies of younger ones, and pervasive imageries of stifling closeness, shallow artifice, aggressive but empty honor, entropy, and decay. Such a view of culture generates a corresponding view of nature as field of mortality, animal drives, fallen innocence, questioned providence. This wintry view qualifies and chills the redemptive catharsis generally attempted at play's end. In the romantic comedies, a younger generation of giddy lovers is allowed to shake off shackles of parental-cultural repression. The old art context dies and flakes like a snake's skin ready to be sloughed off, and a new society is easily born out of the superior vitality of youth that carries with it an implicit definition of creative nature, vexatious and folly inducing—like the forest of Arden or wood near Athens—but benignly ordinant of love.

In the romances, the older generation retains a potentially tragic dominance. The critiques of moribund society and its analogue in nature work more broadly and deeply here than in the comedies. But in each romance the potentially tragic patriarch loses himself, his sense of political place and power, and is revitalized in more familiar and humane terms by his daughter. The post-despairing versions of Pericles, Cymbeline, Leontes, and Prospero are all inseparable from the presence of their restorative daughters. Society and nature are freshly feminized, made nurturant in the promise of new birth.

Only in *Pericles* and *The Winter's Tale*, however, do wives as well as daughters figure in the new harmony, and only in *The Winter's Tale* does the protagonist's wife participate significantly in the complication and resolution of the action. Part of the play's grandeur lies in the way Shakespeare molded Greene's narrative toward a sensitive and sophisticated exploration of regal alienation, misogyny, and unfaith that first challenge and then prompt the assertion of counterforces in nature, human and beyond. A final subject of the play, as we have seen, is the faith that powers love, and Shakespeare nowhere proves more assiduous or detailed in searching out the sources of that faith in all manner of mankind and in the rites due each age, place, and season.

In the line of plays extending from *Hamlet* through *Lear*, *Macbeth*, *Antony and Cleopatra*, and the romances, Shakespeare vastly enlarges the cosmic and spiritual dimensions of his drama. Whereas the comedies and history plays show us men and women more or less confined to a secular plane, only intermittently concerned with and infrequently touched by vertical forces of sub- and super-nature, the great tragedies and romances impel their protagonists to perceive towering vertical influences—demonic and divine—that intersect the thin lines of history and human culture.

In *The Winter's Tale*, the Oracle, Apollo, Time, and "great creating nature" are allied as providential powers. Sacrament signals itself as well in the very texture of the drama. Leontes, in his mistrust, loses all sense of a sacredness in life. He denies that his marriage is a thing of "grace." He thinks that affection stabs the center, leads to unreality, and he seems to go beyond Polixenes in thinking that mankind is fallen, that we cannot answer heaven "not guilty" (1. 2. 74). The hope of his friendship with Polixenes—"The heavens continue their loves" (1. 1. 31)—is vain, for Leontes drains love of faith. Shakespeare is at some pains here, as in *Lear* and *Macbeth*, to suggest the interdependence of human love and belief in creation. Leontes, with his declamations on false women, winds, and waters, on nature betraying itself, on the bawdy planet, on the world as "nothing," on having seen the spider, refuses to see that trust in another person involves trust in life itself, or at least does so in Shakespeare's universe. His jealousy is finally revealed as blasphemy—"There is no truth at all 'i th' Oracle" (3. 2. 140). The rest of the play, as we have seen, sustains an argument for the numinous presence in life of forces that support and give meaning to human love. Shakespeare recharges our intimation that life is not mechanical and atomized but is vital and whole, vibrant with interanimations. Released at last from the closed circuit of Leontes' profane trespass, the spectators witness vast changes in weather and place, a far journey through storm, dream, a savage bear-god, talk of fairies from semi-mythic Shepherds hosting their archetypal foundling, the abstracted appearance of Time benign, the swirling pastoral celebration of metamorphic gods, Nature's Arts, maids and then Satyrs dancing, the wedding drive, and Florizel uninterruptible:

> It cannot fail, but by
> The violation of my faith; and then
> Let nature crush the sides o' th' earth together,
> And mar the seeds within! (4. 4. 477)

This is Shakespeare's essential theme: upon our faith depends all meaning that we find in the natural order of things. If one's generation knows no faith, then none need be sought in nature. Conversely, when we re-establish or "awaken" faith anew, as happens in the statue scene, we not only see and feel more surely what life is but we also take on the power to create, to invest life where it was not before: "O, she's warm!"

"Faith," however, proves itself in Shakespeare more than an informing touch upon life's pulse. Faith is the very inmost principle of proportion and due measure, a principle in love itself, that sets and tells the time of generation ("nor my lusts / Burn hotter than my faith" [4. 4. 34]) and keeps us true to one another. In this sense, faith is art. The touch of Leontes does not awake Hermione. Music does. "Music, awake her; strike!" (5. 3. 98). To know and feel the bond between the touch and the music, between nature's winking glow and art's waking grace, is to approach a central, sustaining mystery in *The Winter's Tale.*

Postscript

At a symposium on Shakespeare's romances not very long ago, one of the speakers alluded to *The Winter's Tale*, quite simply and sincerely, as "Shakespeare's greatest play." The first chapter quoted an example of perhaps equal hyperbole written by a famous critic decades earlier, and we have seen how engagement with the play in the theater has produced, on occasion, similar sentiments of surpassing awe and wonder. From one viewpoint nothing is served by such gratuitous and unverifiable assertions. But from another point of view, these awe-struck evaluations invite us to re-examine our more skeptical and no doubt more prevalent assumptions about the play.

While it is true that *The Winter's Tale* has of late received more, and more flattering, recognition from certain Shakespearean interpreters and even, to some extent, from producers of Shakespeare's plays, still it is by no means true that the general readers of Shakespeare, or most students, or even most teachers of Shakespeare now regard *The Winter's Tale* to be as profound and moving in its way as the great tragedies of Shakespeare are in theirs. The present study stands, therefore, as an invitation, and is offered as a brief and no doubt faulty plea, for continued payment of loving attention to this still much-too-neglected masterpiece. No one, admittedly, can or should want to force others to read or see or study whatever they instinctively and deeply and with some reasons reject. But dismissals of *The Winter's Tale* are generally not of that sort, being not heartfelt and knowing but, rather, casual and uninformed. What the company of the faithful asks, moreover, in the case of *The Winter's Tale*, is not that there should be wholesale conversions to ecstatic praise but only that a few more and then a few more still may find, and find happily, their own paths to appreciation of this astonishing artifact.

What the company of the faithful, in diverse fashions, finds in the play may never, I suspect, be demonstrated out of it like some theorem out of geometrical proofs. One can do no better, perhaps, than to emulate Shakespeare's colleagues who advised readers of the First Folio to "reade him, therefore; and againe, and againe," only, one hopes, readers of *The Winter's*

Tale will also see it again, and again, until its strangeness and the malapert idiosyncrasies of varied productions cancel out, leaving at the center the very face of affection: concerned, reflective, shining.

Index